UNDERSTANDING DEAFNESS
SOCIALLY

UNDERSTANDING DEAFNESS SOCIALLY

Edited by

PAUL C. HIGGINS, PH.D.

Department of Sociology
University of South Carolina
Columbia, South Carolina

and

JEFFREY E. NASH, PH.D.

Department of Sociology
Macalester College
St. Paul, Minnesota

CHARLES C THOMAS • PUBLISHER
Springfield • Illinois • U.S.A.

Published and Distributed Throughout the World by

CHARLES C THOMAS • PUBLISHER

2600 South First Street

Springfield, Illinois 62794-9265

© *1987 by* CHARLES C THOMAS • PUBLISHER

ISBN 0-398-05300-6

Library of Congress Catalog Card Number: 86-23018

With THOMAS BOOKS *careful attention is given to all details of manufacturing and
design. It is the Publisher's desire to present books that are satisfactory as to their physical
qualities and artistic possibilities and appropriate for their particular use.* THOMAS
BOOKS *will be true to those laws of quality that assure a good name and good will.*

Printed in the United States of America
Q-R-3

Library of Congress Cataloging in Publication Data

Higgins, Paul C.
  Understanding deafness socially.

  Bibliography: p.
  1. Deaf--United States--Social conditions. 2. Deaf-
ness-Social aspects. 3. Socialization. I. Higgins, Paul C.
II. Nash, Jeffrey E.
HV2545.U53 1987   305.9'08162'0973   86-23018
ISBN 0-398-05300-6

CONTRIBUTORS

Sharon N. Barnartt, Ph.D.
Department of Sociology and Social Work
Gallaudet University
Washington, DC 20002

Gaylene Becker, Ph.D.
Institute for Health and Aging
University of California, San Francisco
San Francisco, CA 94143

John B. Christiansen, Ph.D.
Department of Sociology and Social Work
Gallaudet University
Washington, DC 20002

Carol J. Erting, Ph.D.
Center for Studies in Education and Human Development
Gallaudet University
Washington, DC 20002

Paul Higgins, Ph.D.
Department of Sociology
University of South Carolina
Columbia, SC 29208

Kathryn P. Meadow-Orlans, Ph.D.
Center for Studies in Education and Human Development
Gallaudet University
Washington, DC 20002

Anedith Nash, Ph.D.
Higher Education Consortium for Urban Affairs (HECUA)
Hamline University
St. Paul, MN 55104

Jeffrey E. Nash, Ph.D.
Department of Sociology
Macalester College
St. Paul, MN 55105

Jerome D. Schein, Ph.D.
Professor Emeritus, Deafness Rehabilitation
New York University
New York, NY 10003

        and

Powrie Vaux Doctor Professor of Deaf Studies
Gallaudet University
Washington, DC 20002

INTRODUCTION

PAUL C. HIGGINS

IMAGINE a child who is deaf. Educators are concerned that the child is appropriately instructed. In what educational setting should the child be placed? What curriculum is best for the child? What educational materials should be used? These and many other concerns are addressed by educators. Audiologists and speech therapists are concerned that the child's auditory and speech capacities and abilities are developed. Is a hearing aid appropriate? If it is, what kind suits the child best? How can the child's speech and speechreading be best developed? These and other issues concern audiologists and speech therapists. The physician is concerned that the child's residual hearing is maintained and, if possible, enhanced. Might medication or surgery be appropriate? Should a special regimen be followed? Medical questions like these concern the physician. The psychologist is concerned that the child's personal and emotional development is not harmed by the hearing loss. Is the child developing any maladaptive behaviors? If so, how should those behaviors be handled? These and similar issues concern the psychologist. And the parents, especially soon after learning that their child is deaf, though sometimes years after, are likely to be bewildered.

Each of the concerned practitioners perceives the deaf child from a particular viewpoint — educational, audiological, medical or psychological. They do so appropriately and counsel the parents accordingly. The child and the child's deafness become partialed among the disciplines used to understand and to treat the child and the deafness. Each of these perspectives provides a means for understanding and "working with" the deaf child and, more generally, with deafness and deaf people. However, by themselves each perspective is certainly not enough. Even together they are not enough, though traditionally they have been the predominant perspectives for understanding deafness. The assumptions, con-

cepts, and knowledge within different disciplines enable us to understand, but they also keep us in ignorance of that which they do not address. Other perspectives are needed.

Each deaf person, child or adult, is an individual. Each's life is
unique. However, we cannot understand each deaf person's life and experiences only in an individualistic manner. In order to understand
deafness and deaf people we cannot look exclusively within individual
deaf people. Instead, we must look outward to the actions, reactions and
interactions between deaf people and others. Deaf people live their lives
among others, and those others influence the lives deaf people live. Even
when those others are not directly encountered, as in social practices and
arrangements brought forth from the past, they and their actions are important. Those others may be other deaf people, but mostly they are
hearing people. They may be concerned practitioners mentioned earlier,
but mostly they are unknowledgeable, though sometimes sympathetic,
citizens. They may be strangers, acquaintances, family members, and
others. In schools, families, businesses, neighborhoods, clubs and many
other social settings and circumstances deaf people live their lives. In
growing up, learning, working, raising a family and many other activities deaf people again live their lives. A social approach to understanding deafness requires that we locate the lives of deaf people within the
larger social world in which they live (Mills, 1959).

OUTSIDERS IN A HEARING WORLD

That larger social world to a great degree is a "hearing world" — and
deaf people are outsiders within it. It is a world of sounds, of all kinds of
sounds — babbling babies, barking dogs, rustling leaves, screeching
sirens, people talking, and much much more. It is a world where we talk
and listen — face to face or by means of telephones, radios, loudspeakers,
and intercom systems. Even television, which is thought to be a very visual medium, often makes little sense without sound. Deaf people live
within that "world of sounds but are not fully part of that world" (Higgins, 1980:22). In a related but more profound sense, deaf people are
outsiders as well. That "hearing world" is not merely one in which people
are assumed to be able to hear, but it is also one, which, to a great degree, is controlled by those who do hear. Deaf people "live within a world
which is not of their own making, but one which they must continually
confront" (Higgins, 1980:22). In doing so, they live their lives.

With a few obvious changes, the following observation of black Americans is applicable to deaf people.

> (Racism is the) single most important source of the developing ethnic peoplehood. Racism has been such an omnipresent reality that the direct and indirect struggle against it makes up the core of black history in America (Blauner, 1972:140-141).

"Handicapism," instead of racism, is the "omnipresent reality" with which deaf people and many others with disabilities continue to contend. Handicapism is:

> a set of assumptions and practices that promote the differential and unequal treatment of people because of apparent or assumed physical, mental, or behavioral differences (Bogdan and Biklen, 1977:14).

Handicapism becomes more specifically "deafism": The set of assumptions and practices which promote the differential and unequal treatment of people because of their deafness.

An important part of that hearing world is the many assumptions that people make. Those assumptions concern all aspects of people's lives. They involve what is thought to be natural and unnatural, right and wrong, acceptable and unacceptable. They concern what people are thought to be like, what is appropriate for them to do, and so on. Based on those assumptions people often act unreflectively. They do without fully considering what it is they have done. Typically unnoticed assumptions of the larger hearing world have had a profound impact on deaf people.

Deafness as a Deficit

Perhaps the most important, certainly the most troubling, assumption made by citizens and by concerned practitioners is that deafness is a deficit (Padden, 1980:90). Deaf people are perceived as lacking an important, even an essential, element of being human. Consequently, deaf people are defective:

> Scholars and ordinary people, in fact society in general, traditionally considered the deaf to be on a subhuman level, incapable of education or culture, bereft of human intelligence (Furth, 1966:7).

Historically, this assumption has taken more or less extreme forms. While it has become less extreme in recent years, it certainly remains. Out of it and related assumptions have developed varied practices which have profoundly influenced the lives of deaf people.[1]

"Deaf and dumb" starkly captures this assumption. Perhaps denoting only the inability of deaf people to speak (which is incorrect), but cer-

tainly connoting their inability to think, this view of deaf people has
greatly influenced their lives. Out of this assumption have come in the
past restrictions on deaf people's right to marry, to vote, and to make
wills. Due to this assumption, deaf people were placed in the same category as fools and minors in early Hebrew law. If cattle entrusted to them
broke away, then the owners were liable for damages because they had
shown so little sense. Some states such as Alabama and Georgia passed
laws to prevent carnivals from bringing deaf people with them and then
abandoning them in local towns (Higgins, 1980:23-27). Based on a related assumption, deaf people have encountered difficulty in obtaining
driver's licenses and insurance at reasonable rates. After all, goes the assumption, one must be able to hear well in order to drive well. Not necessarily so (Schein, 1968)! Due to this assumption that deafness is a
deficit there continues a long tradition of psychologically investigating
the possible (or is it probable?) pathological development of deaf people
(Neisser, 1983:65). Because of this assumption, "deaf education, by definition if not by design, has had a long history of low standards" (Neisser,
1983:144). And due to this assumption, it has only been recently recognized (and certainly not universally so) that sign language is a language,
not a shorthand, a broken-form of English or some other inferior means
of communication.

A self-fulfilling prophecy is potentially at work (Merton, 1957).
Based on assumptions concerning the deficits of deafness, people have
acted in ways which have led deaf people to behave in ways which unfortunately fulfill those assumptions. If educators, employers and significant others such as parents—in general hearing people—typically
believed that deaf people were defective, then it made sense that they did
not provide similar educational, occupational, and other opportunities
and challenges to deaf people as were provided to those believed not to
be defective. It made sense that parents often sheltered their deaf children (many times out of shame), protecting them from (and therefore
depriving them of) the experiences of everyday life. It made sense that
deaf students were greatly praised for very modest accomplishments or
typically trained for manual occupations instead of being encouraged to
prepare for college. It made sense that education for deaf students (and
in general for those with special needs) would be the "stepchild" of the
educational system. It made sense that deaf people were often locked
into low-level jobs, being passed over for supervisory positions. All of
these actions and more made sense if deafness was assumed to be a deficit and deaf people were defective. Consequently, deaf individuals typi-

cally have not achieved as much academically or occupationally as those who hear (Schein and Delk, 1974). Their low achievements became further proof that deafness was indeed a deficit. Yet, was it the "objective" limitations of hearing losses or the social obstacles due to hearing people's assumptions and related practices which led to those putative deficits of deafness?

Given those debilitating assumptions concerning deafness, deaf people have nevertheless typically led ordinary lives. However, in doing so, deaf people have had to continually confront the assumptions and practices of hearing people. Thus, a social understanding of deafness must necessarily confront those assumptions and practices as well. Among other insights, that social understanding provides us the:

> capacity to recognize the content of unexamined assumptions and accepted concepts that is among the most valuable contributions through which social science enables human beings to transcend the conventional and create new approaches and policies (Gusfield, 1976:32).

UNDERSTANDING THOSE WHO HEAR

A social approach to understanding deafness leads not only to a greater understanding of the lives of deaf people, but also to a greater understanding of those who are not deaf. It does so for at least two reasons. Because deaf people live much of their lives within the larger hearing world, contending with the assumptions and practices of those who hear, a social understanding of deafness necessarily provides an understanding of those who are not deaf, of their assumptions and practices.

For example, many deaf people are adamantly opposed to oralism, to the heavy emphasis on speech and speechreading to the exclusion of sign language. They will not use hearing aids even though it may be beneficial for them to do so. They do not speak as often as they might even though to do so may again be beneficial. They perceive themselves and/ or others as the victims of misguided hearing educators and others (often parents) who tried to make them something that they were not. Certainly the educators saw their deaf students signing when outside of the classroom and recognized that their students were progressing poorly, if at all, within the classroom. So, too, with those "others" who emphasized oralism. Did educators simply deceive themselves? Certainly some did. Did educators, like other concerned practitioners and citizens, assume that deaf children could not learn well? Unfortunately, many must have. However, the almost absolute refusal to consider seriously sign language as a powerful means of communication and the cruel and/or petty punishments of students caught signing in school (such as monetary fines or smacks of the hand with a ruler) spoke to another set of concerns among hearing educators and others.

Those practices reflected the dominance of an Anglo-Saxon culture which repressed "all" that was foreign—whether it was sign languge by those who were deaf, Welsh spoken in Wales (which was repressed by England), or Spanish spoken in the southwestern United States (Higgins, 1980:65; Lane, 1984; Neisser, 1983:29). As related to deafness, those practices reflected the concern among some that sign language, along with isolated residential schools, magazines for deaf people, teachers who were deaf, and other circumstances, might lead to marriages among deaf individuals and the creation of deaf communities within, but apart from, the hearing world (Higgins, 1980:64). Alexander Graham Bell (1883) even feared the formation of a deaf variety of the human race as a certain portion of the offspring of the marriages among deaf individuals were deaf themselves.

Once those who heard decided to "help" those who did not, it was to be on the former's terms. Help, of course, is also a means of control, of controlling what the recipients of the help are able to do and to become.[2] For much too long, the help extended by those who hear to those who do not has been designed to mold the latter in the image of the former. Both the goal (i.e., to behave [perhaps even **be**?] as much like a hearing person as possible) and the (limited) successes in achieving that goal are taken as proof in the importance of hearing and speaking for being fully human, for literally being at times God's chosen one. Failure has not become typically grounds for questioning the assumptions and practices but has been an indication of the difficulty to make whole those who were defective. The significance of hearing and the superior social position of those who hear (i.e., the opportunities and resources available to them) have been preserved. More generally, this has been so for those who are able-bodied. In part, they have maintained their privileged position, both symbolically and materially, at the expense of those who are deaf or possess other disabilities.

A social approach to understanding deafness urges us to view critically (not criticizingly) even those practices which seem most motivated by humanitarian concerns. For example, did the recent changes in the education of deaf students and others with special needs as embodied in

P.L. 94-142, The Education for All Handicapped Children Act, and other legislation and judicial decisions arise out of the humanitarian concerns for the development of those who had been neglected in the past? Is it a product of outraged parents and other concerned individuals who mounted a "quiet revolution" (Abeson and Zettel, 1977)? Or might these developments be understood **in part** as the responses of an increasingly financially overburdened government, responses which have led to the "least restrictive environment" which may likely be less expensive than existing programs such as residential facilities or even separate classes within public schools (Sarason and Doris, 1979:369, 371-72; Hartman, 1983)? Might mainstreaming be "integration on the cheap" (Barton and Tomlinson, 1984:71)?[3] To understand deafness, we cannot ignore the activities of those who are not deaf (Lane, 1984).

More importantly, a social approach to understanding deafness enables us to understand those who are not deaf because deaf people are first and foremost **people**. They are people who are also deaf. Deaf people are made of the same "stuff" as are those who hear. Of course, much of the hearing world assumes otherwise. Deaf people's concerns—making a living, raising a family, being a friend, developing one's place in the world, and so much more—are the concerns that we all face. Those concerns do not vanish when people are deaf, though how they are experienced and managed may be altered. How they are experienced and managed by deaf people become variations of a theme—the theme of being human. Thus, a social approach to understanding deafness necessarily becomes an understanding of the social condition of humanity.

SOCIAL CONSTRUCTION OF DEAFNESS

The significance of deafness does not exist in the condition itself. Its meaning is not inherent in the impairment. A social approach to understanding deafness recognizes that its significance is created. The social reality of deafness is constructed through the responses to deafness and deaf people by those who encounter deafness and deaf people, whether they be hearing or deaf people themselves (Berger and Luckmann, 1966). In contending with the assumptions and practices of the larger hearing world as they live their lives, deaf people create the social reality of deafness. As hearing people develop assumptions about and interact with deaf people, they too create the social reality of deafness—the meanings people hold about **deafness** and **deaf** individuals, practices directed toward and done by deaf people as **deaf** people, the social position of **deaf** people in the world, and so on. Those and more constitute the social reality of deafness. It is a reality that is made and can be remade through the individual and the collective action of deaf and hearing people. It is not static, though dominant features of it do not change from moment to moment.

The social reality of deafness is primarily one in which deaf people are outsiders in a hearing world. However, that has not always been so. On Martha's Vineyard, off the coast of Massachusetts, between the late 1600's and the early 1900's, it was not (Groce, 1980, 1982, 1985). Deafness did not set apart much those who were deaf from those who were not. Why not? First, to a great extent, Martha's Vineyard was a "closed society." For approximately two centuries after 1710 there was relatively little contact between the islanders and those who lived off-island. Families lived on the island for generations; islanders married one another and therefore were related to each other; and citizens of the island towns knew one another, often well. Due to the relatively high prevalence of deaf people on Martha's Vineyard there was (greater) necessity for hearing islanders to learn to sign (some) in order to communicate with the sizable deaf segment of the island population.[4] Further, there were few activities in which deaf people could not engage. In a relatively technologically simple society (e.g., one in which there were no telephones and none of the social consequences of telephones such as some occupational dependence upon them), hearing was not as important as it is today. Finally, for not clearly specified reasons, deaf individuals were included in the daily activities of the islanders from early childhood. Perhaps that inclusion developed out of the hearing islanders' skill in signing. The relative number of deaf individuals would encourage such inclusion as would the familial and familiar relations among the deaf and hearing islanders. That early inclusion further supported the development and use of signing among the hearing islanders. The people of Martha's Vineyard from the late 1600's to the early 1900's constructed a vastly different social reality of deafness than has typically been constructed.

The reality of deaf people as outsiders need not be permanent, and it should not be taken for granted. It can be and is being reconstructed. A social approach to understanding deafness seeks to understand that construction and reconstruction and, in doing so, aid in the enhancement of deaf people's lives. However, those features of life on Martha's Vineyard which led to a different reality of deafness are missing in today's world.

While a social approach to understanding deafness is optimistic that deaf people's reality as outsiders can be changed, it is not naive in assuming that to do so is an easy task. That is the challenge of a social approach — to understand the creation by deaf and hearing people of the social reality of deafness and to aid in its remaking. The following chapters take up that challenge.

PLAN OF THE BOOK

A social understanding of deafness usefully builds upon an understanding of the size and characteristics of the deaf population. Jerome Schein explores the demography of deafness, primarily in the United States, but also throughout the world. The deaf population is not static. Instead, its size and shape (i.e., its critical features such as the distribution of the population across age categories) do change over time and from one locale to another. Schein concludes that current, well conducted censuses of deaf populations are needed for appropriate planning and understanding.

Through socialization humans develop skills and understanding, beliefs and behaviors, that are used to navigate through the social world. When children and youth are deaf, their socialization may be more problematic. Kathryn Meadows-Orlans examines how deafness influences socialization from birth through adolescence. The socialization processes of deaf children and youth and the outcomes of those processes are not homogeneous. They are diverse because people's responses to deafness are diverse. Once again we realize that the significance of deafness does not exist within the impairment, but it develops through the interaction between and among those who are and those who are not deaf.

While we often think of socialization as occurring only in childhood and adolescence, it is a lifelong process. Gaylene Becker explores how peer groups, often developed among deaf individuals in childhood and adolescence, enable deaf people to deal with the difficulties of being deaf in a hearing world. Through peer groups, deaf people develop significant social competence. Peer groups facilitate effective communication, the exchange of information, mutual assistance, and the development of friendships and cliques. However, as the deaf community becomes more heterogeneous, peer groups may become more fragmented. Nevertheless, Becker argues that peer groups can be a resource through which services are provided to deaf people.

American Sign Language has been defended and attacked for centuries. While it remains a target of systematic efforts to change it or to eliminate it, Jeffrey Nash shows that it has remained resilient. Not only is ASL a vehicle for exchanging meaning, but it is also a powerful means for establishing and maintaining group identity, for establishing links among people. Ironically, in opposition to oppressive policies that emphasize spoken English and denigrate signs, American Sign Language achieves much of its vitality.

In modern society, according to Anedith Nash and Jeffrey Nash, much of life, including family life, is seen by people as the result of choices. When a child is deaf, choices are still made, but the alternatives among which parents choose may be more limited than what those parents had imagined. Families in which there is a deaf child pass through similar phases as do families in which no child is deaf. However, deafness presents challenges to which parents must respond, but to which typically they are not sure how to respond.

In exploring the cultural conflict between hearing educators and deaf parents in a school for deaf children, Carol Erting uncovers the diverse orientations that participants have concerning the education of deaf children. These orientations have existed for more than one hundred years. Thus, a social understanding recognizes the historical character of the dynamics of deafness. The conflict within the school examined by Erting is an expression of and reproduces the wider conflict between deaf and hearing worlds.

In responding to the difficulties of being deaf in a hearing world, many deaf people become members of deaf communities. However, as Paul Higgins explains, deafness is neither a necessary nor a sufficient condition for membership in deaf communities. Further, while members are similar to one another in significant respects, they also create and maintain differences among one another. Those involved with deaf communities and the communities themselves presently face many challenges.

Deaf people in the United States have historically found themselves in disadvantaged positions. John Christiansen and Sharon Barnartt explore the socioeconomic status of the American deaf population through the twentieth century. They also compare the disadvantaged position of other physically disabled populations to that of deaf folks. Christiansen and Barnartt argue that we should not "blame the victim" in understanding the disadvantaged socioeconomic status of deaf people. Instead, through employing a minority group perspective, we need to examine the practices of the nondisabled society that keep deaf people and others with disabilities down.

FOOTNOTES

1. Increasingly, this assumption that deafness and disabilities in general are individual defects is being challenged, particularly by individuals with disabilities (Gliedman and Roth, 1980; DeJong, 1983).
2. See Tomlinson (1982) for a discussion of the social control consequences of special education.
3. See Scull (1977) for a similar argument concerning the deinstitutionalization of those with mental health problems and to a lesser extent those who have committed crimes.
4. As many as one resident in twenty-five for one small town "up-island" at the end of the 19th century was deaf. In one small neighborhood in that town, one in four residents was deaf. Compare this to approximately one deaf person in every two thousand at that time and approximately one in every 500 people today (Groce, 1982, 1985; Schein and Delk, 1974).

REFERENCES

Abeson, Alan and Zettel, Jeffrey: The end of the quiet revolution: the education for all handicapped children act of 1975. *Exceptional Children, 44:*114-128, 1977

Barton, Len and Tomlinson, Sally: The politics of integration in England. In Barton, Len and Tomlinson, Sally: *Special Education and Social Interest.* London, Croom Helm, 1984, pp. 65-80.

Bell, Alexander Graham: Upon the formation of a deaf variety of the human race. Presented to the National Academy of Sciences, 1883.

Blauner, Robert: *Racial Oppression in America.* New York, Harper and Row, 1972.

Bogdan, Robert and Biklen, Douglas: Handicapism. *Social Policy, 7:*14-19, 1977.

DeJong, Gerben: Defining and implementing the independent living concept. In Crew, Nancy M., Zola, Irving Kenneth, and Associates: *Independent Living for Physically Disabled People.* San Francisco, Jossey-Bass, 1983, pp. 4-27.

Furth, Hans G.: *Thinking Without Language.* New York, Free Press, 1966.

Gliedman, John and Roth, William: *The Unexpected Minority: Handicapped Children in American.* New York, Harcourt, 1980.

Groce, Nora Ellen: Everyone here spoke sign language. *Natural History, 89:*10-16, 1980.

Groce, Nora Ellen: Beyond institutions: the history of some American deaf: an example from Martha's Vineyard. In Higgins, Paul C. and Nash, Jeffrey E.: *The Deaf Community and The Deaf Population,* Sociology of Deafness Series, Washington, D.C., Gallaudet College, 1982, Vol. 3, pp. 97-129.

Groce, Nora Ellen: *Everyone Here Spoke Sign Language: Hereditary Deafness on Martha's Vineyard.* Cambridge, Harvard University Press, 1985.

Gusfield, Joseph: The literary rhetoric of science: comedy and pathos in drinking driver research. *American Sociological Review, 41:*16-34, 1976.

Hartman, William T.: Projecting special education costs. In Chambers, Jay G. and Hartman, William T.: *Special Education Policies: Their History, Implementation, and Finance.* Philadelphia, Temple University, 1983, pp. 241-288.

Higgins, Paul C.: *Outsiders in a Hearing World: A Sociology of Deafness.* Beverly Hills, Sage, 1980.

Lane, Harlan: *When the Mind Hears: A History of the Deaf.* New York, Random House, 1984.

Merton, Robert K.: *Social Theory and Social Structure.* Rev. ed. Glencoe, Free Press, 1957.

Mills, C. Wright: *The Sociological Imagination.* London, Oxford University Press, 1959.

Neisser, Arden: *The Other Side of Silence: Sign Language and the Deaf Community in America.* New York, Knopf, 1983.

Padden, Carol: The deaf community and the culture of deaf people. In Baker, Charlotte and Battison, Robbin: *Sign Language and the Deaf Community: Essays in Honor of William C. Stokoe.* Silver Spring, National Association of the Deaf, 1980, pp. 89-103.

Sarason, Seymour B. and Doris, John: *Educational Handicap, Public Policy, and Social History: A Broadened Perspective on Mental Retardation.* New York, Free Press, 1979.

Schein, Jerome D.: *The Deaf Community: Studies in the Social Psychology of Deafness.* Washington, D.C., Gallaudet College, 1968.

Schein, Jerome D. and Delk, Jr., Marcus, T.: *The Deaf Population of the United States.* Silver Spring, National Association of the Deaf, 1974.

Scull, Andrew T.: *Decarceration: Community Treatment and the Deviant; A Radical View.* Englewood Cliffs, Prentice-Hall, 1977.

Tomlinson, Sally: *A Sociology of Special Education.* London, Routledge and Kegan Paul, 1982.

CONTENTS

UNDERSTANDING DEAFNESS
SOCIALLY

CHAPTER 1

THE DEMOGRAPHY OF DEAFNESS

JEROME D. SCHEIN

K NOWLEDGE of the size and distribution of deaf people in any
given country can contribute importantly to understanding deafness in that milieu. Analysis of additional demographic factors, such as
the deaf population's civil status and economic condition, sheds further
light on the meaning of deafness. The information places deaf people
within a social structure, establishing a context for the actions and reactions of this minority group, and it provides epidemiological evidence
that bears upon the factors giving rise to deafness and, hence, to associated conditions that influence not only its incidence but also its likely
concomitants, such as poverty, disease, and other predispositions to
physical disability.

Implicit in the preceding paragraph is the philosophical stance that
the meaning of deafness is culturally determined, that deaf people in one
society may be at more or less of a disadvantage than those in some
other setting. A corollary to that assumption is that attitudes of a society
are shaped, to some degree, by demographic factors — in this instance,
by the size of the deaf population. Put another way, the relative number
of deaf people influences how the nondeaf majority reacts to them.

A further corollary states that the meaning of deafness can best by
apprehended by seeing it as a social condition rather than a disease or
even a physical disability. Taken from that stance, the demography of
deafness plays a key role in explicating phenomena that might otherwise
be simply esoteric or, worse, misinterpreted.[1] At the same time, we do
not deny that deafness can be usefully studied as a physical disability,
only that the medical description of deafness does not fully anticipate its
social consequences.

SOURCES OF DATA

In what follows, most of the data about deafness come from fairly recent studies done in the United States. This restricted view of the field is not deliberately chauvinistic, but stems from the paucity of demographic studies available from other countries and from the need to establish a consistent basis for comparing data gathered by diverse methods, at different times, from different locales. Of particular interest are accounts from so-called Third World countries, those that are less well-developed economically. These countries, however, are least apt to invest their slender resources in studying their disabled populations. As the minister of an economically depressed African country once said in response to my urging that his nation should undertake a population survey to determine the prevalence of various disabilities, "Why bother counting our disabled children, when we cannot afford to educate all who are able-bodied!" That rhetorical question points up one of many difficulties encountered in seeking demographic information from around the world. To a large extent, then, demographic studies come from well-developed countries, limiting the confidence that can be placed in generalizations drawn from the data that will be presented here. The reader is well-advised to view the inferences emerging from this account with reservations: as more data become available from other countries, its conclusions may prove to be culturally bound beyond present expectations. A properly conservative attitude would be that the conclusions drawn from present studies hold in a particular economic and social context, principally that defined by what is usually called "Western culture."

A second difficulty in cross-cultural comparisons of deaf people is the lack of a uniform definition of deafness. In order to avoid sowing more confusion in a field already beset by varied use of the same word to mean widely different things, the definition of deafness used in this essay is presented immediately below.

DEFINITIONS

Deafness is the common outcome of diverse causes, not the result of a single etiological agent. Accidents, heredity, illnesses, injuries — all can cause deafness. Common parlance tends to use "deaf" to mean any significant loss of hearing. At the other extreme, deafness implies no ability to hear at all. In addition to cause and degree of impairment and depending upon the interests of whatever group coins the definition, it may include other factors (Shein, 1968). Audiologists define deafness in terms of auditory thresholds for pure tones; educators include speech and language development in their definitions; otologists focus on tissue pathology. None of these definitions is **the** correct one; each attests to another viewpoint. Increasingly these semantic variations have given way to a consensus centering on spoken communication, leading to the definition that will be used throughout this chapter: **Deafness is the inability to hear and understand speech through the ear alone.**

The definition specifies that ordinary receptive communication is disordered; thus, it must be noted that the deaf person may **hear** speech but cannot **understand** (i.e., discriminate) it. By the phrase "through the ear alone," the use of vision, as in lipreading, is not considered in determining if a person is deaf, even though most deaf persons find their vision essential to meaningful interpersonal communication. In other words, the definition does not say that deaf people are unable to communicate, only that they cannot communicate by means of audition. By eliminating such other considerations as whether or not the deaf person speaks—a factor largely determined by age at onset and education—the definition facilitates its use in social research. An extended discussion of this particular definition in relation to others prevailing at the time can be found in Schein & Delk (1974).

It is gratifying to note that since its introduction, this definition has gained widespread acceptance, albeit in a variety of linguistic guises (see, for example, Frisina, 1974). An increased uniformity in the use of the term **deafness** means a correspondingly great increase in the value of research that makes use of the term. Apparent contradiction in results are often easily resolved by pointing out that two studies of "deafness" are actually dealing with different phenomena. Once assured that the same definition applies in a variety of studies, their results can be confidently combined—a great advantage to scientists.

Age at Onset

Because a person's age at the time of communicative hearing is lost greatly influences the effects of deafness, the definition's users have adopted a convention to account for it: they either specify age at onset precisely (e.g., deafness occurring at a specific age) or categorically by use of adjectives (e.g., "prelingual" or "senescent"). Including that factor in the definition of deafness makes comparisons to other chronic physical disabilities difficult and obscures trends within data on deafness. Thus, where **deaf** is used without modification, it should refer to all ages at onset. Among the adjectives used, two will appear frequently in this chapter: **prelingual,** by which is meant before age 3, and **prevocational,** by which is meant before 19 years of age.

Degree of Impairment

Another point deserves mention here. Concentrating on one end of the auditory continuum — the extreme of disability — should not obviate the necessity for auditory researchers to determine the functions of whatever factors they deem relevant over the range of hearing impairments. Failure to do so calls into question the validity of the lawful relations they hope to evince from their data. For the time being, however, huge gaps exist in the available information about hearing-impaired individuals. Typical studies do not sample the full range of hearing abilities or do not provide sufficient information about samples that do include persons with hearing impairments from mild to profound. In the final section, this point will be pursued further in relation to understanding deafness through demography.

SIZE OF THE POPULATION

What is the size of the deaf population? Answers depend on (a) how deafness is defined, (b) the time at which the question is posed, and (c) the location of the population.

Early Deafness: Geographical Dispersion

The magnitude of the range of prevalence estimates can be demonstrated by examining data in Table 1. The prevalence rates are from countries that conducted national surveys (censuses) in the last half century. All of the rates in Table 1 are for "deaf mutes," a term that is no longer in favor among scientists, since it implies that there is a **necessary** relationship between early deafness and mutism. As noted above, the preferred way to indicate age at onset is by appending an adjective: thus, prelingual deafness would be preferred over deaf-mute for the data in Table 1, since they refer to deaf persons who do not speak.

Peru reports the highest proportion of prelingually deaf persons in its population, 300 per 100,000, a rate obtained in its 1940 census. Austra-

Table 1

Prevalence Rates per 100,000 Population for Prelingual Deafness[a]
in General-Population Census: Various Countries, 1930-1974

Country	Year	Rate
Peru	1940	300
Honduras	1935	138
Finland	1950	131
Japan	1947[b]	118
	1970	225
Switzerland	1953	94
Sweden	1930	87
Iceland	1948	76
India	1931	66
Canada	1941	63
Egypt	1937	60
Belgium	1950	60
	1974	51
Norway	1930	53
Union of South Africa	1936[c]	49
France	1946	47
United States	1930	47
	1971	100
Northern Ireland	1956	45
Denmark	1940	43
West Germany	1950	43
Mexico	1940	39
	1974	46
Australia	1933	35

[a]Most countries referred to this condition as deaf-mutism. See text for discussion of terminology.
[b]Census limited to persons 3 to 39 years of age.
[c]Only the European population counted.

Source: Adapted from Schein, 1973

lia shows the lowest rate, 35.1 per 100,000, a figure from its 1933 census. The other countries fall between these nearly tenfold extremes. Though some of the discrepancies in the rates may be due to methods of gathering the data, the disparities can hardly be reconciled by reference to methodology alone. To a large extent, they likely approximate true differences in the proportions of their populations that have become deaf in early childhood **at the time of the surveys.**

Table 2

Rates per 100,000 for Prevocational Deafness and Deafness Without
Regard to Age at Onset by Regions: United States, 1971

Region[a]	Deafness[b]	Prevocational Deafness[c]
United States	873	203
Northeast	697	173
North Central	965	242
South	895	196
West	931	194

[a]Regions are those established by the U.S. Bureau of the Census.
[b]Deafness without regard to age at onset.
[c]Deafness occurring before 19 years of age.

Source: Schein & Delk, 1974

Rates within countries also show marked variations. Early studies of
Argentinian and Peruvian census data showed that rates tend to be lowest in coastal regions and highest in isolated mountainous terrain in the
countries' interiors (Schein, 1973). Figures from the U.S. show similar
trends, as shown in Table 2. Consistently, studies of the U.S. have
shown that prevalence rates for deafness are lowest in the Northeastern
and highest in the North Central region. The findings have been ac-
counted for by the summation of a series of vectors:[2] coastal areas tend
to have (a) milder climates, (b) better economic conditions, (c) less consanguinity, and (d) adequate iodine in the diet. Regardless of the explanation, it should be clear that rates established for one region of a
country will probably not be the same for another. Even more emphati-
cally, the proportion of a population that is deaf, regardless of age at onset, in one country will differ markedly from that of another, even
contiguous, country; for example (in rates per 100,000 population),
Sweden's 86.9 vs. Norway's 53.0; Switzerland's 93.7 vs. France's 47.0.
These data demonstrate the fallacy of trying to estimate hearing impairment within one region from rates derived in another region, even when
the regions are adjacent areas of the same country.

Early Deafness: Chronological Factors

Referring again to Table 1, the two figures for the U.S. — 47 and 100
per 100,000 — indicate the likelihood that the prevalence rate for prelingual deafness has increased between 1930 and 1971. The 1930 figure is

based on the instructions that the U.S. Bureau of the Census gave its enu-
merators: to count as deaf those people whose deafness occurred before 8
years of age. The latter rate is for prelingual deafness, defined as deafness
occurring before 3 years of age. Since setting a later age at onset should
lead to larger numbers of persons being classified as deaf, the fact that the
1930 estimate is lower than the 1971 emphasizes the probability that the
relative presence of deafness in the United States has grown substantially
in recent years. Similarly, Japan appears to have an upwardly accelerat-
ing rate for deafness, though the 1947 and 1970 findings are not strictly
comparable; the former applies to only a portion of the population, while
the latter rate applies to all ages. The two estimates for Mexico also shows
the later one to be higher, but not so for Belgium, where the most recent
prevalence rate for prelingual deafness is lower. In general, where two
rates are available for the same locale, the later rate tends to be higher,
suggesting that the prevalence of deafness throughout the world may be
increasing.[3] However, this statement needs considerable qualification before it can be accepted. The dramatic drop in the prevalence of deafness
in Switzerland is a classic epidemiological story (De Reynier, 1959). On
the other hand, major epidemics can greatly increase the amount of deafness in neonates (Fraser, 1976). Also, as will be discussed below, the age-
sex composition of a particular locale bears strongly upon the prevalence
of hearing impairment in that region.

Hearing Impairment Over Time

Since establishment of the National Health Survey (NHS), in 1956,
three special studies of the prevalence of hearing impairment in the non-
institutionalized population of the U.S. three years of age and older
have been conducted (Gentile, Schein, & Haase, 1969; Gentile, 1975;
Ries, 1982). Because NHS does not make use of the term deaf, we compare rates per 1,000 for the broader category that includes all degreees of
hearing impairment. These have grown from 43.7, in 1963, to 69.0, in
1971, and 70.2, in 1977. Since similar (though not identical) methods
were followed in the three surveys, a methodological explanation for the
increases is not reasonable. What is clear is that rates calculated for one
period of time will not hold for another period **even in the same locale.**
Thus, while historical rates have ample value for a number of purposes,
they are not satisfactory for current administration, and their stability
over time should not be taken for granted. Change appears to be more
likely than constancy.

AGE AND SEX

Major factors associated with the prevalence of deafness in a given locale, at a given time are the age-sex distribution of the population at interest. Two generalizations with respect to age and sex can be made at
the onset. First, men experience proportionally more hearing impairment than women. This finding holds across ages, ages at onset, and de-
gress of impairment in almost all studies. The second is that rates for
hearing impairment increase with age.

Table 3

Rates per 1,000 Persons Three Years of Age and Over Reporting
Trouble Hearing, by Age and Sex: United States, 1971 and 1977

Sex and Age (in years)	Rates per 1,000 Population	
	1971	1977
Both Sexes, All ages 3 years +	69.0	70.2
3-16	16.2	16.3
17-24	26.5	20.5
25-44	44.7	41.4
45-64	100.0	107.3
65 and over	274.1	261.9
Males, All ages 3 years +	80.9	83.2
3-16	17.8	18.3
17-24	34.9	22.9
25-44	55.7	56.4
45-64	128.6	141.4
65 and over	326.2	313.4
Females, All ages 3 years +	58.1	58.0
3-16	14.5	14.1
17-24	18.9	18.1
25-44	34.5	27.4
45-64	74.1	76.4
65 and over	235.9	225.7

Source: Adapted from Ries, 1982

Table 3 provides a comparison of rates from the last two NHS reports. In these surveys, the two generalizations about sex and age stand
without exception: proportionally more hearing impairments are re-

ported by men than women, and by older than younger persons.[4] These points hold for all age-by-sex categories. Rates for corresponding categories in the two surveys, however, differ, likely reflecting sampling variability, with two exceptions: the increase for all ages combined and the sizable increase shown in those 45-to-64 years of age. These appear to reflect basic changes in prevalences due to increased hearing impairments from such factors as noise exposure (Miller & Silverman, 1984).

PREDICTED PREVALENCES OF HEARING IMPAIRMENT

What about the future? Do present trends presage what lies ahead with respect to the prevalence of hearing impairment? The strong relation between age and hearing impairment means a continuing increase in the overall prevalence of this disorder. By 2000, the overall prevalence rate is projected to 90 per 1,000. For persons 65 years of age and over, the prediction calls for a rate of 460 per 1,000. These prognostications should be read with the recognition that they are based on the assumption that the current aging trends in the population will continue. At present, 11.6% of the population is 65 years of age and over. By the year 2000, this percent is expected to increase to 13.0%. Since a large share of that 12% increase will be due to greater longevity, and since the longer people live, the greater the likelihood of hearing impairment, the prediction that the relative prevalence of hearing impairment will grow follows logically. Consider further that for 2050, the forecasted rates for hearing impairment are 11.8% for the total population and 59.0% for those 65 years of age and over (Schein, 1985).

RACE OR COLOR

In every decennial census of the United States, from 1830 to 1930, the proportion of white deaf persons has exceeded the proportion of non-white deaf persons (Schein & Delk, 1974). NHS has found similar results for all degrees of hearing impairment in the three special studies it conducted in 1963, 1971, and 1977. In 1963, the rates per 1,000 for bilateral hearing impairment were 23 for whites and 15 for non-whites. The difference has grown; in 1977, it was 39 for whites and 18 for non-whites. While the findings are consistent across studies, attempts to account for them are not. Explanations have varied from genetic (Post, 1964), to economic (Stewart, 1986; Works Progress Administration, 1942), to methodologic (Schein & Delk, 1974). Probably all of these factors contribute in some degree to the substantial discrepancy in rates of hearing impairment for the two groups.[5]

DEGREE OF HEARING IMPAIRMENT

Hearing impairment is one of the most prevalent, chronic physical disabilities in the U.S. Its overall prevalence rate is approximately 70 per 1,000. Deafness, on the other hand, is relatively rare, occurring at a rate of about 8 per 1,000. Prelingual deafness has an estimated rate of 1 per 1,000. Research interest has focussed on the latter group, suggesting that there is a "rule" that research occurs in inverse proportion to the size of the population affected: the fewer persons, the more studies. With respect to hearing impairment, the rule further specifies that as age at onset increases, research interest declines: the earlier the onset of deafness, the more studies. In what follows, then, much of the evidence on the psychological, social, and economic consequences of hearing impairment derive from studies of persons deafened at birth or in early childhood. This evidential skew should be borne in mind, since, as noted above, degree of impairment and age at onset determine, to some extent, hearing impairment's effects.

The frequency of occurrence of deafness is of social-psychological importance, because the relative rarity of early deafness means that those who are so characterized form a minority group in the population. As will be pursued in the various sections, the point is that many aspects of the behavior of early deafened people would be differently construed, if they were not such a small proportion of the population.

THE DEAF FAMILY

Nine out of ten deaf children come from nuclear families that have no deaf members (Schein & Delk, 1974). This fact means that the deaf child will be raised by parents who were unprepared for her or his deafness, who cannot depend upon their own experiences for critical decisions about the child, who will not have natural empathic responses to guide them in rearing the child. The consequences of that parent-child mismatch have been boldly outlined by Schlesinger & Meadow (1971). By contrast, deaf children born to deaf parents tend to be better adjusted to school and to develop language more readily (Meadow, 1980).

When early deafened people marry they tend to choose deaf spouses (Schein & Delk, 1974). The rates vary somewhat by the age at onset and other factors, but deaf-by-deaf marriages occur approximately at a ratio of 9 to 1. So far as research has been concerned with this topic, it shows that the choice of a deaf marital partner by deaf people is a matter of preference for someone who will be compatible, shares a common background, and is easy to communicate with (Rainer et al., 1963).

On the average, marriages involving deaf people result in **normally hearing** offspring in about 9 out of 10 live births. Again, the rates vary by ages at onset of the parent, with two prelingually deaf parents more apt to have a deaf offspring than two postlingually deaf parents. The fact remains that, insofar as deafness is concerned, the typical deaf person is isolated from his or her own parents and children. The odds favor parents of deaf children being normally hearing, and the children of deaf-by-deaf marriages being normally hearing. These facts have interesting consequences for the sociological development of deaf people, though their implications have not had the study they deserve. In part, the isolation imposed by these circumstances may contribute to the relative strength in the development of the Deaf Community. Finding communication difficult with their parents and their offspring, deaf adults may turn more readily to their deaf peers for the bulk of their social lives, enhancing the importance of the Deaf Community.

EDUCATION OF DEAF CHILDREN

Until recently, the education of deaf children in the U.S. has largely been with other deaf children. Furthermore, the bulk of deaf students attended residential schools. The passage of federal policy opposing "segregated" educational facilities for disabled children (P.L. 94-142) has altered that trend. By 1980, the majority of deaf students have been found in day classes. A small proportion of deaf students are in regular classes ("the mainstream"), though determining this number is difficult, due to diagnostic vagaries. A child who is deaf and mute may be classified as "speech impaired." Conversely, children with relatively mild degrees of hearing impairment may be classified as "hard of hearing." Despite these confounding factors, the broad outlines of the change that has occurred in the education of U.S. deaf students are clear: they are increasingly dispersed within the educational system. Studies probing the effects of dispersal are now underway. Until their results become available, the effects of this public policy will remain in doubt.

One welcome change that has occurred since 1970 is the increase in the proportion of deaf students who pursue their higher education. From 1900—when they attended colleges and universities at about the same rate as the general population—through 1960, the proportion of deaf students who went to higher-education institutions remained virtually constant, while the corresponding proportion for the general population dramatically increased (Schein & Bushnaq, 1962). While far from catching up with their nondeaf peers, deaf students appear to be reducing their relative disadvantage, since Section 504 of the Rehabilitation Act of 1973 requires all institutions receiving federal support to make their facilities accessible to disabled persons. For deaf students, this law has meant the removal of restrictions against their admission solely because of their deafness and the ready availability of interpreters and other important educational accommodations in institutions that they choose to attend.

OCCUPATION AND INCOME

Early deafened people work in all United States industries, holding positions that span the occupational hierarchy from laborers to professional and technical workers. On the average, however, deaf persons tend to have been concentrated in the craftsmen and operative categories, far more so than the general population (Schein & Delk, 1974). Their labor-force participation, rates of employment, and average earnings are below those of comparable groups in the general population. A detailed discussion of these and additional points will be found in Chapter 8.

COMMUNICATION

An important demographic aspect of deafness is communication. How do deaf people communicate with each other? with members of the larger community? Table 4 presents some data on these critical questions. In their daily contacts, deaf people make use of speech almost half the time, and those who direct messages to them do so vocally about the

Table 4

Percent Distribution[a] of Communication Methods Used by Respondents
with Various Categories of Persons: United States, 1972

Communication Methods	To Sales Clerk	To Super-visor	By Super-visor	To Others at Work	By Others at Work
Speech	32	26	26	28	27
Manual	1	2	2	3	3
Writing	37	25	22	18	15
Gesture	4	4	4	3	4
Speech + Manual	*	2	3	5	5
Speech + Writing	13	17	13	9	11
Speech + Gesture	3	2	4	3	3
Writing + Gesture	5	4	6	5	5
Other Combinations	6	12	20	26	26

*Less than 0.5%

[a]% rounded to nearest whole number.

Source: Adapted from Schein & Delk, 1974.

same amount of time. The second most frequent form of communication to and by the deaf person is writing. Sign language plays the least part, being used less frequently than gestures **in the situations described.** However, in interactions with other deaf people and with the small portion of the nondeaf population that knows it, sign language is the prevocationally deaf person's preferred mode of communication.

To clarify what this discrepancy is apt to mean to deaf people, the data in Table 5 are offered here. Deaf people judge their own ability to speak as good less than half the time. For those without college education, from 1 to 12 to 1 in 6 do not speak at all. A little over half of the college-educated deaf persons regard their lipreading skills as good, the majority of those with less than 13 years of education consider their lipreading to be fair, poor, or non-existent. By contrast, the majority of deaf respondents rated their signing ability as good. Very few claimed no signing ability. Thus, it would appear that in their daily contacts with the general population — whether at work or in commerce — deaf people must depend upon skills with which they are uncomfortable and for which many have inadequate competence.

The cement that binds the Deaf Community is American Sign Language (Ameslan). Like other minority-language communities, deaf people have had to struggle to maintain their unique system of com-

Table 5

Percent Distribution of Communication Ability as Judged by Respondent,
by Highest School Grade Completed for Respondents 25 to 64 Years
of Age: United States, 1972

Rating by Communication Mode	Highest School Grade Completed[a]			
	1-8	9-12	13-16	17+
Speech				
Good	18	31	47	54
Fair	42	41	39	27
Poor	25	19	12	13
None	16	9	2	6
Lipreading				
Good	24	41	55	54
Fair	40	37	37	33
Poor	26	15	4	10
None	11	7	4	2
Signing				
Good	66	70	59	65
Fair	22	17	18	10
Poor	7	6	4	6
None	7	8	21	21

[a] % rounded to nearest whole number.

Source: Adapted Schein & Delk, 1974

munication (Lane, 1976; Schein, 1984). Ameslan is not "English on the hand," not just another code for the spoken language. It is a language in its own right. Those who use it are usually those who were born deaf or lost their hearing in childhood. Persons deafened in adulthood usually do not become members of the Deaf Community. Those who do join use manual communication (Higgins, 1980; Schein & Delk, 1974). Ameslan is the lingua franca of the Deaf Community.

How many people in the U.S. use manual communication? To answer that frequently asked question requires taking advantage of bits and pieces of information, for no specific study of its use by the general population has been made. First, the terms **use** and **sign language** must be defined. Anyone who communicates manually for more than one hour per week is a "user;" e.g., interpreters and people who work with deaf clients. This definition is different from one that asks, How many people **know** sign? That question would be difficult to investigate, because communicating a definition of knowledge in a household survey require a great deal of explanation. In place of sign language, **manual communication** is substituted, in order to avoid having to distinguish its various forms, of which Ameslan is only one. Next users are divided into two groups: deaf people and the general population. The results are displayed in Table 6, which shows that somewhat over 2 million people are probably using manual communication in the U.S.

Table 6

Estimated Number of Persons Who Use Manual Communication, by Group: United States, 1980

Group	Total Number in Group[a]	Percent Who Use Sign[b]	Number Who Use Sign
All Groups	226,534,000	1.0	2,121,428
Deaf, age at onset before 19	480,000	86.0	413,500
Deaf, age at onset 19 +	1,350,000	10.0	135,000
Nondeaf persons	224,704,000	0.7	1,572,928

[a]Rounded off to whole numbers

Additional support for this estimate can be inferred from related activities. Local classes of instruction in manual communication began with a grant to the National Association of the Deaf, in 1963. Since that time, colleges, universities, high schools, church groups, and private organizations have sponsored sign-language instruction. It is possible to take a sign class in virtually every part of the U.S. Sales of books on sign language have dramatically increased from 1960 to the present, with no indication of abatement. Television programs teaching sign date back to the mid 1960s, when the U.S. Office of Education sponsored a program series shown on PBS. In the 1970s, "Speaking with your Hands," a program of 10 lessons in sign, was shown on over 100 NBC stations, and it continues to be displayed occasionally. Federally sponsored programs to train sign-language interpreters have been in existence since 1974, with ten currently funded. Altogether, then, it would appear that the estimate is reasonable (Schein, 1984).

METHODOLOGICAL CONSIDERATIONS

This section confronts the problems that face demographers and epidemiologists in studying deafness. Some difficulties affect the study of any morbid condition; some are specific to deafness. As noted earlier, these issues are introduced here as an antidote against too ready acceptance of interpretations of population data, and also to encourage the kinds of programs that are needed to correct gaps and defects in our present data. It is sad to find that, demographically, the United States is among the underdeveloped countries of the world. During the period from 1960 through about 1975, strides were being made to obtain adequate information about the disabled population of the United States. However, the era of budget-cutting and the cry for less government interference in the lives of citizens have drastically slowed the efforts to maintain a clear picture of the nation's health — or more accurately of the health of its citizens.

The Decennial Census

From 1830 to 1930, the U.S. decennial censuses reported on the numbers and principal characteristics of deaf, blind, and deaf-blind persons. After the eleventh decennial, the Bureau of the Census asked Congress to relieve it of this responsibility. Table 7 shows the rates of deafness per 100,000 obtained over that period. They vary from 32.1 to 67.5, a range of estimates that led the author of the Bureau's report to conclude, "No high degree of accuracy is to be expected in a census of the blind and of deaf-mutes carried out by the methods which it has been necessary to use thus far in the United States" (U.S. Bureau of the Census, 1932).

Table 7

Prevalences and Prevalence Rates per 100,000 for Deaf-Mutism:[a]
United States Decennial Census, 1830 — 1930

Census Year	Number	Rate per 100,000
1930	57,084	46.5
1920	44,885	42.5
1910	44,708	48.6
1900	24,369	32.1
1890	40,592	64.8
1880	33,878	67.5
1870	16,205	42.0
1860	12,821	40.8
1850	9,803	42.3
1840	7,678	45.0
1830	6,106	47.5

[a]Term used by the Bureau to indicate deafness of onset before 8 years of age

Source: U.S. Bureau of the Census, 1931

The principal difficulty encountered by the Bureau in its enumeration of deaf persons was its failure to operationally define what it meant by "deaf-mutism." How were census takers instructed to identify such individuals? Without specific, objective criteria, decisions would be left to the whims of thousands of individuals, an obviously unsatisfactory situation. That this problem can be solved economically has been demonstrated (Schein, Gentile, & Haase, 1970; Schein & Delk, 1974). That the Bureau opted to leave the field rather than solve it, displays its lack of interest, not its lack of expertise.

While preparations were being made for the 1980 decennial census, the Bureau was again requested to reinstitute enumerations of disabilities. Those making the request were unmindful of the earlier history of this activity. They were impressed by the Bureau's former reputation as one of the world's great statistical organizations, a reputation that has declined due to budget cuts and intimations of political interference.

Fortunately, the Bureau did not carry out the plan it proposed in response to the pressures it was getting. The Bureau offered to initiate a voluntary survey; i.e., persons identified as disabled in the Census would be given a form that they could complete, if they wished to do so. From such data accurate prevalence rates could not be calculated. Indeed, whatever information was gathered would not have been directly interpretable, since the non-response rates could not be determined by the procedures proposed. Advocates of such haphazard methods sometimes argue that "some data is better than none." In fact, the opposite is more often true. Data gathered by the Bureau would be treated as gospel. Most people would assume that whatever was released as part of the Census was conducted in the same painstaking manner as applied to the overall effort. Thus, little could be done to correct the misinformation. Any attempts to mount a proper study would be met with the complaint that it had already been done by the Bureau. As the Bureau's own statements attest, it is capable of producing inaccurate information, and unlike lesser data gatherers, its missteps almost totally impeded corrective efforts.

Incidence vs. Prevalence

Most of the preceding data have been what demographers and epidemiologists call prevalences or prevalence rates which differ from incidences or incidence rates.

Incidence refers to the number of new cases of a particular condition arising in a given period of time.

Prevalence is the number of all cases of the condition existing at a particular time.

A moment's reflection should convince the reader that these are distinct concepts, incidence measuring the rate at which cases are accruing, and prevalence the number of afflicted individuals living at a specified time. Except under special circumstances, the incidence of a chronic condition cannot be determined from successive prevalences, because affected people may die, move from the area being studied, or recover from the condition. Therefore, the difference between two prevalences for any condition may reflect mortality, migration, or remission, rather than the incidence of the condition, masking the addition of new cases (if the rates are the same) or overestimating an increase in the condition (if the increase results from afflicted persons moving into the area.) To gather each kind of information requires specifically designed procedures. It is also worth noting that incidence and prevalence are numbers. Incidence and prevalence **rates** are determined by dividing the numbers by the appropriate population at risk.

With respect to hearing impairment in the United States, almost no reliable incidence data are available. Occasional crude estimates have been made, but determining the number of **new** cases has not captured the attention of investigators of hearing impairments. For 1935-36, the National Health Survey (ad hoc predecessor to the present organization of the same name) attempted to arrive at the incidence of deafness by taking the differences between successive age groups (Beasley, 1940). That strategy overlooks the fact that incidence is apt to vary with both cause and type of impairment, a fact not taken into consideration in deriving the estimates and, thus, invalidating them.

Usefulness of Incidence Data

Illustrating the importance of obtaining incidence, changes in incidence rates have been highly dramatic in Switzerland. From 1915 to 1922, the number of deaf neonates ranged from 120 to 170 per 100,000 births. The rate dropped to 40 per 100,000 in 1925 as a result of preventive measures introduced (Trotter, 1960). While the substantial decrease in the incidence rates stands out, the corresponding changes in overall prevalences would not immediately reflect the declines, since infants are only a small fraction of the population. Emphasizing the independence of incidence and prevalence should support the importance of having both kinds of information.

Spectacular events, like the rubella epidemics which affect fetuses whose mothers are infected, also call attention to the value of incidence data. In the 1963-65 rubella epidemics in the United States, numbers of deaf and deaf-blind children were added at a far greater rate than would be normally expected. An estimated excess over normal expectation of 35-40,000 deaf children occurred during those years, which represents a rate for the period of about 360 deaf neonates per 100,000 live births, as opposed to the rate of 50 to 90 per 100,000 that has often been estimated for deafness at birth in the United States.

This marked increase in the incidence of deafness in newborns created what has been referred to as the "rubella bulge." The term emphasizes the greater-than-usual number of affected children born. The U.S. Congress reacted to the huge increase in the number of deaf children with legislation that has provided more funds with which to deal with the problems created by the bulge as it passes from age group to age group. However, studies of data from 1900 to 1950 make it clear that other epidemics have occurred from time to time in various parts of this country, leading to sharp fluctuations in the numbers of born-deaf children (Fraser, 1976). The search for **one** incidence rate for deafness in a given region makes no sense: periodic variations in incidence should be expected and carefully examined.

Opposition to Programs Yielding Incidence Data

Why are not incidence rates collected? The answer appears to be a lack of interest, not a lack of methodology. Infant screening programs could provide incidence data for neonates. Such programs would enable intervention to be undertaken early, a strategy urged by most experts on the care of hearing-impaired children. Yet routine neonatal auditory screening has been opposed by some audiologists on the grounds that present procedures yield too many false positives. This peculiar argument implies that practitioners would upset parents by incorrectly advising them about their children's hearing instead of properly alerting them to the **possibility** of such a problem and urging them to obtain follow-up testing. Expense has also been raised as an objection to routine screening. Again, however, that argument exaggerates the modest amount required, while underplaying the benefits that would be derived from earlier identification (Campanelli & Schein, 1969). Critics point to the fact that the low incidence of hearing impairment might mean testing 1,000 children to identify one in need of treament. However, these critics do not object to putting silver nitrate in every child's eyes, even though the rate for maternal syphillis is less than 1 per 3,000. Against the expenditure of a dollar or less per child should be weighed the benefits of early detection of unanticipated hearing impairment.

Other potential sources of incidence data are the screening programs in public schools. Reporting the results of such annual efforts would provide useful data, provided they adequately met the standards for such procedures (Martin & Sides, 1985). Even rates of failures to pass audiometric screening levels are seldom found in the literature, indicating lack of interest in incidence data. Such neglect impedes research, misleads planners, and ultimately damages the provision of services.

Additional Disabilities

Any study of deafness that does not attempt to account for the presence of additional disabilities must be considered methodologically flawed. A study cannot logically contend that its results solely reflect the influence of deafness, unless it controls for other disabilities that might account for the results. How likely are early deafened people to have other disabilities? Almost 1 of 3 deaf students have been found to have an additional educationally handicapping condition (Schein, 1979). Most critically for their education, these students have far greater rates of visual impairments than are found in the general population. Since deafness makes one visually dependent, this finding should particularly concern administrators of educational programs (Schein, 1980). The national study of prevocationally deaf adults also found that 1 of 3 reported an additional disability. For the social scientist, then, these statistics signal a clear warning to include procedures to identify additionally disabling conditions among prevocationally deaf people being studied.

SUMMARY AND CONCLUSIONS

A major stumbling block to research on the demography of deafness has been the lack of a uniform definition of the condition. Using a functional definition of deafness, one that focuses on spoken communication, resolves much of the difficulties that have plagued demographers who have tried to combine data from different studies. This resolution has gained increasingly wide acceptance among a variety of professionals involved in the field. As consensus on terminology is achieved, it contributes to improved understanding of deafness.

Analyses of available data make clear that incidence and prevalence rates for deafness vary by locale and time. Some factors associated with geography have been identified (e.g., diet, economics, and consanguinity), but more may be uncovered by intensive analysis of particular regions. Three factors appear to contribute the major portion of the variation in prevalence rates over time for a particular region: age, sex, and epidemics.

Race also seems to be a contributing factor in determining the prevalence of hearing impairment. No answers as to why whites tend to have greater prevalence rates for deafness than non-whites have been widely accepted. With respect to hearing impairment from otitis media, non-white populations have higher prevalence rates, generally attributed to poorer medical care. But lower prevalence rates for deafness, especially among negroes, remains a perplexing result open to competing explanations.

Some interesting relations emerge when deafness is considered in terms of family life. The majority of deaf children have normally hearing parents; when grown, the majority choose deaf spouses, and the offsprings of these marriages are typically normally hearing. The full meaning of these facts about family life for the typical deaf person have not been realized by researchers. In general, however, they appear to have a strong bearing on the social structure of the Deaf Community.

Another factor that is apt to have a substantial impact on the Deaf Community is the changed educational settings from which U.S. deaf students are now emerging. Earlier in this century, the majority attended residential schools with other deaf students. Today, the majority are in day classes or in regular classes, greatly increasing their daily contacts with normally hearing age peers. This fact, along with the increased opportunities for deaf students to attend colleges and universities other than Gallaudet College and the National Technical Institute for the Deaf, has the potential for greatly altering the character of the Deaf Community.

Economically, prevocationally deaf adults have not done as well as their normally hearing age peers. Employment rates and earnings have tended to be comparatively low. Furthermore, the recent trends suggest that, whenever economic conditions worsen, deaf workers will suffer disproportionately, at least in terms of their earnings.

While no one familiar with deafness would be surprised to find that deaf people must accommodate to the communication preferences of the majority, rather than the other way around, it is nonetheless of interest to estimate the extent to which that fact holds. Considering the emphasis on spoken communication, deaf persons' self-estimates of their speaking and lipreading abilities provide a further testimony to the disadvantages that they face in daily commerce.

Taken together, the findings with respect to geographical and temporal dispersion of deafness should impress administrators of programs for deaf people with the necessity to obtain up-to-date, information specific to their area of operations. Lack of current information about the deaf population of their particular region will hamper the planning, administering, and evaluating of their programs. Sound administration and fruitful research also call for both incidences and prevalences of deafness. The importance of incidence data deserves special attention in view of its paucity. Much information on the occurrence of deafness could be made available without great expense, especially in view of the value of the data in relation to the cost of gathering it. Data-gathering costs, however, should be balanced against the waste of badly planned, poorly administered, mistakenly evaluated programs. Inaccurate information can be far more wasteful of public and private resources than the amounts needed to collect accurate data.

FOOTNOTES

1. Two brief examples illustrate the application of demographic facts to other phenomena. The ancient notion that born-deaf children could not be educated arose from the rarity of surviving deaf adults who would have revealed the lie. So knowing the low prevalence of prelingual deafness assists in understanding, albeit only partially, why society responded as it did to deaf people. As another example, affiliation patterns depend upon the achievement of a "critical mass" (to borrow a term from physics), i.e., a sufficient number of persons must be in contiguity to form a socially significant group. Thus, the changes in the status of deaf persons in the U.S. occurred after the first school was established in Hartford, CT. Within a decade after the school brought together numbers of deaf children, the first organization of deaf persons came into being, and within six decades the National Association of the Deaf emerged as the first group of its kind. Again, the demography contributes to understanding such events.

2. The term **vector** is intended in the epidemiological sense of a factor which, though not directly causing a disease, promotes it. Mosquitoes, for example, do not cause malaria, but they transmit the parasite that does. Similarly, poverty does not cause deafness, but poor people's environments and diets that make them more prone to disease and, when poor people do become ill, they generally have less adequate medical care. In this sense, then, poverty is a vector for deafness.

3. What about methodological improvements in morbidity surveys? So far as deafness is concerned, no foreign census known to this author has taken advantage of the survey techniques developed for the U.S. National Health Survey. However, improvements in sampling design and in interviewing techniques generally might uncover more deaf persons, while not necessarily increasing the rate of deafness, since the same technical improvements would assist in enumerating other disadvantaged groups in the population.

4. The reader is cautioned to recall the distinction made throughout this paper between hearing impairment (all degrees) and deafness (the most severe form of hearing impairment). In the National Census of the Deaf Population (Schein & Delk, 1974) the prevalence rate of prevocational deafness increased markedly in persons 45 years of age and older compared to those under 45 years of age. The proportionally greater prevalence of prevocationally deaf persons relative to their age groups should not be confused with a greater incidence of the condition in the first 19 years of life. For instance, prevocationally deaf males, with rare exceptions, were not accepted in military service and, therefore, were not subject to the same mortality rates as unimpaired males. Many other factors, of course, contribute to the differential prevalence rates at any given age. The generalization about **prevalence** rates holds regardless of corresponding incidence rates, if for no other reason than that people are living longer, including deaf persons.

5. A multifactorial explanation of racial differences in the prevalence of hearing impairments appears most likely to account for the findings. Post may be correct in assuming that there is some genetic predisposition among white persons to diseases of the ear and subsequent hearing impairment. Right or not, that explanation would not contradict the arguments that non-white persons, especially in the U.S., tend to be economically less well-off and, hence, to suffer more diseases and to suffer more from the diseases they do contract because of poorer medical care and substandard nutrition. Consequently, non-white persons do not live as long as white persons and, in particular, they tend to die from diseases, like meningitis, that the white population survives, though suffering deafness as a result. The methodological argument that non-white persons, especially those who are disabled, are less likely to be enumerated in censuses also fits with the remaining arguments. The three explanations summate, leading to the same conclusion that non-white hearing-impaired persons are relatively less frequently found in population surveys. Of course, this resolution leaves unresolved the amount to which each vector contributes to the overall outcome, a question deserving of further intensive study.

REFERENCES

Beasley, W. C.: Characteristics and distribution of impaired hearing in the population of the United States. *Journal of the Acoustical Society of America, 12:*114, 1940.

Campanelli, P. A., and Schein, J. D.: Inter-observer agreement in judging auditory responses in neonates. *Eye Ear Nose Throat Monthly, 48:*697, 1969.

De Reynier, J. P.: La surdi-mutite en Suisse en 1953. *Bibliographie Otorhinolaryngologica, 5:*1, 1959.

Fraser, G. R.: *The Causes of Profound Deafness in Childhood.* Baltimore, Johns Hopkins University Press, 1976.

Frisina, D. R.: *Report of the Committee to Redefine Deaf and Hard of Hearing for Educational Purposes.* 1974. Mimeo.

Gentile, A., Schein, J. D., and Haase, K.: Characteristics of persons with impaired hearing: United States, July 1962-June 1963. *Vital and Health Statistics,* Series 10, No. 35, 1967.

Gentile, A.: Persons with impaired hearing, United States, 1971. *Vital and Health Statistics,* Series 10, No. 101, 1975.

Higgins, P. *Outsiders in a Hearing World.* Beverly Hills, Sage, 1980.

Martin, F. N., and Sides, D. G.: Survey of current and audiometric practices. *Asha, 27:*29, 1985.

Meadow, K. P.: *Deafness and Child Development.* Berkeley, University of California Press, 1980.

Miller, M. H., and Silverman, C. A. (Eds.): *Occupational Hearing Conservation.* Englewood Cliffs, Prentice-Hall, 1984.

Post, R. H.: Hearing acuity variation among negroes and whites. *Eugenics Quarterly, 11:*65, 1964.

Rainer, J. D., Altshuler, K. Z., and Kallmann, F. J. (Eds.): *Family and Mental Health Problems in a Deaf Population.* New York, New York State Psychiatric Institute, Columbia University, 1963.

Rawlings, B. W., Karchmer, M. A., King, S. J., and Brown, S. C.: *Gallaudet College Alumni Survey, 1984.* Washington, D.C., Research Institute, Gallaudet College, 1985.

Ries, P. W.: Hearing ability of persons by sociodemographic and health characteristics: United States. *Vital and Health Statistics,* Series 10, No. 140, 1982.

Schein, J. D.: *The Deaf Community.* Washington, D.C., Gallaudet College Press, 1968.

Schein, J. D.: Hearing disorders. In Kurland, L. T., Kurtzke, J. F., and Goldberg, I. D.: *Epidemiology of Neurologic and Sense Organ Disorders.* Cambridge, Harvard University Press, 1973.

Schein, J. D.: Multiply handicapped hearing-impaired children. In Bradford, L. J. and Hardy, W. G.: *Hearing and Hearing Impairment.* New York, Grune and Stratton, 1979.

Schein, J. D.: How well can you see me? *Teaching Exceptional Children, 12:*55, 1980.

Schein, J. D.: The demography of deafness. In Higgins, P. and Nash, J.: *The Deaf Community and the Deaf Population.* Washington, D.C., Gallaudet College, 1982.

Schein, J. D.: *Speaking the Language of Sign.* New York, Doubleday, 1984.

Schein, J. D.: Hearing impairment among elderly people. *Soundbarrier, 1:*4, 1985.

Schein, J. D., and Bushnaq, S. M.: Higher education for the deaf in the United States: a retrospective investigation. *American Annals of the Deaf, 107:*416, 1962.

Schein, J. D., and Delk, M. T.: *The Deaf Population of the United States.* Silver Spring, National Association of the Deaf, 1974.

Schein, J. D., Gentile, A., and Haase, K.: Development and evaluation of an expanded hearing loss scale questionnaire. *Vital and Health Statistics,* Series 2, No. 37, 1970.

Schlesinger, H. S., and Meadow, K. P.: *Sound and Sign.* Berkeley, University of California Press, 1972.

Stewart, J. L.: Hearing disorders among the indigenous peoples of North America and the Pacific Basin. In Taylor, O. L.: *Nature of Communication Disorders in Culturally and Linguistically Diverse Populations.* San Diego, College-Hill Press, 1986.

Trotter, W. R.: The association of deafness with thyroid dysfunction. *British Medical Bulletin, 16:*92, 1960.

U.S. Bureau of the Census. *The Blind and Deaf-Mutes in the United States: 1930.* Washington, D.C.: U.S. Government Printing Office, 1931.

Works Progress Administration of Georgia. *Georgia's Deaf.* Atlanta, 1942.

CHAPTER 2

UNDERSTANDING DEAFNESS: SOCIALIZATION OF CHILDREN AND YOUTH

KATHRYN P. MEADOW-ORLANS

A LL CHILDREN must learn to operate within the context of their own social groups. The knowledge—or sense—of appropriate ways of behaving and of fulfilling expectations of those around them— comes from observation, from teaching, from the incorporation of manners, modes, beliefs, and values of family members, peers, cultural heroes. This complex understanding which develops over the course of an individual's life, but particularly in the childhood years, has been called "socialization." The term is intended to summarize learning that occurs informally as well as through formal training and teaching. It includes understandings that are arrived at through conscious observation as well as intuitive, long term shifts, and imitation that is done with awareness or without awareness. It includes the processes by which children acquire "knowledge, skills and dispositions that make them more or less able members" of their society (Brim & Wheeler, 1966:3).

In most cultures, parents are the most important socializing agents for a new or infant member of the culture. Parents have both the opportunity for socializing their child in directions they see as appropriate and the responsibility for providing the rules, norms, and avenues for optimal development. There is the notion of a cumulative process, so that new roles, skills and definitions build upon those already acquired. The process has been defined as including the establishment of social ties, the development of language, the achieving of a self-image separate from that of others, learning motivations necessary for social participation, and generally, the social orientation of a child or the reorientation of an adult (Clausen, 1966:250).

It is assumed, in discussions of childhood socialization, that parents will have at their disposal the linguistic means for communicating this complex system of cultural expectations to their young children. It is this crucial assumption that is problematic when severe deafness is present in a young child, and which creates a totally new picture or set of options for socialization.

More than ninety percent of the parents of deaf children have normal hearing themselves (Rawlings & Jensema, 1977). Most of these parents have never known a profoundly deaf individual. For them, two related problems are immediately confronted when deafness is diagnosed in their young infant. First, they must cope with the shock of the presence of an unexpected handicap. Second, they must face the difficulties of socializing their child in the absence of a common—that is, a spoken—linguistic system. This is the central feature of the socialization of deaf children: the language available (or unavailable) to parents for the easy communication of all the skills, values, rules, and games which parents of other children can take for granted.

One group of parents does have command of a linguistic system enabling them to communicate easily with their deaf children. These are parents who are deaf themselves and who therefore are fluent in a sign language system. The socialization of deaf children from these two kinds of families is very different indeed. There are wide variations in socialization patterns and problems of the deaf children in these two groups (that is, the group with deaf parents and the group with hearing parents), but this one dimension helps to explain and underline some of the most basic social processes at work in the lives of deaf children.

For deaf parents, deafness is a familiar condition. They have a wide circle of deaf friends. They probably participate in a community comprised primarily of deaf people (Padden, 1980). They know the educational opportunities available for deaf children, and the vocational possibilities that lie ahead. They can anticipate socializing their deaf child as they themselves were socialized, or perhaps with modifications based on experiences they wish to avoid. For parents with normal hearing, all of these areas provide unknown vistas. Their own socialization experiences may give them few guidelines for the socialization of their deaf child. From their first suspicion of their child's condition, through their contacts with medical, audiological and educational specialists, into the child's preschool, elementary, high school, college or technical training experiences, the deaf parents and the hearing parents of deaf children will have differing understandings and differing expectations. Contrasting the hopes and fears, the expectations and the obligations of deaf and hearing parents of deaf children, it is possible to come to a deeper understanding of the socialization process as it is influenced by the condition of deafness.

THE DIAGNOSIS OF DEAFNESS: A CONTEXT FOR SOCIALIZATION

For most parents with normal hearing, the diagnosis of deafness in a young child comes as a profound shock. Often, the diagnosis confused deafness with other kinds of impairments such as mental retardation or emotional disturbance. The very struggle to achieve a firm medical diagnostic opinion of the child's condition may be debilitating for parents, and interfere with early socialization practices. Parents sometimes are made to feel incompetent to deal with their child's needs, particularly when they are told by medical professionals that their suspicions of "something wrong" are false (Williams & Darbyshire, 1982).

Thus, the very earliest experiences of a hearing parent around their child's deafness may create strong feelings of inadequacy in them. Their own feelings of stress and helplessness can be communicated to the child with resulting spirals of tenseness and helplessness that can contribute to general family chaos. This unhappy scenario is even more likely in families where the deaf child is first-born. Confidence that other parents gain from prior parenting experience cannot emerge in these parents. Sometimes they can look to a supportive extended family for help. For others, this support may come from educational professionals or from other parents with similar experiences. However, many families face the dark days of diagnosis alone. Failure of medical professionals to provide a helping hand is an experience which many parents describe. Here is one example:

> When Sally was about four months old (was when) I discovered it. . . when she started to cry, I couldn't calm her down by talking to her. She would never look at me when I called her. I just knew there was something wrong, only I couldn't put my finger on it. I kept taking her to my doctor, about three or four times, and he thought I was bugs! He said he couldn't see anything wrong with that baby. . .I tried everything I could. He finally sent me to an ear specialist. And he thought I was nuts. He said to me, don't you dare bring that baby back until she's at least fifteen months old because there's no way in the world that you can tell whether she can hear or not. Well, I knew that she was deaf. . .(and) when I knew

she was a deaf mute, I knew there was nothing that could be done for her, like chasing around after doctors and all that. And we couldn't afford it anyway. So I just did the best I could (Meadow, 1968b:301).

In this particular example, the result of the two medical consultations was especially unfortunate. First, the mother was given the message that she was an incompetent observer; second, the child was denied early intervention which might well have given her an important head start in overcoming the handicap of hearing loss. A second example illustrates a similar experience with a different maternal response:

I had a friend who's an ear specialist, so I took Billy to him. He walked behind him, and Billy's head was like a swivel. "Wait till he's three," he said. . . .when he was almost three we took him for (another) hearing test. The doctor ran his thumb across a balloon—Billy can hear that sound to this day. The doctor got the idea he was spoiled: Billy cried and said "Mama" when the doctor slapped his hand. "All he needs is a firm hand at home." We were crushed. My husband stopped on the way home at a store and said he was going to get him a hearing aid. The salesman said she couldn't sell us one over the counter, but she gave us the name of another doctor. When that doctor told us Billy was deaf, I rejoiced. At last I found somebody who understands and doesn't tell me that all he needs is a "firm hand at home." . . .simply to find out that he was deaf. . .Before I was never really sure what to do. Once you know, then you can start to work. At last I found something I could get hold of (Meadow, 1968b:301).

Billy's mother illustrates an important human response that is often evident among the parents of handicapped children: she found the ambiguity of his condition more difficult to bear than the firm diagnosis of the handicap itself. Also, she found it especially difficult to be told by the first physician, a good friend, that she was wrong about her son (an incompetent mother).

Several professionals who have worked extensively with parents and children believe that the diagnosis of a handicap in a young child evokes a response of grief in the parents which is similar to the grief that is felt for the death of a loved one.

Most parents find disability to be the great spoiler of their dreams and fantasies about who or what their child was to be. Most dreams require an unimpaired child; therefore, the initial diagnosis of disability often marks the point when a cherished and significant dream has been shattered (Moses, 1985:86).

The particular processes experienced by many parents of handicapped children have been discussed by several professionals who are experienced in counseling with them. The response to the diagnosis of hearing loss has been described as similar to the reaction to other kinds of crises: shock, recognition, denial, acknowledgement, followed by constructive action (Kubler-Ross, 1969; Luterman, 1984). Although parents may not experience these emotions in any particular order, most hearing parents probably feel this way about their hearing-impaired children at various times and in various ways. Some of the "states of grief" identified by Moses include denial, guilt, depression, anger, anxiety, and coping.

Another response observed by Schlesinger (1985) is a sense of powerlessness in parents of a newly diagnosed deaf child. That is, parents may feel that they should be able to do something to reverse the unwelcome diagnosis. When they are told by medical specialists that "nothing can be done" their sense of being incapable of influencing the destiny of their young child is overpowering for them. Schlesinger believes that the sense of powerlessness continues beyond the child's infancy, and becomes particularly intense when parents begin to try to communicate with the child and are unsuccessful. They then become more and more domineering as they try harder and harder to break through the communication barrier.

The responses of deaf parents to the diagnosis of deafness in a young child may have quite a different quality, compared to those of hearing parents.

Deaf Mother: If we had hearing children, maybe we would worry about speech development, because we can't hear and we're not talking. With deaf children, you don't have to worry about that. That's one advantage of having deaf children. We're able to share more fully with deaf children.

Deaf Father: I can share and discuss things with Steven easier. . .because I've had those same experiences. . .I was deaf and I had deaf parents. You share similar experiences, so it's easier to communicate and share with the children (Erting, 1985:232).

Expectations about a child's hearing status clearly have a major influence on parental responses. However, many factors can influence those expectations.

A deaf couple tells a particularly striking story of the effect of their child's diagnosis of hearing impairment. Both husband and wife had believed their deafness to be the result of non-genetic causes, and therefore assumed their children would have normal hearing. When their first child was two years old, the director of a nursery program for hearing-impaired children urged them to enroll him as part of a "reverse main-streaming" project. One month later, they were shocked to receive a call saying a hearing loss was suspected in the child. The wife reports that "I remember my shock and disbelief when (my husband) came home to tell me the news. It just couldn't be. It was as if someone we loved had died. Certainly something in us died." The husband agreed:

> Yes, it was a shocking blow. I remember all too well how casually the program director notified me of the findings. I fear the error was made of assuming that because we were hearing impaired we would be able to take the news in stride, but the shock was just as great. Not only that, we were, for the first time, forced to look at our own deafness and the defenses we had built up. . . (Thompson, Thompson & Murphy, 1979:338-339).

These first-person accounts illustrate, more dramatically than any theoretical formulations might, the forceful role played by parental expectations in creating their definition of the child's diagnosis. The meaning this situation has for parents is influenced by their own hearing status, by their prior experiences with deafness, the expectations and attitudes of family members about hearing loss, and whether the diagnosis reflects a shift in a prior understanding about the child's hearing status. All of these help to create a context for parents' definitions of the diagnosis. This definition, in turn, creates a context for the socialization of the child at successive stages of life. For parents who know very little about deafness (primarily parents who themselves have normal hearing), the manner in which they are informed of the hearing loss may have an important influence on later behavior as well.

LINGUISTIC ORIENTATION: CONTEXT FOR SOCIALIZATION

Just as the diagnosis of hearing loss creates a context for socialization, cutting across the childhood and adolescence of the deaf child, so does the linguistic orientation of the parents. For hearing parents, decisions about use of sign language versus cued speech versus only spoken English are the ones that will probably be most critical. Nash and Nash have proposed a typology for describing hearing parents of deaf children, in terms of their orientation to language mode (1981:47-61).

They describe oralists as "recruiters" who see the use of sign language as a last resort "used only when a child is hopelessly handicapped" (p.48). These parents proselytize others to their views and follow an active strategy of convincing parents of other deaf children that theirs is the preferred way. The second group of oralists is called "the searchers"—not completely convinced that oral-only education is the complete answer, but continuing to search for medical remediation to normalize their child. The third group, "the aloof," rely on special schools and teachers to "make oralism work" for their deaf child, while they engage in other kinds of activities.

Hearing parents who support the use of sign language are also divided into three types: the first is resigned to its use, feeling that this is the best that can be expected for deaf children, even though it is second best to oralism. The second type of sign language users are called "sign changers." They try to become familiar with the experiences of deaf people, but they prefer to change the sign language of deaf adults into a more English form—one of the artificial sign languages which follows the grammar and syntax of spoken English. The third group of signers among hearing parents, in terms of the Nashes' typology, are the "friends of the deaf." These parents attempt to participate in the deaf community to a greater extent than any of the other hearing parents. Although they probably will not become fluent in American Sign Language, they are sympathetic to the experiences of deaf people, and to their attachment to their own language as an expression of culture or ethnicity.

Regardless of hearing parents' linguistic orientation, if they are committed to the use of sign language, there will be times when the use of a new and unfamiliar language with their child will become taxing. For example, these parents of a four-year-old deaf child describe some of their frustrations around the use of language:

> *Mother:* Most of the time I talk to her and sign at the same time. But there are times I get angry and I talk. Or, there are other times I want her to lipread, so I don't use it. . .
>
> *Father:* If we know she can lipread it, we'll just talk to her. Other times we'll fingerspell because we're trying to get more fingerspelling in (Erting, 1985:232).

There is variation in the linguistic orientations of deaf parents as well as in hearing parents of deaf children. Much of the variation is related to their own childhood experiences. Erting (1985) has described in rich detail the ideas and linguistic attitudes of a group of deaf parents in a school for deaf children in which she was closely involved (see Chapter 6). Memories of their own childhood frustrations in the rote learning of speech and English at school, contrasted with their own feelings of freedom in communicating with other deaf people in sign, contributed to linguistic philosophies for their own children.

THE SOCIALIZATION OF DEAF
CHILDREN DURING INFANCY

Because of the difficulties of diagnosing hearing loss in young infants, few are known to be deaf before they have reached twelve months of age. Thus, there is little information about their socialization during the early months of life, and we can only speculate about how limited auditory contact with the environment may change their responses to their parents or their surroundings. Likewise, we do not know how parents may change their ways of interacting with their infants at this early age. From what we know of hearing parents about the impact of the diagnosis on them, and about their anxieties when they realize that something is "different" about their infant, we can assume that their behaviors are also influenced.

A primary task of very young babies is that of differentiating the "primary caregivers" from other people — of learning that someone dependable is usually available for nurturance, for warmth, for the provision of comfort. We are beginning to appreciate more and more the importance of positive interaction between mothers (or fathers) and their babies in this very early period. Babies respond positively to gentle, rhythmic sound and handling, and they become expert in eliciting positive attention from their parents. They are able to provide comfort for themselves when unexpected stress is encountered. It seems clear that babies can learn to substitute one form of sensory comfort for another. For example, blind babies respond to their mothers in ways that are similar to sighted babies, but their responses are interpreted differently by the mothers. Unless the parents of these babies are taught the meaning of their infant's different responses, their own expectations for interaction are disappointed and they tend to pay less attention to the infant than responding appropriately to a different kind of cue.

Again, it should be instructive to observe the interaction between deaf mothers — accustomed to interact primarily in a visual mode — and their infants. A limited number of research studies have been completed that give us some notion of how socialization may differ for deaf or hearing infants who have deaf parents. Deaf parents have been observed to use touch in a variety of ways to reinforce interaction, to sensitize their infants to basic aspects of space and time in signing and fingerspelling, and to help the infants to attend visually (Maestas y Moores, 1980). They often sign on the infant's body, mold or physically guide their infant's hands, sometimes in shapes that approximate sign language.

For hearing mothers, concerned about the nature of the "difference" they feel in their hearing-impaired infants, and worried about the implications, it is likely that normal early interaction would also be impaired. The results of one study of two deaf infants with hearing mothers (Nienhuys & Tikotin, 1983) suggest that some differences between these sets of mothers and infants and others with normal hearing were attributable to the mothers' depression. The mothers were observed to "play" less with their infants compared with mothers of hearing babies studied previously. Clearly, it is difficult for parents to engage in normal socializing behavior when they are deeply concerned and depressed about the health and normal development of their infant.

Implications for Parents and Teachers of Deaf Infants

Both the evidence of hearing parents' responses to the diagnosis of deafness and speculations about the effect of stress on parent-child interactions in the infant's first year of life would lead to the conclusion that early counseling of families could be exceedingly important for future socialization of these children. Although parent groups with a focus on education are a usual part of parent-infant programs, most educational specialists do not have special training in dealing with parents' emotions. Some experienced professionals believe that parents of handicapped children are less capable of utilizing complex information about communication modes, hearing aids, speech and lipreading training until they also have an opportunity to express their feelings of disappointment and loss about their child's handicap. If educational specialists have not received training in listening and responding, they are likely — and perhaps appropriately so — to avoid opening up parents' feelings too quickly.

A second implication for those who work with older hearing impaired children and their families is that of reaching a deeper understanding of what may have been a very hurtful early trauma for the family and therefore for the child. Unresolved, these traumas may continue to fester, creating angry, uncooperative, overprotective or unrealistic parents at many stages of the educational process. Another important lesson from information about responses of parents to childhood hearing loss is the very different nature of deaf parents' reactions. Teachers (most of whom are not deaf or hard-of-hearing) tend to forget that deafness seems quite normal for this group of parents. The assumption that it need interfere with normal development in all cases can be a disparaging one for those who have learned successfully to cope with it.

SOCIALIZATION IN THE PRESCHOOL YEARS

In the years from one to five, many important socialization processes are expected. Most children develop a total mastery of their native language, including a vocabulary of several thousand words. Secure attachment to parents, and an ability to operate independently of a caretaker for increasing periods of time are expected. Mastery of body processes — that is, control of body elimination — occurs. Cognitive understanding of complex environmental events and gross and fine motor development take place at a rapid rate. Most of these developmental tasks need not be affected by a child's hearing loss. In point of fact, most of them can be affected by parents' expectations and their techniques of coping with a hearing-impaired child.

Attachment

The important task of attachment to caregivers has been the focus of much attention from psychologists, and several theories have been developed to explain the process of the child's identification with and positive feelings toward parents during the first four years of a child's life (Bowlby, 1969; Ainsworth, Blehar, Waters, & Wall, 1978). A great deal of laboratory research has been undertaken, much of which involves asking the child's mother to leave the room where they have been playing, and observing how children of various ages respond to this separation and to a subsequent reunion. After the age of two, most children do not show acute distress when they are separated from their mothers for brief periods of time (Maccoby & Feldman, 1972). Until some time after their third birthday, they do show a desire to be close to their mother when she returns after a brief separation, and they may appear to be angry with her. By the time they are four years old, most children will be able to discuss their mothers' announcement of an impending separation, and will agree that this is acceptable to them (Marvin, 1972; 1977).

Because of the delay in language acquisition among most deaf children, and the supposed lessened abilities of these children to reach verbal agreement with their mothers or to understanding the mother's explanation for her leave-taking, Greenberg and Marvin (1979) hypothesized that their deaf subjects would be delayed in their achievement of the most advanced phase of attachment (that is, the ability of the mother-child pair to reach agreement about the mother's leave-taking). However, they found that deafness *per se* did not lead to such a delay; instead they found that if the deaf child was able to communicate in any way with the mother, their attainment of mature attachment was not delayed.

It would seem that an understanding of this aspect of the socialization of deaf children might also be enhanced by considering those with both deaf parents and hearing parents. One important consideration of any comparison of these two groups is the realization that many deaf adults (including those who are the parents of deaf children) have experienced reduced educational opportunities, depressed academic achievement, and lack of access to information and community resources. In addition, the primary communitive mode for most of these adults (American Sign Language) was not until recently seen as "acceptable" by the wider community, and by the educational establishment especially. Thus, the social and economic resources available to deaf and hearing families could be expected to differ widely.

It might not seem surprising that a group of psychoanalysts reported some negative findings on the early socialization practices of a group of four deaf parents of young deaf children (Galenson, Miller, Kaplan & Rothstein, 1979). They say that "during the second year. . .severe separation anxiety appeared and persisted. The clinging to the mother was of course aggravated by the deaf child's need to keep his mother in view in order to maintain contact with her. . .The severe separation anxiety suggested that there was considerable difficulty in the establishment of a stable maternal mental representation" (p.136).

A later study of 17 deaf children with deaf parents, all of whom were associated (as students, alumni, faculty or staff) with a liberal arts college for deaf students, reported quite different results in a study of attachment behavior. The later study found that these deaf children with deaf parents exhibited attachment patterns almost exactly the same as those reported for hearing children of similar ages. Half of the children younger than age 3 showed signs of distress when separated from their parent in the laboratory setting; the majority wanted to be near their mothers and were sociable when she returned to the room. Five of seven children older than age 3 had achieved the "partnership" or agreement phase of attachment development (Meadow, Greenberg & Erting, 1985).

The authors propose that an explanation for these discrepant results lies in the very different socialization or sociolinguistic environments experienced by the two sets of families. Data for the first reported observations were collected in a school widely-known for its commitment to oral-only education for deaf children, whereas data on deaf mothers and children reported in the second study were collected on the campus of a college widely associated with support for American Sign Language and Sign English.

Language Development and Interaction Patterns

The socialization of children assumes a commonly accessible language for parents and child. This is the case for deaf parents who use sign language with their young deaf children. It is not the case for hearing parents. Until the early 1970's, the use of sign language by hearing parents with young deaf children was absolutely unprecedented. At that time the theoretical approach to deaf education began to change, and many hearing parents were encouraged to learn some form of signed English to use. This new approach is widely referred to as Total Communication, to indicate that parents and teachers are encouraged to use speech and sign language simultaneously, and to utilize hearing aides and speech training as well. However, even when hearing parents enroll their deaf children in a preschool program with a total communication orientation, there is an inevitable lag in their ability to learn and use sign language effectively. While any number of studies of deaf children with deaf parents indicate that these children acquire sign language at the same rate and in the same progression as hearing children acquire spoken language, deaf children of hearing parents are inevitably delayed in their language acquisition.

Apparently this delay has a pervasive effect on interactions between parent and child. The seven studies of interactions of deaf children and their mothers published between 1970 and 1983 report a consistent set of findings (Goss, 1970; Greenberg, 1980; Henggeler & Cooper, 1983; Hyde, Power & Elias, 1980; Meadow, Greenberg, Erting & Carmichael, 1981; Schlesinger & Meadow, 1972; Wedell-Monnig & Lumley, 1980). Hearing mothers of deaf children were clearly found to be more dominating of and intrusive with their children. They tended to spend more time teaching their children and to be rated as tense and antagonistic. The deaf children, on the other hand, were described as less compliant, less attentive, and less responsive than were the hearing children with whom they were compared. Perhaps the conflict between teachers' imperatives to communicate more and the deaf child's inability to communicate orally created pressure on mothers to try harder and harder to elicit responses. Thus, deaf children may be bombarded increasingly with messages they do not understand; they then become less attentive of their mothers and less compliant. The very behaviors which are sought appear less frequently than they otherwise might (Meadow, 1980; 1985).

Granting Independence to the Deaf Preschooler

When communication between parents and a preschool child is dramatically reduced, parents become more protective of that child. The parents' definition of a child's fragility may be the critical factor, rather than the child's actual ability to perform a developmental task. One study of English families with deaf children reported that more than half of the mothers said they made concessions to their deaf children that were not made to siblings with normal hearing. For example, they were less strict about bedtimes and overlooked rule infractions that would have been punished in the other children. Of some significance is the fact that mothers of deaf children seemed more likely to make concessions than did a comparison group of mothers whose children had cerebral palsy. Kinds of punishment utilized with deaf children also were different from those used with hearing siblings (Gregory, 1976). A laboratory study of hearing mothers and deaf children indicated that demands were relaxed for performance of simple tasks (Stinson, 1974; 1978).

Parents feel it necessary to supervise their preschool deaf child more constantly than they would if the child had no hearing loss. One group of parents reported a narrower range of disciplinary techniques, a heavier reliance on spanking, and more frustration around child-rearing techniques generally than did a comparison group of parents of children without hearing impairments (Schlesinger & Meadow, 1972).

Deaf parents with deaf children appear to be much less anxious about their deaf preschoolers' abilities to navigate within their neighborhoods independently, about environmental dangers, and generally about their ability to care for themselves.

The Deaf Preschooler's Educational Experience

For all children, parents are certainly the most important agents of socialization. For most deaf children, a teacher assumes an earlier importance, and is probably more significant than may be the case for most non-handicapped children. It is an accepted tenet of the educational establishment that early intervention is an important element for later success in overcoming the handicaps of a hearing impairment.

Early intervention ordinarily includes the application of a hearing aid, with some educational exercises or training in the use of residual hearing. Teachers work with the child in developing speech sounds (as well as teaching parents how to work with the child).

A third area is training in the recognition of speech sounds on the lips, or speechreading. Finally, for educational programs that utilize some manual communication mode, teachers will work with children and parents in the development of skills in systems of Cued Speech, Signed English, or American Sign Language. All of these special areas of training help to provide the socialization environment for a young deaf child. He or she (with the parents) must cope with many special areas of learning as well as with those socialization tasks that are taken for granted for other (non-handicapped) children.

Because a hearing-impaired child's "career" as a deaf individual begins only after diagnosis has been accomplished, and is also somewhat dependent on the availability of educational services and the parents' willingness or ability to take advantage of those services, there is much variability in the kinds and the timing of intervention. Because of the wide variation in acceptance of visual communication supplements, and disagreements on the optimal type of these supplements, the nature of the early intervention to which deaf children are exposed varies widely. Again, the diagnosis often provides the context for the amount and the kind of early training received by individual deaf children. The first diagnostic specialist with whom the parents are in contact exerts a tremendous influence on parents' acceptance of particular kinds of intervention.

Implications for Parents and Teachers

The anxieties of hearing parents that emerge in the first year of life (or at the time of the diagnosis of the child's deafness) continue to have an impact on the child's socialization during the preschool years. Both parents and teachers tend to feel that it is extremely important for the deaf preschooler to "catch up" in the linguistic and developmental experiences he may have missed because of the hearing loss. Pressures may unwittingly be placed on parents to work very hard with the child; the parent may pass this stress on to the child. One researcher has suggested that hearing-impaired preschoolers, especially those who are exposed to oral-only educational programs, may begin to "burn out" even before they start kindergarten or first grade (Musselman, Lindsay & Wilson, 1985). To find a balance between the extra help and work needed by both parents and hearing-impaired children and the benefits of a more relaxed approach to the special aspects of development is an important goal for both the families and for educators.

Some of the prevalent child-rearing patterns in hearing families with deaf children tend to curtail opportunities for independence in deaf children. These early patterns may bear the fruit of less mature deaf teenagers and adults. It has often been observed that only those who have the opportunity to take responsibility for themselves become capable of doing so. Although it is difficult for hearing families to provide these opportunities for deaf children, it seems to be very important.

SOCIALIZATION IN MIDDLE CHILDHOOD

As children move from preschool settings to kindergarten and then primary grades, many new skills and behaviors are expected of them. Less of the day is at home and with parents, more at school with teachers and classmates. Although a teacher is an important part of the deaf child's life from the time of diagnosis onward, full days at school mean a big change. The "work" of speech training, speechreading lessons, auditory or listening practices have been a part of the deaf child's life for several years. Now the additional expectations for academic achievement — reading, writing, arithmetic — also become important.

Different kinds of decisions must be made by parents about school placement for their children. Sometimes these decisions influence the communication mode to which the child will be exposed. Although some deaf preschoolers attend classes with hearing classmates, most special nursery settings are designed for hearing-impaired children only. Since the passage of Public Law 94-142 (the Education for All Handicapped Children Act) in 1975, many more deaf children attend classes in neighborhood schools rather than traveling to a school with a special class for hearing-impaired children.

This trend toward mainstreaming adds a new dimension to the picture of the deaf child's socialization, and creates an additional option about which parents must make decisions. For an understanding of various pathways that the socialization of deaf school-age children may take, we must add this possibility (mainstreamed vs. self-contained classroom) to the dimension of parental hearing status which provided the framework for looking at socialization during infancy and in the preschool period.

Expanding Horizons of Social Interaction

As the socialization environment enlarges from home and small preschool group to wider areas, deaf children must learn to interact with children and adults who do not understand the consequences of hearing impairment. Hearing loss is seen as a handicap by most of this wider community, so it is of some importance to learn about the developing attitudes of children toward those who are different from them. A summary of recent research on this topic includes the following points:

1. Non-handicapped children first become aware of physical handicaps in other children at about age four. It is likely that awareness of other, less obvious types of handicaps occurs somewhat later.
2. Non-handicapped children tend to have a negative attitude toward the handicapped. In the case of the physically (that is, the visibly) handicapped, this attitude seems to make its first appearance at about age five. Emergence of this attitude toward other types of handicaps would presumably be dependent on a prior ability to perceive such handicaps.
3. Older children have a more negative attitude toward the handicapped than younger children do.
4. Contact with handicapped children does not necessarily reduce negative attitudes toward them. In some instances this contact may intensify rather than diminish these attitudes (Levitt & Cohen, 1976).

A group of researchers followed the progress of eleven hearing-impaired children in mainstreamed classrooms over a three-year period, beginning when the children were in grade 1 (about age 6). Sociometric instruments were used to determine the level of social acceptance the children were given. During the first year of mainstreaming, they were selected as friends by classmates significantly more often than chance; in the second year there was no difference; in the third year the hearing-impaired children were chosen significantly less often. Observational data indicated that the hearing-impaired children interacted more frequently with peers (Kennedy & Bruininks, 1974; Kennedy, Northcott, McCauley & Williams, 1976).

Socialization of deaf children in a mainstreamed setting produces both benefits and pain. Many parents (especially hearing parents) are anxious for their hearing-impaired children to be placed in classrooms with normally hearing children, in the belief that they will practice their speech and speechreading skills more consistently, that their teachers will have higher expectations for them than would be the case in classrooms where all the students have hearing handicaps, and that they will learn to interact more comfortably with hearing peers. These possible advantages may be offset by lack of acceptance from those hearing peers that can lead to loneliness and feelings of isolation. The results of one study showed that for the six- to ten-year-olds participating in a partial mainstreaming program, they were more likely to use their oral skills in the self-contained classroom than they were in the class with hearing peers (Antia, 1982).

The choice between a self-contained classroom for deaf students and a mainstream program in a neighborhood school is quite different from the choice which other parents face for their deaf children in the middle years: between a State residential school and a local special education program. This was much more likely to be the situation for families 20 years ago than it is today, when about three-quarters of deaf students are enrolled in local mainstream programs. Today, enrollment has declined in the residential schools, and they are more likely to serve deaf children with additional handicaps than they were two decades ago. When the choice between residential and local programs is possible, deaf parents are more likely than hearing parents to feel favorably inclined toward the State schools. The reason for this is that many deaf adults were themselves educated in the State schools. Many of their life-long friends were made in those schools, and they entered the deaf community or sub-culture at the time of their enrollment there.

Interviews conducted with deaf and hearing parents of deaf students enrolled in State residential schools twenty years ago illustrate differences in the attitudes of the two groups. Almost half of the hearing parents felt that the decision to send their deaf child to the residential school was an extremely traumatic one: "the worst thing we had to face." Fewer than ten percent of the deaf families felt that any degree of trauma was involved. Some deaf families had moved to the area specifically because they wanted their deaf children to attend that particular residential school. The homesickness experienced by many of the young children was accepted by most of the deaf families as a fact of life (they themselves had lived through it); for the hearing families this was a continuing source of grief:

> He was terribly homesick at first. . .I felt I was punishing him for his handicap. . .He never wants to go back to school, always begs not to. At Christmas he wouldn't get on the bus, then when I got him on, he braced his feet against the seats on each side of the aisle and wouldn't sit down. Screaming. Finally, I thought they'd put him off the bus, but a man came over from where he was sitting and sat with him and I left. He screamed a while. I could hear him outside. One of the other boys on the bus wrote to his mother from school. He said, "That little Sam boy screamed a little while and then stopped" (Meadow, 1967:292).

For students in residential settings, it is clear that teachers and dormitory counselors assume a major role in their socialization.

Socialization for Academic Learning and Performance

Erikson's theory of socialization refers to the period from ages six to eleven as a time for gaining competency in the completion of tasks through "a free exercise of dexterity and intelligence" (Erikson, 1964:124). This can be translated to the child's need to perform well in school. Motivation is closely linked to success, and for deaf children, whose language competency is likely to be less than that expected of other children of this age, successes in this area may be few. In turn, their teachers may become discouraged with their potential, and begin to expect less, furthering the spiral of low expectation, and low achievement (see Schlesinger's formulation, Schlesinger & Meadow, 1972:18-20). The differing linguistic environments of deaf children with deaf and hearing parents can again be utilized to speculate about the consequences of these for academic performance.

A recent review (Meadow-Orlans, in press) of a series of studies comparing the academic achievement of deaf children with deaf parents with that of those whose parents are hearing surveyed five different reports using that comparison (Stuckless & Birch, 1966; Meadow, 1968a; Balow & Brill, 1975; Vernon & Koh, 1970; Brasel & Quigley, 1977). In each of these studies the deaf children with deaf parents were found to perform at a higher level on tests of academic achievement than did the deaf children with hearing parents. The study by Brasel and Quigley (1977) utilized two additional dimensions in their comparison. They separated the children with hearing parents into two groups, one exposed to very early and intensive oral-only training before they were two years old, the other group receiving less intensive oral training (before the age of four). Likewise they divided the children with deaf parents into two groups: one whose parents routinely used Manual English with them at home, the other who routinely used American Sign Language with them. On the four language-related subtests of the Stanford Achievement Test, the group whose deaf parents used Manual English performed at a level significantly above that of the three other groups: the group with hearing parents and later intervention consistently ranked lowest. This study illustrates an important principle for understanding the socialization of deaf children: no matter what the dimension being examined, there is great variation within each "type" of family and environment.

Another illustration of this important point is found in a study of family environment and achievement of deaf students (Bodner-Johnson, 1986). Based on interviews with 125 families with deaf children, and on school performance scores of the children, the author concludes that children who were the most proficient readers had parents who were involved with their academic and recreational activities and had adapted to their children's deafness. Those who performed best in math had parents with high educational and occupational expectations and who reinforced their academic successes. Finally, those who performed best had parents who were informed about their child's school progress and encouraged independence in their deaf children.

Socialization for Independence

Like most other tasks of childhood and adolescence, development of independence begins in the preschool years, if not in infancy. When a child starts to elementary school, however, he/she is generally expected to be able to operate in many situations without parents. As hearing parents tend to shield their deaf children in the early years, this carries over into middle childhood. The ability to care for oneself and to act independently influences many classroom behaviors as well as educational achievement, in addition to the impact it has on social relationships. Deaf children seem to have more difficulty in demonstrating independence than do children without hearing handicaps. Teachers tend to describe their deaf students as dependent on others for help, as giving up quickly and expecting to fail; as demanding attention and help constantly and taking a disproportionate share of their teachers' time (Zwiebel, Meadow & Dyssegaard, 1986).

An early study of deaf children with deaf parents reported that their teachers saw them as more mature, independent and capable of taking responsibility, compared to deaf children with hearing parents, whether the children were enrolled in residential or in day schools (Meadow, 1968a; Schlesinger & Meadow, 1972).

A recent study utilized Scales of Independent Behavior (Bruininks, Woodcock, Weatherman & Hill, 1984) which utilizes parent interviews for the collection of data (Klansek-Kyllo & Rose, 1985). Interviews were conducted with 25 (hearing) parents of deaf children and 25 (hearing) parents of hearing children. The deaf children were found to have scores very similar to those of the hearing children on items comprising subscales involving gross and fine motor skills and a set of subscales labelled personal living skills, and community living skills. The deaf students were deficient in items comprising scales called social interaction, language comprehension, language expression, money and value, and home-community orientation. The authors suggest that the kinds of independence reflected in the ability to make a dental appointment and to fill out an application form for a savings account are directly influenced by communicative ability, and that it is these activities in which the deaf students are deficient.

Socialization for Empathy and Impulse Control

Two other areas in which many deaf children seem to need special help are those of the acquisition of empathy and impulse control. The ability to think about the consequences of action before impulsively rushing to an act or a conclusion are important to the success of many interactions. The ability to understand the feelings of others as a possible basis for their actions, as well as one's own emotions is also important for the successful growth to adulthood. One psychologist studied impulsivity in deaf children with deaf parents and with hearing parents and found those with deaf parents more capable of impulse control (Harris, 1978).

As in other areas where deaf children are sometimes seen as being deficient, lack of communication skill rather than auditory deprivation are the major basis for lacks. A group of psychologists interested in the whole area of deafness and development have formulated the complex links between communication ability and impulse control in a useful way. They propose that misbehavior on the part of deaf children is punished not by verbal admonishment or by denial of privilege related to the misdemeanor, but by removal from a situation or physical discipline. This is the case because too often parents do not have the level of communicative ability that would allow them to do otherwise. As a result of this general situation at home (and perhaps at school as well), deaf children have few experiences in which they learn exactly what was wrong about their behavior, how it affected other people, and what substitute behaviors would be more acceptable. In addition, parents are demonstrating that avoidance and physical action are acceptable ways of solving problems and the children have few opportunities to learn from past difficulties. "Quite simply, the impact of these limited explanations and restricted experiences is to deny them their rightful opportunity to understand others" (Greenberg, Kusche, Gustafson, & Calderon, 1984:245).

Implications for Parents and Teachers

Increasingly, educators are becoming more aware of some of the social difficulties created by communicative deficiencies, and more committed to remediating them. Social skills are seen more and more as creating either barriers or as facilitating academic learning. In recent years a number of programs and techniques have been devised for and by teachers that have been found to improve the social skills of deaf children.

One of these is a curriculum called PATHS (Providing Alternative Thinking Strategies) consisting of 75 lessons in three sections. The first section includes 12 lessons directed toward the development of self-control, teaching children the "Turtle Technique." This is designed to help them stop and think when they feel angry and want to lash out.

Another section with about 30 lessons is divided into 8 steps: (1) stop and realize that a problem exists; (2) identify the problem; (3) identify one's feelings; (4) decide on a goal; (5) generate a list of alternative solutions; (6) consider the consequences of each solution; (7) select and implement a plan; (8) monitor the outcome (Greenberg, et al., 1984:249).

Another example is a program called "language for adaptive interaction" or "adaptive dialogue." This gives students phrases to be used in communicative situations where they do not understand what is expected of them (Gawlik, McAleer & Ozer, 1976). A curriculum for elementary school age students called "career education" includes units designed to help deaf children learn to make positive decisions for themselves, to recognize their own feelings, to develop goals, and to resolve interpersonal conflicts. In addition to being developmental or socialization directed activities, they are rightfully conceptualized as necessary abilities for future career success (Fitch, LeNard, Neuman & Richardson, 1981).

While these remedial programs have been used effectively and would seem to be a positive response to language deficiencies which are widespread, the preferable course would be prevention of linguistic deficiencies through early intervention and better communication between deaf children and their parents.

SOCIALIZATION OF DEAF ADOLESCENTS

Each of the areas of socialization discussed thus far remains important for the growth of adolescents. Work on the tasks emphasized here leading to the ability to engage in productive and satisfying work and to form intimate loving relationships began long before the ages of twelve to eighteen. As young people look toward adulthood, it becomes more important to them to be ready for the kind of intimacy that is necessary for the establishment of a happy family, and to be ready to use skills and competencies in the world of work. Both of these areas require a strong and positive sense of self. This is the basis for Erikson's proposal that adolescence is a time when the focus of individual development is on identity (Erikson, 1968; Schlesinger & Meadow, 1972).

Socialization for Positive Self-Identification

Several studies of the self-image or self-concept in deaf children and adolescents suggest that generally they may have less positive ideas about themselves than do comparable groups of hearing peers. Of more interest to us, perhaps, are differences among various sub-groups of deaf children. Again, there have been reported differences between groups of deaf children with deaf parents and those with hearing parents. One study sub-divided the deaf children in each of these groups (that is, the group with deaf parents and the group with hearing parents), in terms of rankings for what was termed "family climate" (Meadow, 1969). This took account of socio-economic factors as well as intactness of the family and interpersonal problems within the family. In the group of deaf children with deaf parents, those from the most positive family climates had highest scores for positive self-image, followed by those with intermediate family climate ratings, with those in the lowest family climate group having most negative self-image scores. However in the group of deaf children with hearing parents, those with intermediate ratings for family climate received the highest scores for self-image. A possible explanation for this reversal of the expected finding was that hearing parents expectations for their children's achievements were more closely tied to successful performance in the academic arena, and in the development of oral skills. The inability of the deaf child to meet parental expectations led to a poor self-evaluation.

In this same study, it was reported that children with hearing parents who had better oral communication skills had more positive self-image scores, while communication skill level made no difference in the self-image scores of children with deaf parents. The effect of school achievement on self-image scores was similar to that of communication skill acquisition. For the deaf children with deaf parents, school achievement had little relationship to self-image. For the deaf children with hearing parents, those with higher achievement test scores also had higher self-image scores. This illustrates the complexity of self-image or self-esteem, and how it is related to a wide range of experiences, situations, and individual or group comparisons.

Identity, Social Development, and Mainstreaming

As deaf children reach high school age, it becomes more and more likely that they will be found in mainstream school situations. For adolescents who are in the process of learning "who they are" and who want badly to fit in with their peers, this can be an isolating, negative experience for students who are "different" in an important way, and whose communication skills set them apart from the group.

One study has been reported of social interactions of high school aged mainstreamed hearing-impaired students with their normally hearing peers. This research was carried out with students who were mainstreamed in vocational courses only. During a three-year period of time, increasing rates of interaction between deaf and hearing students were observed, and the deaf students received average ratings on sociometric measures. Parents and teachers felt that the social situations of sixty percent of the hearing-impaired students was positive. Nevertheless, more than half of the hearing-impaired students had difficulty making friends with their hearing peers at school and had almost no contact with them outside of school hours (Ladd, Munson & Miller, 1984).

Moores and his colleagues recently completed an in-depth review of the social and educational effects of mainstreaming placement on hearing-impaired students. They concluded that the amount of social interaction taking place in mainstream environments is directly related to structured activities involving both deaf and hearing students. They also believe that the provision of support services can be an important influence (Moores, Kluwin & Mertens, 1985:35).

The Acquisition of Social Norms in Deaf Adolescents

Learning social expectations and the dimensions of socially approved behavior is another of the tasks of socialization that is continuous throughout childhood and adolescence. This is an area that psychologists often describe as social adjustment. Students who are at the extreme end of the continuum of social maladjustment might be considered to be emotionally or behaviorally disturbed. If the disturbance takes the form of acting out or aggressive behavior, and disrupts the classroom, the student would probably be excluded from school. Thus, this topic has been the focus of a good deal of attention from educators as well as psychologists and others who deal with deaf students.

Deaf children generally are reported to show more problems of social adjustment than do hearing children (Meadow, 1980). Deaf children with deaf parents are less frequently identified as exhibiting problems of emotional and behavioral adjustment than do deaf children with hearing parents (Stokoe & Battison, 1981). A study of students between the ages of ten and fifteen compared deaf students in residential and public schools with hard-of-hearing public school students and public school students with normal hearing in terms of their social and emotional adjustment. It was reported that deaf students in public schools received lower ratings from teachers than did students in any of the three other groups. Hard-of-hearing students were significantly below the two remaining groups on items reflecting self-esteem (Farrugia & Austin, 1980). Another study indicates that integration (or mainstreaming) appears to be beneficial for academic achievement of deaf students, but that personal and social problems of mainstreamed deaf students may increase (Reich, Hambleton & Houdin, 1977).

Implications for Parents and Teachers

As children become older, it is expected that peers and the wider community will gradually become more important to their socialization. Because of the special difficulties of hearing parents in communicating with their deaf children, it may well be that this trend is exacerbated for them.

One professional who has worked closely with parents of deaf adolescents described them as having many concerns not expressed by parents of hearing adolescents, most related to communciation:

> There is a well-known communication gap between parents and adolescents, but. . .with deaf adolescents this can amount to a chasm. It's a very painful, shocking and sad experience for parents to realize that the child they nurtured is becoming. . .a virtual stranger in the house. . .Lack of communication skills and apprehension increased the difficulty experienced by parents who tried to answer the adolescent question: "Why am I deaf?" Parents also discussed their concerns about letting go, some dreading the adolescent's separation from family, particularly if they felt their youngster might choose the deaf world (Aldridge, 1984:126).

At a national conference on adolescence and deafness, two parents of deaf adolescents made the very important point that the range of responses by parents is extremely broad. They describe the experiences of a large number of families. One describes concerns for a deaf daughter whose language skills prevent her from learning social skills that other children in the family learned effortlessly. Another family realized for the first time when their daughter was fifteen that she was barely able to read. Some parents finally realize that perfect speech will never be a reality for their deaf child, and that electronic implants will not provide an "answer" for deafness. "When the reality of adolescence hits there are no more fantasies, no more pretenses, no magic" (Mendelsohn & Fairchild, 1984:113).

CONCLUSION

As deaf children move closer to adulthood, it becomes more apparent that their acceptance in the wider community is important to their continued or increased happiness. Acceptance of deafness and an understanding of the potential contributions of deaf people to their community is a goal toward which parents, educators, and deaf people themselves continue to work. The increasing visibility of sign language, the increasing availability of sign language interpreters, and the growing interest in and respect for the deaf community are positive signs that deaf children and deaf adolescents will have the opportunity to take their place as adults in the larger community. The goal of broad acceptance, of alternatives for adult functioning, of a range of options in all areas, is the aim of socialization by parents of all children, not just for those who are deaf.

REFERENCES

Aldridge, Lita D.: Surviving adolescence. In Anderson, Glenn B. and Watson, Douglas: *The Habilitation and Rehabilitation of Deaf Adolescents*. Proceedings of the National Conference on the Habilitation and Rehabilitation of Deaf Adolescents, Wagoner, Oklahoma, April 17-20, 1984, pp. 123-133.

Ainsworth, M. D. S., Blehar, M. C., Waters, E., and Wall, S.: *Patterns of Attachment*. Hillsdale, N.J.: Lawrence Erlbaum, 1978.

Antia, S. D.: Social interaction of partially mainstreamed hearing impaired children. *American Annals of the Deaf, 127:*18-25, 1982.

Balow, I. H., and Brill, Richard G.: An evaluation of reading and academic achievement levels of 16 graduating classes of the California School for the Deaf, Riverside. *The Volta Review, 77:*266-276, 1975.

Bodner-Johnson, Barbara: The family environment and achievement of deaf students: a discriminant analysis. *Exceptional Children, 52:*443-449, 1986.

Bowlby, John: *Attachment and Loss, Vol. 1., Attachment*. New York: Basic Books, 1969.

Brasel, Kenneth E., and Quigley, Stephen P.: Influence of certain language and communication environments in early childhood on the development of language in deaf individuals. *Journal of Speech and Hearing Research, 20:*96-107, 1977.

Brim, Orville, G., Jr., and Wheeler, Stanton: *Socialization after Childhood: Two Essays*. New York: Wiley, 1966.

Bruininks, Robert H., Woodcock, R. W., Weatherman, R. F. and Hill, B. K.: Scales of Independent Behavior. Allen, TX: DLM Teaching Resources, 1984.

Clausen, John A.: Research on socialization and personality development in the U.S. and France: Remarks on the paper by Professor Chombart DeLauwe. *American Sociology Review, 31:*248-257, 1966.

Erikson, Erik: *Insight and Responsibility*. New York: Norton, 1964.

Erikson, Erik: *Identity, Youth and Crisis*. New York: Norton, 1968.

Erting, Carol J.: Cultural conflict in a school for deaf children. *Anthropology and Education Quarterly, 16:*225-243, 1985.

Farrugia, David, and Austin, Gary F.: A study of social-emotional adjustment patterns of hearing-impaired students in different educational settings. *American Annals of the Deaf, 125:*535-541, 1980.

Fitch, B., LeNard, J., Neuman, D., and Richardson, J.: *Model for the KDES Career Education Program*. Washington, D.C.: Pre-College Programs, Gallaudet College, 1981.

Galenson, Eleanor, Miller, Robert, Kaplan, Eugene, and Rothstein, Arnold: Assessment of development in the deaf child. *Journal of the American Academy of Child Psychiatry, 18:*128-142, 1979.

Gawlik, R., McAleer, Marlene, and Ozer, M. N.: Language for adaptive interaction. *American Annals of the Deaf, 121:*556-559, 1976.

Goss, R. N.: Language used by mothers of deaf children and mothers of hearing children. *American Annals of the Deaf, 115,*93-96, 1970.

Greenberg, Mark T.: Social interaction between deaf preschoolers and their mothers: the effects of communication method and communicative competence. *Developmental Psychology, 16:*465-474, 1980.

Greenberg, Mark T., Kusché, Carol A., Gustafson, R. N. and Calderon, R.: The PATHS Project: a model for the prevention of psychological difficulties in deaf children. In Anderson, Glenn B., and Watson, Douglas: *Habilitation and Rehabilitation of Deaf Adolescents.* Proceedings of the National Conference on the Habilitation and Rehabilitation of Deaf Adolescents, Wagoner, Oklahoma, April 17-20, 1984.

Greenberg, Mark T., and Marvin, Robert S.: Patterns of attachment in profoundly deaf preschool children. *Merrill-Palmer Quarterly, 25:*265-279, 1979.

Gregory, Susan: *The Deaf Child and His Family.* London: George Allen and Unwin, 1976.

Harris, Robert I.: Impulse control in deaf children: research and clinical issues. In Liben, Lynn S.: *Deaf Children: Developmental Perspectives.* New York: Academic Press, pp. 137-156, 1978.

Henggeler, S. W., and Cooper, P. F.: Deaf child-hearing mother interaction: extensiveness and reciprocity. *Journal of Pediatric Psychology, 8:*83-95, 1983.

Hyde, M. B., Power, D. J., and Elias, G. C.: *The use of verbal and nonverbal control techniques by mothers of hearing-impaired infants* (Research Report No. 5). Australia: Mt. Gravatt College of Advanced Education, Centre for Human Development Studies, 1980.

Kennedy, P., and Bruininks, R. H.: Social status of hearing impaired children in regular classrooms. *Exceptional Children, 40:*336-343, 1974.

Kennedy, P., Northcott, Winifred, McCauley, R., and Williams, S. M.: Longitudinal sociometric and cross-sectional data on mainstreaming hearing-impaired children: implications for preschool programming. *The Volta Review, 78:*71-81, 1976.

Klansek-Kyllo, Valerie, and Rose, Susan: Using the scale of independent behavior with hearing-impaired students. *American Annals of the Deaf, 130:*533-537, 1985.

Kubler-Ross, Elizabeth. *On Death and Dying.* New York: Macmillan, 1969.

Ladd, G. W., Munson, H. L., and Miller, J. K.: Social integration of deaf adolescents in secondary-level mainstreamed programs. *Exceptional Children, 50:*420-428, 1984.

Levitt, E., and Cohen, S.: Attitudes of children toward their handicapped peers. *Childhood Education, 52:*171-173, 1976.

Luterman, David: *Counseling the Communicatively Disordered and Their Families.* Boston: Little, Brown, 1984.

Maccoby, E. E., and Feldman, S. S.: Mother-attachment and stranger-reactions in the third year of life. *Monographs of the Society for Research in Child Development, 37,* 1972 (3, Serial No. 148).

Maestas y Moores, Julia: Early linguistic environment: interactions of deaf parents with their infants. *Sign Language Studies, 26:*1-13, 1980.

Marvin, Robert S.: Attachment-exploratory and communicative behavior in 2, 3, and 4-year-old children. Unpublished doctoral dissertation, University of Chicago, 1972.

Marvin, Robert S.: An ethological-cognitive model of the attenuation of mother-child attachment. In Alloway, T. M., and Krames, L.: *Advances in the Study of Communication, Vol. 3, Development of Social Attachments.* New York: Plenum, 1977.

Meadow, Kathryn P.: The effects of early manual communication and family climate on the deaf child's development. Unpublished doctoral dissertation. University of California, Berkeley, 1967.

Meadow, Kathryn P.: Early manual communication in relation to the deaf child's intellectual, social, and communicative functioning. *American Annals of the Deaf, 113:*29-41, 1968a.

Meadow, Kathryn P.: Parental responses to the medical ambiguities of deafness. *Journal of Health and Social Behavior, 9:*299-309, 1968b.

Meadow, Kathryn P.: Self-image, family climate and deafness. *Social Forces, 47:*428-438, 1969.

Meadow, Kathryn P.: *Deafness and Child Development.* Berkeley: University of California Press, 1980.

Meadow-Orlans, Kathryn P.: Impact of a child's hearing loss on the family. Presentation at the biennial meeting of the Society for Research in Child Development, Toronto, Ontario, Canada, April, 1985.

Meadow-Orlans, Kathryn P.: An analysis of the effectiveness of early intervention programs for hearing-impaired children. In Guralnick, Michael J., and F. Curt Bennett: *The Effectiveness of Early Intervention for At-Risk and Handicapped Children.* New York: Academic Press, in press.

Meadow, Kathryn P., Greenberg, Mark T., and Erting, Carol: Attachment behavior of deaf children with deaf parents. In Chess, Stella, and Thomas, Alexander: *Annual Progress in Child Psychiatry and Child Development, 1984.* New York: Brunner/Mazel, 1985, pp. 176-187.

Meadow, Kathryn P., Greenberg, Mark T., Erting, Carol, and Carmichael, Heather: Interactions of deaf mothers and deaf preschool children: comparisons with three other groups of deaf and hearing dyads. *American Annals of the Deaf, 126:*454-468, 1981.

Mendelsohn, Jacqueline Z., and Fairchild, Bonnie: Years of challenge: parents, adolescence and deafness. In Anderson, Glenn B. and Watson, Douglas: *The Habilitation and Rehabilitation of Deaf Adolescents.* Proceedings of the National Conference on the Habilitation and Rehabilitation of Deaf Adolescents, Wagoner, Oklahoma, April 17-20, 1984, pp. 110-122.

Moores, Donald F., Kluwin, Thomas N., and Mertens, Donna M.: *High School Programs for Deaf Students in Metropolitan Areas, Progress Report: Year 1.* Washington, D.C.: Center for Studies in Education and Human Development, Gallaudet Research Institute, Gallaudet College, 1985.

Moses, Kenneth L.: Infant deafness and parental grief: psychosocial early intervention. In Powell, Frank, Finitzo-Hieber, Terese, Friel-Patti, Sandy, and Henderson, Donald: *Education of the Hearing Impaired Child.* San Diego: College-Hill Press, 1985, pp. 85-102.

Musselman, Carol L., Lindsay, Peter H., and Wilson, Ann: *Linguistic and Social Development in Preschool Deaf Children.* Toronto. Ministry of Colleges and Universities, 1985.

Nash, Jeffrey E., and Nash, Anedith: *Deafness in Society.* Lexington, Mass: Lexington Books, 1981.

Nienhuys, Terry G., and Tikotin, Jennifer A.: Pre-speech communication in hearing and hearing-impaired children. *Journal of British Association of Teachers of the Deaf,* 6:182-194, 1983.

Padden, Carol: The deaf community and the culture of deaf people. In Baker, Charlotte, and Battison, Robbin: *Sign Language and the Deaf Community, Essays in Honor of William C. Stokoe.* Washington, D.C.: National Association of the Deaf, 1980, pp. 99-104.

Rawlings, Brenda W., and Jensema, Carl J.: *Two Studies of the Families of Hearing Impaired Children.* Series R, Number 5. Washington, D.C.: Gallaudet College, Office of Demographic Studies, 1977.

Reich, Carol, Hambelton, D., and Houdin, B.: The integration of hearing impaired children in regular classrooms. *American Annals of the Deaf,* 122:534-543, 1977.

Schlesinger, Hilde S.: Deafness, mental health, and language. In Powell, Frank, Finitzo-Hieber, Terese, Friel-Patti, Sandy, and Henderson, Donald: *Education of the Hearing Impaired Child.* San Diego: College-Hill Press, 1985, pp. 103-116.

Schlesinger, Hilde S., and Meadow, Kathryn P.: *Sound and Sign: Childhood Deafness and Mental Health,* Berkeley: University of California Press, 1972.

Stinson, Michael S.: Maternal reinforcement and help and the achievement motive in hearing and hearing-impaired children. *Developmental Psychology,* 10:348-353, 1974.

Stinson, Michael S.: Effects of deafness on maternal expectations about child development. *Journal of Special Education,* 12:75-81, 1978.

Stokoe, William C., and Battison, Robbin M.: Sign language, mental health, and satisfactory interaction. In Stein, Laszlo K., Mindel, Eugene D., and Jabaley, Theresa: *Deafness and Mental Health.* New York: Grune & Stratton, 1981, pp. 179-194.

Stuckless, E. Ross, and Birch, Jack W.: The influence of early manual communication on the linguistic development of deaf children. *American Annals of the Deaf,* 111:452-460, 499-504, 1966.

Thompson, Richard E., Thompson, Arlene, and Murphy, Albert T.: Sounds of sorrow, sounds of joy: the hearing-impaired parents of hearing-impaired children-- a conversation. In Murphy, Albert T.: *The Families of Hearing-Impaired Children. The Volta Review,* 81:337-351, 1979.

Vernon, McCay, and Koh, S. D.: Early manual communication and deaf children's achievement. *American Annals of the Deaf,* 115:527-536, 1970.

Wedell-Monnig, Jacqueline, and Lumley, J. M.: Child deafness and mother-child interaction. *Child Development,* 51:766-774, 1980.

Williams, D. M. L., and Darbyshire, John O.: Diagnosis and deafness: a study of family responses and needs. *The Volta Review,* 84:24-30, 1982.

Zwiebel, Abraham, Meadow-Orlans, Kathryn P., and Dyssegaard, Birgit: A comparison of hearing-impaired students in Israel, Denmark, and the United States. *International Journal of Rehabilitation Research,* 9:109-118, 1986.

CHAPTER 3

LIFELONG SOCIALIZATION AND ADAPTIVE BEHAVIOR OF DEAF PEOPLE

GAYLENE BECKER

SOCIALIZATION is a lifelong process of personal development. Individuals learn the norms and values of their society from the time they are born, and live out their lives according to personal idiosyncracies and the resulting cultural patterns. Socialization is not simply a launching process. Although we tend to think of the socialization process as primarily being one of parents raising their children, socialization is in fact a much more complex process that is also carried out throughout life by peers (Brim and Wheeler, 1966). It is intrinsic to ongoing personal development, and influences subsequent life experience and behavior.

Peer socialization is a significant part of the learning process individuals undergo in becoming cultural beings and in the adaptations they make in response to cultural change over time. This process of socialization by peers begins in childhood, escalates in intensity for the period of adolescence, then continues in a more subtle manner for the remainder of the life course. It has been suggested that ongoing socialization is an active part of adult life (Mead, 1970), as we continuously anticipate the tasks we must learn for the next stage of life (Pearlin, 1982).

Despite its central importance in shaping people's lives, ongoing socialization is largely unacknowledged by the general population because it is experienced primarily in the context of daily interactions and routines. Indeed, once the rudiments of learning have been established in the individual, informal peer learning becomes largely an unconscious process (Martin, 1986). Nevertheless, socialization, peers, and the

59

learning process form a linkage that profoundly affects personal development. This linkage is important within the deaf population for it enhances the ability of deaf people to effectively cope with deafness.

Socialization never ceases. Deaf people must actively work to keep abreast of trends in the hearing world because they cannot automatically monitor it. The peer learning process thus diminishes the effects of the sensory and social learning deficit deaf people experience. This chapter will discuss how the peer learning process that originated within the deaf community to meet basic needs of life in childhood and young adulthood may ultimately lead to greater self-awareness and self-acceptance. The peer learning process may have significant consequences for the adaptive behavior that deaf people develop over the life course, and may uniquely affect their experience of old age.

Despite variations between and within generations, the phenomenon of socialization appears to have been equally significant for deaf persons of all ages. Indeed, it is one of the main threads of cultural continuity in understanding the nature of deafness, and is the vital link that perpetuates the deaf community and its culture.[1]

In the pages that follow, we first examine the dynamic processes that have led up to lifelong socialization becoming such a significant aspect of deaf people's lives, followed by a discussion of the specific ways in which peer socialization continues to be pivotal to individual well-being.

SOCIALIZATION AND LANGUAGE

In all societies parents socialize their children by communicating cultural norms through language. Language is instrumental in the development and maintenance of identity and facilitates life cycle transitions (Coleman, 1985), as well as in learning the values of society. Most researchers who study early child development assume that the child is spontaneously learning the language of his or her culture, and that the parents' language is the means by which the child is socialized (Brown, 1962). The family functions as a cultural unit, a microcosm that reflects family-specific cultural beliefs and values (Henry, 1965). This cultural richness is thus experienced by most children, for whom language acquisition and socialization proceed together. Parents' behavior towards others is also an important factor in socializing children, since children overhear what their elders say to each other and combine what they learn with their observations of adult behavior to develop norms for social behavior.

Deafness that occurs at birth or early in life interferes with the linguistic means of transmitting culture, and without language, the rich
cultural content of the socialization process is lost on deaf children.
Since culture is transmitted through language, some aspects of the socialization process are delayed until language is acquired. Moreover, the
emotional bonding between parent and child that accompanies the socialization process is often lost. Among deaf persons who are now in
adulthood this delay in beginning the process of socialization lasted until
the child began his or her education at the age of five or six years, retarding not only social development but emotional development at well
(Schlesinger and Meadow, 1972). Thus, the great majority of deaf persons have hearing parents with whom they cannot communicate and
whose value system differs in subtle but significant ways from their own.

The language barrier thus significantly interferes with relationships
between parent and child. This phenomenon has few parallels cross-
culturally. Lack of parent-child socialization coupled with poor communication and fragile emotional bonds has created a weak link between
the deaf person and his or her family of origin that has culminated in
further separating the deaf individual from the hearing world in adulthood.

INSTITUTIONAL SOCIALIZATION

The processes of socialization and education occur together for most
deaf children, a unique situation in complex societies (Cohen, 1971).
Most deaf persons who are now adults were socialized in institutions. In
the United States, institutionalization is generally seen as the last resort,
whether it be commitment to a mental hospital, a nursing home, or an
orphanage. It is a value of American society that children should be
reared within the family, preferably by two parents. The family is seen
as the optimum environment for the normal development of children, in
contrast to the value placed by Israelis on communal education (Spiro,
1965). When early childhood development takes place within an institution in the United States, the child is perceived as lacking the benefits
that nurturance by the family provides and, consequently, as both
vulnerable and incomplete in the eyes of society (Yarrow, 1964).

Institutionalization is a stigmatizing experience for anyone, with its
implicit assumption of rejection by one's family and by society. A stigma
connotes a mark or moral taint that is deeply discrediting to the individ-

ual (Goffman, 1963). Stigmas are defined in the context of culture and reflect culture as well. Beliefs held in common with others about the cultural meaning of a given attribute dictate the nature of the stigma associated with it, and the responses of stigmatized persons (Becker and Arnold, 1986). Individuals' experience of stigma arise from social attitudes that are both subtle and pervasive, and individuals quickly become aware of the way that others view them. Failure to possess attributes viewed as important by a social group is experienced as a stigma, such as the failure to hear. Individuals experience such culturally dictated stigmas as failures to conform to society, and may consequently experience a deep sense of personal responsibility for their stigma.

The feeling of personal responsibility for stigma is often passed from one generation to the next (Freidson, 1966). Children are socialized by their parents to internalize negative attitudes about certain stigmas, even when these are directed against themselves. Parents, in their guilt over having produced a child they consider imperfect, pass their own sense of stigma onto the child (Davis, 1963; Ablon, 1984). Persons who are stigmatized in this way find themselves in a continual struggle with negative attitudes and with the devalued status that accompanies them and must constantly develop strategies for dealing with the stigma. The degree to which the individual feels stigmatized, the degree to which the stigma is shared with others in society, and the degree to which the stigma can be miminized, will all affect the process of adaptation that the individual undergoes in dealing with the stigma.

When language barriers prevent the development of parent-child rapport and are compounded by institutionalization of the child, an aura of social marginality surrounds the child that is difficult for the individual to dispel once he or she becomes an adult. The sense of stigma that people describe in adulthood in retrospective accounts of childhood is the glue in the formation of strong peer groups in the institution. During these formative years the peer group emerged, and the child learned to rely heavily on other children for emotional support and information about the world, a pattern that is maintained in adulthood. As we will see, the phenomenon of peer group socialization that began under this cloud of stigma has been transformed over the life course for many persons into a source of ongoing nurturance and positive reinforcement of identity. These positive aspects of identity assuage the deaf person's perception of self as being different from others.

The residential school has a strong influence on the individual. Integration into society is difficult for any individual who has been removed to a closed environment that teachers about the outside world without offering experience of it directly. The institution itself develops its own culture (Goffman, 1961), that invariably differs in some ways from the rest of society. Most deaf persons who are now adults have stayed in school until they were 18 years old, spending 12 years in an institution. In the past, older persons usually spent the entire year at the institution, going home only in the summer. The separation of the child from the family has weakened the parent-child bond in many instances, a factor that places limits on deaf individuals' resources in adulthood.

As a child, the deaf person was both nurtured and given an identity within the institution, while the perceptual force was on the social group. In cultural terms, the group becomes a major part of the individual's perception because of its significance as a surrogate family. The focus on the group is part of a variant view of culture that is presented to deaf children in institutions and continually reinforced. It thus becomes part of the socialization process. Like that of the Hopi (Lee, 1959), the world view of deaf people is of people in groups rather than as individuals. Therefore, the group becomes an organizing element in the social world of deafness.

As Schlesinger (1972:22) points out, children are expected to make the transition from communal living in the institution to the outside world, where the emphasis is on individualism. An orientation toward the group, taken for granted early in life, continues throughout the life course. This lifelong focus on the group rather than on the individual is in direct conflict with those American core values that emphasize individualism as good and collectivity as bad. In adult life this orientation simultaneously poses difficulties and offers advantages. As a result of their need for face-to-face interaction, deaf people develop a high degree of social interdependence that modifies core values. Deaf children of hearing parents must discover for themselves workable variations of American core values in order to survive as social beings once they leave school.

The remainder of this chapter explores the process of lifelong socialization through which deaf people develop workable solutions to the dilemmas posed by deafness. We will examine the various ingredients of this process as individuals grope through the period of adolescence and young adulthood and are gradually immersed in the life of the peer group. This process, including the way that peer learning is put to work, has significant consequences for the way in which people experience life. We will explore the key elements in this process as people grow throughout their lives.

THE TRANSITION TO ADULTHOOD

The transition to adulthood in American society almost invariably provokes an identity crisis, as the young person develops autonomy from his or her family and rethinks family values in relation to his or her own life goals. This first major transition of adulthood is characterized by the time of upheaval that encompasses philosophical questions such as, "What is the meaning of life?" as well as everyday concerns, such as leaning how to budget money. Young adults become immersed in the discovery of personal freedom and the realization that there are choices to be made in life about self-definition. Most young people are anchored to some extent in this process by having had role models for how adults live. Even if the individual dimishes the significance of role models such as parents in the search for self, however, most young adults unconsciously utilize some of the social tools they have been socialized with in making this transition. Later on, when they have a stronger sense of themselves as persons, they gradually integrate those aspects of their family's cultural patterns that they wish to preserve into their own lives.

In contrast to this portrait of the discovery of self, deaf youth have only glimmers of the possibilities in this life transition. The acquisition of adaptive behavior is a process of cultural learning. As deaf individuals reach the brink of adulthood, they are ill-prepared by their familial, educational and social experiences to function effectively in the hearing world. Deaf youth experience the brunt of difficulties emanating from delays in language acquisition and socialization at this time because they contribute to delayed personal and social development. The deaf individual thus spends early adulthood trying to "catch up" with American society. This process is probably completed in middle age, and undoubtedly contributes to the sense of shared life experience that deaf persons have in later life.

Preparation prior to the assumption of a new role is important throughout life and eases the transition into the role, thus reducing the stress of the transition (Albrecht, 1975). The clearer the norms of the new role, the easier the task (Mortimer and Simmons, 1978). The individual's capacity to imagine his or her own future is an important aspect of this process (Atchley, 1975). For example, students who take college preparatory classes in high school are preparing socially as well as academically for a new role.

The period of early adulthood among deaf persons is often highly stressful because of lack of preparation. As deaf individuals grow up, leave school, and begin to take on the roles of adult life, communication barriers continue to intervene in their adaptation. Despite the multiple roles that they must fulfill in life, deaf persons often manage without the emotional and social supports available to others. In describing this time of life, deaf persons often characterize themselves in retrospect as ignorant of the ways of the world, stating that no one explained what life outside the institution would be like.

Preparation for adult family roles in our society usually occurs in the family in which one grows up. Deaf persons often struggle to develop and maintain family cohesiveness without adequate preparation for marriage and parenthood, and their responsibilities in these roles. Although there is no comparative data on the subject, it is likely that because of the limited communication experienced between deaf persons and their hearing families, deaf people rely significantly less than hearing persons do on their parents and other relatives for information, help, and emotional support. In contrast to this general pattern, one women reported that her mother had taught her everything she knew. Her mother even took her with her when she was planning her husband's funeral because "someday this will happen to you." She contrasted her own experience favorably with those of her friends, who were "lost" when they were first forced to handle such matters. The lack of role models and familial supports forces deaf persons to turn to each other to meet their needs.

THE PEER GROUP

Peers serve crucial lifelong developmental functions as they facilitate social competence (Norris and Rubin, 1984). Social competence is an outgrowth of social interactions that are high in quality. Social relationships such as these allow for the development of intimacy with others. As such relationships develop, they provide a critical avenue for the development of interpersonal skills and personal development. The elements involved in cooperating with others, in resolving conflict, and developing flexibility in relation to others all heighten individual maturity and further individuals' capacity for greater intimacy. Moreover, such relationships provide emotional support and nurturance that further enhance personal development. When a person feels that others care about him or her, the potential for self-reflection and self-acceptance is enhanced. Socially competent people have a behavioral repertoire of some breadth, are sensitive to situational factors, and are successful in meeting their goals through culturally acceptable means (Norris and Rubin, 1984). These qualities are important in developing the flexibility to deal with critical life events (Hultsch and Plemons, 1979), and have important implications for coping and adaptive behavior over the life course.

The peer group provides deaf persons with the potential to develop social competence through a variety of means. The broad base of friendship developed in school early in life forms the basis for social support that helps to sustain the individual amidst the ongoing difficulties of daily life. While young deaf adults usually lack social skills in relation to the hearing world, if they have been raised in an institutional setting their social skills in relation to other deaf people are usually well developed, especially with regard to age mates. The peer group is thus uniquely equipped to meet many of the social and emotional needs of deaf people in specific ways that facilitate the development of social competence. They are (1) language and communication; (2) information exchange; (3) friendship; (4) cliques; and (5) reciprocity.

Language and Communication

Language is a key ingredient in the glue that contributes to the peer socialization process. While deaf people are undergoing the transition to adulthood, they are simultaneously being challenged about issues basic to their identity, such as their language. Language is such an important channel for expression of the self and identity, for thinking and feeling, that to abandon or be asked to abandon one's native form of expression may require the denial of a central component of the self (Coleman, 1985). Throughout life deaf persons find their language challenged, first as children when they develop a language different from that of their parents, and later as young adults when they leave the sheltered confines of the institution. These challenges to the language profoundly affect identity and critically affect participation in social activities with peers in adulthood.

American Sign Language is a symbolic badge of identity in the deaf community, yet a knowledge of English is an important part of life in American culture. Despite the effort to learn English, reading and writing remain a problem for most deaf persons in adulthood. The signs themselves often tell a story about the frustrations of ineffective education. For example, one composite sign stands for "Too many big words."

There are signs that indicate negative self-image, such as "dummy" and "pea-brain," and deaf people often apologize to hearing persons or to more highly educated deaf people with comments such as "Me dummy—know nothing."

During the course of research in the deaf community, a recurrent pattern was observed. When individuals were in a group of deaf people they were talkative, confident, outgoing, and relaxed. When they were interacting with people with normal hearing, whether alone or with only a few deaf people present, they became quiet and hesitant. Their self-perceptions shaped two different kinds of behavior, one convivial, sociable, and gregarious, the other wary, timorous, and withdrawn. For this reason, deaf people seek out other deaf people in their social relationships, as comfort in social interaction is a necessary prerequisite for the development of social competence.

Negative feelings about oneself and the language are countered by the tremendous symbolic significance of the language. Since many persons were starved for a means of communication in childhood before they learned sign language, there is immense pride in the language. Its resilience is a testimony to individual perserverance. While language is the vehicle through which all people establish and maintain social relations, language has an added emotional significance for deaf people. The symbolic meaning and richness of the language greatly enhances the ongoing process of socialization.

One important aspect of the development of social competence is the ability to tailor communication to the demands of the social context and to communicate effectively (Norris and Rubin, 1984). Becoming an adept communicator is an important aspect of the development of mastery, and high value is placed on it in the deaf community. Within the context of deaf social events in the deaf community storytelling and debate often take place. People typically arrange their chairs in a big circle. If many persons are present, two circles may form, one of men and one of women. Men and women both participate, and cover a broad range of topics. A battle of wits may take place between two persons telling puns, as they attempt to "out-pun" each other. Or a discussion may ensue of a national political problem, or of some issue within the deaf community.

The use of sign language in the development of social competence makes it a potentially powerful tool in symbolically transforming the overall content and quality of interactions. The potential for sign language to become a conveyer of a sense of mastery and control over the environment is profound. Not only is the stigma attached to sign language negated through this process, sign language as a symbolic badge of identity is reinforced. The act of communication itself is thus symbolically laden with positive reinforcers of self so that the potential for self-actualization through deaf identity is enhanced.

Information Exchange

One purpose of sociability is to exchange information of both a personal and an impersonal nature. Everyone does this as a matter of course. Deaf people, however, underline the importance of information exchange out of a sense of urgent necessity. Deaf persons are not privy to information that has become commonplace to many others because of the linguistic and communication differences that exist. These, in turn, affect deaf persons' level of sophistication on various subjects. For example, the changing status of the birth control pill as a health risk is a subject that assumes considerable knowledge of health and health practices, yet many deaf persons have little information on such a topic.

In interchanges with each other, deaf persons do not limit themselves to information, however. Thoughts, feelings, reactions, and opinions are all a part of the learning process. Interchanges are complex, not simply informational. For example, in the course of a discussion about how to rent an apartment, the individual can talk to peers not only about the "nuts and bolts" of apartment rental but about the frustrations and fears he or she has in carrying out such an undertaking. Feelings of inadequacy that arise from trying to communicate with landlords may emerge in such a discussion, and others may volunteer similar experiences they have had. Such a discussion not only reduces the sense of social isolation that deaf people may experience in their interactions with persons in the hearing world, the problem of the moment is shared with others, thus reducing it in size to something more manageable. In this lifelong process of countless discussions about everyday life, the individual gradually moves from a position of lack of knowledge about the ways of the world to one of considerable knowledge, with a concomitant increase in self-esteem.

Peer learning has become a formalized mechanism for coping with the informational vacuum. For example,

> Mrs. Atkins slipped into her bus seat next to me and said, "Good morning. . .What's the news?" When I apologized for not having anything

new to tell she said, "Well, I just glanced at the paper this morning— there was a drug raid in Oakland yesterday. That's about all."

The emphasis on news is a direct outcome of the lifelong information lag that deaf people experience. It has been channeled and patterned in such a way as to have become an institutionalized part of life. For example, one form of greeting is the sign idiom for "good news." People share both personal and impersonal news at their social gatherings.

Didactic monologues among people with normal hearing are usually limited to special circumstances, such as the formal teaching situation. Within the deaf community didactic monologues are common. One of the ways deaf people receive and communicate information to others is through "telling," a form of didactic teaching that is continually used for relaying information.

Learning also takes place through gossip. Deaf people depend on a variety of sources for information, of which gossip is one. Reliability is a desirable but impossible quality to maintain. When the details of the story are missing, people speculate, and rumor abounds. The information that does get through is often incorrect and is subject to further modification as it is passed from one person to the next. Nevertheless, gossip is social glue. It provides subjects of mutual interest and simultaneously serves peer informational functions. Gossip provides the individual with a broader basis for the social comparison of oneself with others and indirectly provides information about the management of social situations. For example, if an individual has had an embarrassing social interaction with a hearing person that becomes known by his or her peers, it may lead to discussion among peers of how to handle such situations more effectively.

Within the safety of this group of peers, individuals can work at the development of a public self. They can improve their social skills by observing others, and try out new ideas without the fear of being laughed at. They can develop and mature their talents as public speakers and take leadership roles in the community if they chose. These persons are often at the hub of information exchange. Moreover, in taking on these roles, they are not only learning to work cooperatively with others, but they may move on to increasing levels of authority. The gratitude of others and the prestige related to being a spokesperson for the group contribute to self-esteem and balance out other areas of life in which individuals may have little voice, for example, in one's daily job. In this long-term process they develop an appreciation for their own and each others' talents and simultaneously reaffirm their deaf identity.

Friendship

The importance of primary relations throughout the life course for health and well being is one of the most significant findings to come out of the social science literature in recent years. From their review of the literature on social support and health, Schulz and Rau (1985) conclude that intimate contacts buffer the individual both physically and psychologically from a wide variety of health problems. Intimacy, with old and new friends alike, has been found to influence strongly well-being among older people (Lowenthal and Haven, 1968; Weiss, 1979).

Deaf persons' ties to the peer group are striking. These primary relationships often last sixty or more years, extending over the entire course of life. Such long-term relationships are unusual in the United States today, where a pattern of social and geographic mobility is the norm. Life-long peer relationships are more often found in non-industrialized societies. When individuals go through life together as an age-graded group, as do deaf persons, they will experience scheduled life transitions together, such as marriage and the onset of parenting, and will sometimes experience unscheduled transitions such as divorce and the death of relatives as well. These shared experiences take on particular importance as people age.

In old age, deaf people acknowledge changes that have occurred in their behavior over the life-span, and the development of a repertoire of coping behavior that most of them lacked in early adulthood. The coping behavior deaf people exhibit in later life is the result of lifelong socialization. The efforts of older deaf people to achieve mastery over the environment, an American value (Kalish, 1975:85), have thus been relatively successful.

The importance of the peer group may be cyclical across the life span for deaf people in relation to socialization issues. Crucial in early adulthood, it may become less important in mid-life once people have embarked on rearing their families. Once children grow up and start their own families, however, peer socialization reasserts itself and appears to have critical importance in preparing people for old age. Despite the ebb and flow of the peer group in people's lives, sociability continues unwavering throughout life and serves a vital function.

Friendship fulfills a variety of functions for deaf people: it reinforces deaf identity, it draws recognition to the positive aspects of deafness, and it reduces feelings of being "different." This process is very important in fostering self-esteem. Ultimately, friendship becomes a social coping mechanism among deaf people that positively affects their life adjustment and directly influences the aging process.

Deaf individuals often average five or six close friends. In contrasts, Babchuk (1965) states that the model number of close friends in the United States is two. Friendship in the deaf community is initiated by either partner. Friends of both sexes are almost invariably recruited from the peer group of childhood or young adulthood. While intimates are invariably the same sex, many close friendships exist between men and women in the group. Single individuals tend to have their closest friends among the same sex, but socialize with both sexes.

Whether a deaf person has one close confidante or several close friends depends on the individual. Some people have one special friend and a clique, while others have several close friends, having different relationships with each one. For example, one single women's best friend lives in a nearby city. They arrange intensive social interaction over events in the two cities, staying overnight at each other's homes about once a week. This woman also has extremely close relationships with several other women who live near her home. She differentiated her best friend from her other close friends on the basis of confidentiality. She can only maintain her personal privacy by reserving secrets for the best friend.

Men, too, develop intimate relationships with other men. One man mentioned two men with whom he spends most of his time. He said, "You know, we have been great friends for fifty yeas. Of course, there are all these other people who are good friends [indicating a room full of people with a sweeping gesture]. But they [the two men] are my best friends."

The content of relationships such as these is not only informational, it is self-reflective. Over time these exchanges become increasingly intimate. Because the individual is limited to the deaf community for meaningful communication, intense relationships develop and are carried on over the life cycle with the same people. These life-term relationships allow the person freedom of self-expression, enhance personal development, and provide continuity to life.

Peer relationships ensure that individuals will have ample opportunity to reflect on the issues of their particular time of life. Issues change as people age. In their early 20s people are concerned with establishing themselves—where to live, what kind of work to do, who to date, who to marry. In old age the issues are different—coping with the loss of a spouse, with poor health, making the most of retirement. The presence of the same people throughout life ensures an ever-present group of persons with a similar set of concerns with whom these issues may be discussed.

Cliques

Relationships intertwine in complex social networks. A socially active person may have more than one set of primary relationships which may, in turn, overlap with each other. An individual may maintain a complex network without continual interaction. These intense, overlapping relationships are related to the development of cliques. Cliques are defined on the basis of frequency of contact, or on the basis of shared knowledge which excludes others to a certain degree. Both of these factors are important in defining cliques among deaf people.

Cliques are widespread in the deaf community. The most frequent factors determining the make-up of a clique are related to similarities in background, such as attendance at the same school in childhood, and use of sign language versus use of "oral" skills. Other factors such as shared interest and close geographic proximity are also important. The atmosphere of the clique is conducive to discussions of problems of living. The informality and warmth of clique contact provides an optimal environment for on-going socialization. The clique may help the individual to adjust to a new situation. The clique may also fulfill an important role in helping the individual to make life adjustments. It has undoubtedly played such a role in the lives of deaf people. Deaf men and women both participate in cliques. If they are married, they usually participate as a couple. Widowed, divorced, and single men and women are sometimes in mixed cliques and sometimes in sex-segregated cliques.

The overlapping social ties within the group and the public nature of communication results in age peers having considerable knowledge about the lives of most others their age with whom they socialize in large gatherings. Secondary relationships are activated often, especially when members of the primary group are unavailable. These relationships, significant throughout people's lives, attain particular significance in old age. As the community decreases in size through death and immobility, those who remain rely increasingly on secondary relationships for social and emotional nurturance. These relationships, which have demonstrated strength and endurance, are thus able to take over many of the functions of the former primary relationships. They are able to provide strong support because they are so well developed.

Reciprocity

Reciprocity is an important part of social life in the deaf community and is reinforced by deaf identity. Mutual aid takes place most often with neighbors and close friends, and takes many forms — from participation in car pools to care during sickness. As so much social life takes place in large groups, it becomes commonplace to share rides. Ultimately, it becomes a duty. The cliche in the deaf community, "My car is my phone," assumes new importance in old age. As people grow older and less mobile, assistance with transportation becomes more and more important in their lives. People who have cars transport those who do not have cars or those who can no longer use public transportation.

Perhaps the most important kind of mutual aid is group support in time of crisis. As people age, group support becomes a viable, sustaining force that enables individuals to deal with all kinds of problems. During the time I was carrying out research on older people, there were numerous muggings of deaf persons in one urban area. In each case deaf elders responded immediately with a shower of attention and a display of group solidarity. If a person had been an integral member of the group for many years, he or she could count on this kind of support from peers. It takes a lifetime to develop group-wide solidarity, but as its momentum builds, such ongoing support from the peer group reinforces deaf identity and is a sustaining force that helps individuals to cope with the realities of daily life.

LIFELONG ADAPTATION

The symbolic ties between the individual and the group, those **felt** bonds that the individual has for members of the group, have a strong hold on deaf people throughout life. Deaf identity injects every other part of life with meaning. The presence of the deaf community offers assurance that the individual will be able to express himself or herself in language. The need for self-expression is so great that the peer group becomes emotionally charged since it symbolizes the ability to express oneself. Consequently, much of the interaction that takes place in the peer group has ritual significance that reinforces the symbolic bonds that tie individuals to one another.

Deaf people must continually reinforce the symbolism of their collective identity since American Sign Language is a threatened language.

Unlike other languages that evolve down through the generations, sign language is passed on horizontally, through peers (Meadow, 1974:5) since there are few kinship ties between the generations. The deaf children of deaf parents are the linguistic links between the generations, and these persons give a sense of continuity to the language and to the culture itself. The culture is passed on from one generation to the next, however, not only because of these individuals, but because the generations are linguistically mutually intelligible and share a collective identity.

The culture of deafness is thus carried on by the peer group rather than by an enduring institution such as the family. Deaf people must work overtime to sustain and promote the peer group because it exists in an uneasy truce with kin ties. Allegiance is divided between kin and nonkin, a factor that is a lifelong source of stress in the deaf community.

By the time individuals reach adulthood, deafness has become the principle component of identity. Deaf identity continues to strengthen with time, through continual reinforcement from personal experience and from one's social interactions. Throughout adult life the individual's identity as a deaf person directs thought and action and dictates statuses and roles. Identity provides a sense of connectedness and fends off feelings of worthlessness, alienation, and isolation. By late life, the wealth of social relationships many deaf people have has enabled them to achieve considerable social and psychological integration. The development of social competence has facilitated self-knowledge and self-acceptance. The peer support system has thus played a central role in both their adaptation to deafness and their adaptation to old age.

Although intimacy, reciprocity, and primary relationships develop mainly within peer groups, individuals also participate in the broader social system of the deaf community. The nature of the community encourages a certain degree of intergenerational interaction. In contrast to many other sectors of society, older people play an important role in the deaf community. They are part of its historical development, and as an age group they are the most stable. Generally speaking, they have the bulk of the power in the deaf community. Their money supports deaf causes. They provide role models for younger deaf people. The elderly are concerned with their language and their culture, and they have a vested interest in passing them on to younger generations. Younger people, in turn, often view older people as carrying the heritage and traditions of the deaf community. Community leaders, when speaking about the problems of deafness, frequently cite the contrast in coping ability between young and old, and acknowledge the arduous process of life adjustment that deaf people undergo. Despite generational differences in social behavior and the effects of ongoing social change, deaf people gain a sense of continuity from their participation in the deaf community that is often the sustaining link in an otherwise difficult life.

IMPLICATIONS OF SOCIALIZATION

The development of a strong deaf identity is critical to the development of a sense of personal well-being, even though deaf identity incorporates negative self-perceptions (Becker, 1981). Deaf identity is shaped to a large extent by peer socialization. The commonality of shared experience, the frequency of interaction with other deaf people, and successful communication about the meaningful, intimate aspects of everyday life all contribute to the development of a sense of self-esteem that grows with time. The collective identity of deafness defines roles, validates identity, involves people in meaningful interaction, and facilitates the development of autonomy. As society changes, and as the educational structure in which deaf persons grow up evolves, peer socialization remains a central component of the deaf community.

Although most deaf people now in old age have lived out their lives in a fairly homogenous community of peers, there are indications that the peer group has become more fragmented among deaf youth. Educational changes and increased ethnic heterogeneity have contributed to this emerging trend. Ethnicity is an important marker of identity. Attitudes held by society toward ethnic minorities are reflected in the deaf community, and affect interpersonal behavior. Members of ethnic minorities are often excluded from group activities on the basis of ethnicity. As a result, they have a smaller peer support system because of exclusion from the activities of the larger group.. There has been a great increase in the number of ethnic minorities in California since World War II. Immigrant families from other countries as well as families from other parts of the United States have moved to California, and contribute to the cultural diversity of this area, in contrast to other areas of the United States that may reflect greater homogeneity. The deaf children of these families frequently have difficulty in learning their family's traditions. Members of ethnic minorities are often unable to reconcile their ethnicity with their deafness. Moreover, they often experience prejudice and have difficulty in being assimilated by the deaf community. This dilemma results in conflict with the family, social isolation from the peer group, and perpetuates their marginal status in society, in their ethnic group, and in the deaf community. The identity conflict between deafness and ethnicity may be difficult for many persons to overcome.

These strengths and dilemmas of peer socialization have implications for the education of deaf persons, for interactions between deaf and hearing persons, and for existing systems of social support deaf people have developed.

1. Education for daily life. Deaf youth could benefit from training in daily living skills. Training that covers the basics of survival and addresses the gamut of problems of everyday life would help to make the transition to adulthood smoother and ease the stress of this period of life. For example, professionals working with deaf persons in employment and vocational training may be unaware of the extent to which the difficulties persons experience in attempting to manage other parts of their lives may adversely affect their job performance. Education should also be easily accessible to deaf persons in subsequent transitions, such as classes on childbirth and care of the newborn baby. In addition, continuing education that is widely available to and utilized by the general public on topics of health, family life, and the like should be specially tailored for deaf persons, using the peer group as a resource for recruitment. Such training would not detract from the important function the peer group plays but would enhance individual functioning and the peer group's ability to support individuals in their efforts to be independent adults.

2. Interaction with the hearing world. In spite of the self-assurance deaf persons often develop as members of a peer group, they are often wary and unsure of themselves in encounters with the hearing world, especially in formal situations with professionals. They are easily intimidated when communication with hearing persons does not proceed well. In an effort to avoid appearing ignorant they may say they understand something when they do not. If interactions become too difficult, they may withdraw and fail to return, even when a need clearly exists, such as medical care or job counseling. In formal interactions, interpreters should be provided. In certain situations it may be appropriate to also invite the deaf person to bring a friend if the person desires it, for example, to a stressful medical appointment, or to an introduction of a community agency's services.

3. Integration of deaf persons into agencies serving the general population. Participation in the activities of the hearing world is often perceived as unimportant by deaf persons when they are immersed in a strong peer group. Segregation from the hearing world, however, perpetuates minority group status and may prevent access to services and information available to the general population that is critical to well-being. Integration of persons into agencies serving hearing persons is possible with thought and effort and should be encouraged. The most successful way in which to extend services to the deaf population may be through the peer group. It has been found that integration of deaf peer groups into agencies serving the general population enhances self-determination and boosts self-esteem (Becker and Nadler, 1980).

4. Using the peer group as a resource. While groups of deaf peers are in the community, not every deaf person may be linked to them. Indeed, persons who require considerable intervention by professionals may be those very persons who are isolated from the peer group and the deaf community. Professionals working with such persons can facilitate the process of integrating the deaf individual into a peer group through appropriate referrals. For example, the presence of a program for deaf students should be a major consideration in planning an individual's vocational training at a junior college. Linkages can also be established through consolidation with community leaders, introductions to other deaf persons at the same age and background, and through attendance at community events.

CONCLUSION

The deaf community provides an example of how a strong system of social support can alter the course of people's lives. The peer support system influences self-perception and enhances coping ability. The more embedded such a system is in the fabric of everyday life, the greater impact it will have, and the more profoundly it will influence individual health and well-being. Whether the linkages that form this system will remain as strong over time despite cultural changes both within and outside of the deaf community is as yet unknown. Nevertheless, perpetuation of this system is essential to the well being of deaf persons. The peer support system is invaluable to deaf people in the process of adaptation. It has important implications for other Americans in combatting the stress of life in our complex society.

FOOTNOTE

1. The observations in this paper are based on the author's experiences in the deaf community of the San Francisco Bay Area. Two one-year research projects were conducted. The first project, carried out with 200 deaf persons over the age of 60, was concerned with the impact of lifelong deafness on old age. Data was gathered through daily participant-observation and through in-depth interviews with 60 persons. The second project was carried out with deaf persons between the ages of 20 and 60 and focused on adaptation to deafness over the life course, with particular attention to the development of coping behavior in early adulthood. In addition to extensive participant-observation in the deaf community, 40 in-depth interviews were carried out.

REFERENCES

Ablon, Joan: *Little People in America.* New York, Praeger, 1984.

Albrecht, Gary: Adult socialization: ambiguity and adult life crises. In Datan, Nancy and Ginsberg, Leon H.: *Life-Span Developmental Psychology: Normative Life Crises.* New York, Academic Press, 1975, pp. 237-251.

Atchley, Robert C.: The life course, age grading, and age-linked demands for decision making. In Datan, Nancy and Ginsberg, Leon H.: *Life-Span Developmental Psychology: Normative Life Crises.* New York, Academic Press, 1975, pp. 261-278.

Babchuk, Nicholas: Primary friends and kin: a study of the associations of middle-class couples. *Social Forces, 43:*485-493, 1965.

Becker, Gaylene: *Growing Old in Silence.* Berkeley, University of California Press, 1980.

Becker, Gaylene: Coping with stigma: lifelong adaptation of deaf people. *Social Science and Medicine, 15B:*21-24, 1981.

Becker, Gaylene and Arnold, Regina: Stigma as a social and cultural construct. In Ainlay, Stephen, Becker, Gaylene, and Coleman, Lerita: *The Dilemma of Difference: A Multidisciplinary View of Stigma.* New York, Plenum, 1986, pp. 39-57.

Becker, Gaylene and Nadler, Gay: The aged deaf: integration of a disabled group into an agency serving elderly people. *Gerontologist, 20:*214-221, 1980.

Brim, Orville and Wheeler, S.: *Socialization After Childhood.* New York, Wiley, 1966.

Brown, Roger W.: Language and categories. In Bruner, J. S., Goodnow, J. J. and Austin, G. A.: *A Study of Thinking.* New York, Wiley, 1962, pp. 247-312.

Cohen, Yehudi A.: The shaping of men's minds: adaptations to imperatives of culture. In Wax, Murray L., Diamond, Stanley, and Gearing, Fred O.: *Anthropological Perspectives on Education.* New York, Basic Books, 1971, pp. 19-50.

Coleman, Lerita: Language and the evolution of identity and self-concept. In Kessel, F.: *The Development of Language and Language Researchers: Essays in Tribute to Roger R. Brown.* Hillsdale, Erlbaum, 1985.

Davis, Fred: *Passage Through Crisis.* Indianapolis, Bobbs-Merrill, 1963.

Freidson, Eliot: Disability as social deviance. In Sussman, Marvin B.: *Sociology and Rehabilitation*. Washington, D.C., American Sociological Association and Vocational Rehabilitation Administration, USDHEW, 1966, pp. 71-99.

Goffman, Erving: *Asylums*. Garden City, Doubleday, 1961.

Goffman, Erving: *Stigma: Notes on the Management of Spoiled Identity*. Englewood Cliffs, Prentice-Hall, 1963.

Henry, Jules: *Pathways to Madness*. New York, Random House, 1965.

Hultsch, Davis F. and Plemons, Judy K.: Life events and life-span development. In Baltes, Paul and Brim, Orville, G.: *Life-Span Development and Behavior*. New York, Academic Press, 1979, vol. 2, pp. 1-26.

Kalish, Richard: *Late Adulthood: Perspectives on Human Development*. Monterey, Brookes/Cole, 1975.

Lee, Dorothy, *Freedom and Culture*. Englewood Cliffs, Prentice-Hall, 1959.

Lowenthal, Marjorie Fiske and Haven, Clayton: Interaction and adaptation: intimacy as a critical variable. In Neugarten, Bernice: *Middle Age and Aging*. Chicago, University of Chicago Press, 1968, pp. 390-400.

Martin, Larry G.: Stigma: a social learning perspective. In Ainlay, Stephen, Becker, Gaylene, and Coleman, Lerita: *The Dilemma of Difference: A Multidisciplinary View of Stigma*. New York, Plenum, 1986, pp. 145-161.

Mead, Margaret: *Culture and Commitment: A Study of the Generation Gap*. New York Natural History Press, 1970.

Meadow, Kathryn P.: The quiet worlds of deafness — A sociological description of the deaf subculture. Faculty Workshop, California State University, Hayward, October 15, 1974, mimeo.

Mortimer, Jeylan T. and Roberta G. Simmons: Adult socialization. *Annual Review of Sociology, 4:*421-454, 1978.

Norris, Joan E. and Rubin, Kenneth H.: Peer interaction and communication: a life-span perspective. In Baltes, Paul, and Brim, Orville: *Life-Span Development and Behavior*. New York, Academic Press, 1984, vol. 6, pp. 355-391.

Pearlin, Leonard I.: Discontinuities in the study of aging. In Harevan, Tamara: *Aging and Life Course Transitions: An Interdisciplinary Perspective*. New York, Guilford Press, 1982, pp. 55-74.

Schlesinger, Hilde S.: Responsiveness of the environment — residential school living. In Naiman, D. W.: *Inservice Training of the Afterclass Staff in Residential Schools for Deaf Children*. New York, Deafness Research and Training Center, New York University, 1972.

Schlesinger, Hilde S. and Meadow, Kathryn P.: *Sound and Sign*. Berkeley, University of California Press, 1972.

Schulz, Richard and Rau, Marie T.: Social support through the life course. In Cohen, Sheldon and Syme, L. Leonard: *Social Support and Health*. New York, Academic Press, 1985, pp. 129-149.

Spiro, Melford: *Children of the Kibbutz*. New York, Schocken, 1965.

Weiss, Lawrence J.: Intimacy and adaptation. In Weg, Ruth: *Sexuality in the Later Years: Roles and Behavior*. Menlo Park, Addison-Wesley, 1979.

Yarrow, Leon J.: Separation from parents during early childhood. In Hoffman, Martin L. and Hoffman, Lois W.: *Review of Child Development Research*. New York, Russell Sage Foundation, 1964, pp. 89-136.

CHAPTER 4

WHO SIGNS TO WHOM?
THE AMERICAN SIGN LANGUAGE
COMMUNITY

JEFFREY E. NASH

FOR AT LEAST one hundred and fifty years, deaf people in the United States of America have been signing among themselves and to hearing people who happened to be members of their families or communities (Groce, 1980; Lane, 1980; Washabaugh, 1981; Woodward, 1978). But, because of the absence of adequate empirical data, a detailed answer to the question "Who Signs to Whom?" has been very difficult to find. At one level the question seems narrow, requiring only that we count people who report they can sign. However, when we expand the scope of the question to include a description of types of signers, the varieties of signs they use and the social conditions under which they used them, the question becomes more complex and sociolinguistic.

In this paper, I want to take a first step toward a complete sociolinguistic description of the American Sign Language Community, and in doing so, connect our understanding of this "language community" with more general sociolinguistic principles. When we do this, we see that the relationship between American Sign Language and English is particularly interesting, since American Sign Language users appear to be especially resistant to language use policies aimed at shifting them to English. To what degree has there been a shift from signs to English among deaf people, then, becomes a question of general sociolinguistic importance.

While the reasons for efforts to depict the composition of the Sign Language Community may be understandable, the task itself requires considerable guess work. Historical data are nonexistent and even current census data do not include ASL as a language "other than English" (cf. Veltman, 1983). There is, however, a rich literature on deaf educational policy that allows an indirect assessment of shift and maintenance questions. These educational policies have waxed and waned in terms of promoting and retarding shift from signs to English. In this paper, I review briefly this literature, working under the conviction that ASL is the preferred and dominant language of American deaf people (Woodward, 1980; Stokoe, 1978). I also describe language policy in deaf education, and set forth an explanation of the apparent resilience of sign usage which connects ASL maintenance with the character of the deaf community.

AMERICAN SIGN LANGUAGE

Over the past two decades, there has been a great deal of research attempting to depict and explain the linguistic character of American Sign Language. While we need not review the intricacies of this research, we can draw on it to give the reader an idea of what we mean when we refer to American Sign Language.

Generally, American Sign Language is a visual, natural language. This means that it can be described according to its structure and function as a rule governed communicative system. It has rules which define its basic elements, rules which permit users to combine these elements into larger meaningful units, and it is sufficient for a full range of social applications (Stokoe, 1978). In short, American Sign Language (ASL) exists as a minority, natural language within the larger language environment of the United States of America.

Not only has ASL been ignored as a minority languge, there are many stereotypes about it. For example, many people think of it as simply "writing in the air," "like Indian Sign Language," as a kind of "signal system," or a "complex set of gestures." While it is true that American Sign Language has many distinctive features (Fischer, 1978), linguistic research has established what sign language users have known all along—that their visual language is a fully developed language which allows for a full range of human activities, from complex problem solving, and social relationships to delicate and beautiful story telling.

The contrast between what recent linguistic research says about ASL and policies toward it is startling. On the one hand, ASL takes its place among the languages of the world, and the other, it has been and remains a target of systematic efforts to either change or eliminate it. To understand this contrast, and its sociolinguistic significance we turn to a brief review of language policy.

LANGUAGE POLICY IN DEAF EDUCATION

Building on Lane's (1980) work, three definite phases in efforts to replace American Sign Language with English can be identified. The first phase is the early period during which the extreme tendencies promoting and oppressing signs were first articulated. In this phase, Lane cites such important events as Pereire's appearance before the French Academy of Science, the establishment of Epee's school and Sicard's lectures at the first Normal School.

The second phase from the early 1800's to the turn of the century shows the mixed effects of educational philosophy, medical opinion and technological developments. Lane points to Itard's influence, the establishment of The American Asylum and other schools for the deaf in America as well as the emergence of oralism and the involvement of A. G. Bell, Horace Mann and other educators. This period ends with the International Conference supporting oralism, a policy which promotes replacement of signs with a dominant spoken language.

The final phase includes the professionalization of educational services for the hearing impaired and the era of the sign linguist. The most important social forces relevant to replacement of signs are: the certification of teachers — a process which required that teachers be trained in techniques of instruction in lip reading and speech production, but not in sign language; the popularization of oralism with the success of the Tracy clinic; and, finally, the emergence of linguists as experts on matters of language and the influence that they are able to exert on educational policy and practice. Each of these historical occurrences has implications which either promote or retard the replacement process.

The events of the first phase and of early phase two retarded the replacement of signs while in the final stage of phase two replacement policies prevailed. In phase three, dating from 1960 to present, replacement seems once again to be retarded. In the most general terms possible, the process which Lane and others depict is a shift from signs to English. This process entails either outright oppression of signs, as in the case of the establishment of the Clark School, or it took the form of a linguistic cooptation in which signs became a kind of dialect (a visual variety) of the dominant spoken language (cf. Kloss, 1963).

Signs and whatever systematic expression deaf people gave to them were being replaced through negative evaluation and powerful political and economic pressures to adopt the techniques of the British and other educators who had developed techniques to teach the deaf to speak the dominant language of their native country. According to Lane, replacement in the United States and in Europe really gained ground after 1900 until in American schools English became the sole "vehicle of instruction" (Lane, 1980:158).

While Lane's history is restricted to information available on the status of the replacement of sign in educational systems, Groce (1980) and Woodward (1978) underscore the imperative nature of understanding the disparity which existed between whatever native gestural communicative system deaf people employed and the majority language of the communities within which they lived. This disparity requires attention because it helps to account for why in one realm, such as the educational, replacement can be rather complete while in another, the everyday lives of deaf people, signs are maintained.

LINGUISTIC UNDERSTANDINGS OF SIGN SYSTEMS

Whereas the literature on policy and the history of policy are rather complete, there are virtually no systematic examinations of signs until William Stokoe published his short structural analysis of signs in 1960. Stokoe (1960) discovered that the gestural system used by deaf people living in the Washington D.C. area could be understood according to the same principles which were said to distinguish human languages from other communicative systems. Just as spoken languages universally manifest an atomic system — they can be described as systems of finite elements which combine into seemingly infinite expressions — so does American Sign Language. Stokoe showed that signs can be likewise depicted. In his early work, he presented a sketch of elements of signs based on the minimal pair technique. He identified these elements as the shape of the hand (dez), the direction of movement the signer gives the sign (sig), and where the hand is located on the signer's torso (tab). Since his first publication, he and others have added a fourth class, the orientation of interlocutors. Stokoe and the research he fostered made a clear case for the proposition that sign systems are not merely nonverbal or paralinguistic phenomena, but are systems governed by rules much the same as those that govern spoken languages.

Other researchers (Bellugi and Fischer, 1972) demonstrated that signers make mistakes which are similar to the mistakes speakers make. This "slip of the hand" idea also pointed to the same discovery, but it was Stokoe who pushed the analogy between spoken and sign language to its logical conclusion: Sign in general and American Sign Language in particular is a natural language. As Stokoe indicated in an interview conducted by James P. Spradley in 1976, his discovery was not initially appreciated. Some of his colleagues at Gallaudet College thought he was misguided, or that he was wasting his time studying sign since the education of deaf people bore no relationship whatsoever to sign language. Moreover, his detractors reasoned, what difference could it make to describe sign as if it were a spoken language since it obviously is not.

Soon, however, linguists took note of Stokoe's work. They had regarded vocal articulation as a universal feature of human language (Hockett, 1978). Stokoe and the work of his associates seemed to demand a revision in the definitions of language, a revision which reinforced structural conceptions of language. There can also be little question that Stokoe's discovery called for a serious reconsideration of the role of sign language in every aspect of the lives of deaf people, including educational settings, and, therefore, a consideration of its maintenance and shift along lines hitherto unsuspected.

A major impetus for the replacement of signs in the classroom had been the widespread belief that signs were merely gestures, or at best a primitive language. Correspondingly, pedogogic techniques were developed to exclude and oppress the use of signing among children. Over a one hundred and fifty year period such pedagogy had the dramatic effect of eliminating sign language from educational institutions as a medium of instruction. Now, after Stokoe's discovery, signs could still be oppressed, but the professional grounds on which this oppression was to take place had to change. It is at this juncture that Stokoe and the sign linguists influenced by his work changed their research emphasis. As Fischer (1978:309) wrote, in the past

> Those of us working on ASL had a special psycholinguistic or sociolinguistic ax to grind. This ax very easily evolved into a political one as well. We were all interested in showing that ASL really was (and is) a real, live natural language—that just because it is produced in space and perceived by the eyes makes it no less a language. . .It became apparent all too soon, however, that it was difficult to maintain that ASL was totally parallel to oral language, and the pendulum began to swing to concentrating on differences between the two modalities rather than the similarities.

While sign systems may well be natural languages, that fact in and of itself does not justify changes in educational efforts. The work of the sign linguists does have implications for the processes of replacement and maintenance which are clearly in favor of maintenance. Sign linguists, I should note, were not working alone in the battle against efforts to replace sign language. Although less explicit in design, several psychological researchers (Stuckless and Birch, 1966) helped retard replacement by conducting studies which showed that children who never learned signing but received exclusively oral training did not necessarily have better English language skills than bilingual children (those children who both signed and received instruction in speaking and lip reading skills).

Once the ideological battle began to shape up, some sign linguists, including Stokoe, who had shifted their work to dissimilarities renewed their emphasis on similarities. What seems to have happened is that sign linguists realized that the implications of the dissimilarity approach seemed to foster replacement. They, then, tried to find a way to think again in terms of similarities. Presumably, this shift would shore up maintenance efforts. Fischer (1978:310), for example, suggests using creoles which are "unofficial languages" composed of elements of both a minority and majority language rather than "established languages" as the basis for comparison. Although creoles are not often afforded a high status in their speech communities, perhaps the status of creole could become a starting point. After all, New Guinea Pidgin has been elevated to the status of language as Neo-Melonesian.

Sign linguists, it appears, are aware of the implications for replacement and maintenance in the way they conceive of signs. Two of the ways to conceive of signs have already been mentioned. They are to think of signs as structurally similar to spoken language and to think of signs as a kind of creole. To think of signs as a visual spoken language means, among other things, that like speakers of minority languages in the United States, sign users should have the right to use their native language.

However, as Llanes (1981) has pointed out, most bilingual programs in the United States are aimed at facilitating English language learning. They are transitional rather than maintenance programs and are ultimately aimed at the replacement of the minority language with the dominant English language. Like other minority language speaking children, the young deaf signer typically does not do well in English compared to children whose native language is English. As Erting (1978) shows, the language deaf children use in the classroom, even if that language is designed to be a visual version of English, is not actually English, but a kind of sign pidgin.

The analogy of sign language as a minority language is strengthened by observations which link deaf children's performances in English and signs with those of other minority children, like Hispanics, and by the realization that sign English is not English. Erting (1978) calls for a binlingual policy in education which, of course, would not only promote maintenance but also spread as children, their parents and others might learn ASL. However, the programmatic aspects of this policy are linked to support for bilingualism in general. Fischer's work on signs as creole is likewise affected by the success or failure of bilingual policy, and by the strategies proponents and detractors of such policy might devise. Whether ASL is conceived as "language" or "creole" could become a variable in determining the outcome of bilingual policy.

Other ways to conceive of signs have been suggested by Stokoe and by Washabaugh. Stokoe believes that sign language is an important phenomenon to understand in terms of the role it played in the evolution of human communication. He has expounded the view that sign languages preceded spoken language in man. Of course, he in no way means that modern sign languages like ASL are primitive. Such a view would obviate his powerful demonstration of the structure of signs. The significance of his work on signs as symptomatic of human symbolic communication is that apparently signs are learned in a qualitatively different way than spoken languages. The implications of this position for maintenance of ASL are provocative: even if replacement policies were totally successful in the educational setting, as they nearly are, it may be the case that visual languages trigger the language acquisition process in deaf children in a way that spoken languages do not. Hence, the replacement processes do involve offering a different language and incentives to learn it, but they amount to a suppression of language itself.

Conceiving of primordial character of a signing capacity in the human species may not appear to be a solid footing for maintenance processes since it implies that visual languages are "underdeveloped." However, it can help account for the survival of ASL under social conditions which do not seem conducive to maintenance.

SIGN PRACTICE IN THE DEAF COMMUNITY

To appreciate this line of reasoning, one must first understand the distinctive character of the sign community. As Table 1 shows, the sign community differs in some basic ways from other minority language communities. In conventional ethnic groups, members of the first generation have the ethnic mother tongue as native, and, according to which group is being examined, second and third generations shift from the ethnic to the dominant language. In the sign community, there is a peculiar relationship between nativity and generation. The proportion of the community who are first generation, native signers is very low (7%), while the overwhelming majority of the community is comprised of people who learn sign rather late in life, usually in late adolescence and early adulthood. The sign community, then, does not fit the shift trends for minority languages in the United States. A full appreciation of why this is the case and why ASL seems so resilient requires attention to questions of practice—the uses to which deaf people put signs in their social lives.

Prevailing theories of language acquisition imply that there should be striking deficiencies and significant differences between the ways in which native and late signers sign. Stokoe and others who have researched these questions have not discovered such deficiencies. Surely, there is room for much more careful testing of observations about the lack of deficiencies. Qualifications must be made for children with behavioral, emotional and even physical impairments which might impede the acquisition of language. Still, the experiences of field researchers who recognize the power and proficiency of late signers means Stokoe's view warrants serious consideration. He claims that sign language learning taps a learning process grounded in the human brain that may lie in a kind of parallel mode to learning spoken language. Since most people (including those born deaf) never tap fully this mode in childhood, it lies dormant, ready to activate when exposed to the proper stimulus. Of course, the implication is that learning a spoken language during the so called critical period may suppress this system which, however, has no critical period of its own.

Insofar as implications for maintenance are concerned, Stokoe's conceptions argue against any suspicions that because no strong numerical base of native language users exists, the language is in danger of extinction. Rather, his conceptions support the idea that when deaf people are exposed to signs, they will learn them effortlessly.

Washabaugh (1981, 1982) has advanced the notion of signs as a contact language. While he, like Stokoe, supports the similarities analog with spoken language, his approach differs in emphasis. Perhaps because his field studies allowed him to view closely the early development

Table 1
Demographic Composition of Sign Community*

Native Signers	n and % of Community	Late Signers	n and % of Community
		Deaf Child, Both Parents Hearing (only child)	n = 60,000 13%
		Deaf Child, Hearing Parents and Hearing Siblings	n = 250,000 56%
		Interpreters	n = 10,500 2%
		Hearing Siblings	n = 5,000 1%
Both Parents Deaf	n = 36,000 8%		
		Teachers of Deaf (Includes Staff)	n = 14,500 3%
One Parent Deaf	n = 14,000 3%		
		Hearing Parents	n = 50,000 11%
		Ministers of Deaf	n = 1,000 2%
		Others	n = 6,000 1%
Total Native Signers	= 50,000 11%	Total Late Signers	= 397,000 89%

*These figures are estimates derived either from actual official counts (teachers of the deaf) or extrapolated from other sources (for example, only children late signers is a direct proportion of the single child families in the United States as reported in the 1980 census). In no way should these numbers be construed as parameters. They are intended to convey the distribution of demographic features which compose the sign language community in the United States and to underscore the need for an official sociolinguistic survey of the community.

Sources: Schein 1982; Woodward 1978; Cokely 1981; *American Annual of the Deaf,* Services Issue 1982.

of a sign language (he studied a small group of deaf people and their nascent sign language on the Providence Islands), he has a full appreciation of the social functions of signs built into his conception. He writes

> While sign language and oral languages are essentially alike, deaf and hearing communications are different. Specifically, deaf communication. . .makes use of the two cofoundational communicative processes (meaning exchange and presence manipulation) to different degrees (1982:249).

Washabuagh is explicit about the "cofoundational" processes. By meaning exchange he refers to traditional conceptions of language which include all the devices contrived and conventionalized to transmit meanings from person to person. Of course, this aspect of a communicative system includes, among other things, grammar, vocabulary and "rules" for the efficient use of them.

"Presence" manipulation is another sort of process. He argues that the primary function of these communications is not the exchange of information but the establishment of CONTACT. Some contact is physical, other kinds are more concerned with symbolic or identity linkages among people. He suggests that careful linguistic analyses of sign support the hypothesis that sign language functions "to 'remind' interactants of the cultural ground on which they all stand" (Washabaugh, 1982:247).

Washabaugh cites evidence which demonstrates that the ratio of meaning to presence manipulation differs among different communities. For example, in traditional ethnic communities like those found in large, urban "ghettos" when people get together, they use their native language, not so much to "encode" messages, but to establish their distinctive identity as a group. Hence, we find a strong emphasis on story telling, gossip and the re-enactment of events, often ritualistic, which are shared by the group.

Such social occasions provide us with sharp example of the ways language function to establish and maintain group identity. According to Washabaugh, in sign language communities, this ratio favors presence as it does in some spoken language communities. In other words, deaf people may sign to each other less to find out about what is happening in the larger, hearing society and more to establish for themselves a distinctive sense of belonging to a group.

Efforts at replacement of signs, if Washabaugh's thesis of "contact" language is correct, are, in effect, efforts at the destruction of the community of deaf people. That community is strongly grounded in shared competencies in the use of sign (Nash and Nash, 1981). If signs were replaced by English, the quality of interactions among deaf people would be changed and the very existence of deaf communities would be challenged.

The implication for language maintenance is straightforward, if not simplistic. Sign language is the cement of the deaf community. Its appeal derives from the contrast it provides to the dominant language. However, as Groce (1980) has shown, signing alone may not be sufficient to produce a sign community. In her research on Martha's Vineyard, she found that hearing and deaf people alike signed but a strong, distinctive "sign community" apparently did not develop. Probably, other sociological factors like discrimination, social and geographical isolation are also necessary to the formation of a true "community."

As far as replacement policy is concerned, the vitality of sign depends upon its opposition to the dominant spoken language. If signs were to become an official language of deaf education, for example, this might change the ratio of meaning to presence functions in favor of meaning and might weaken the contact function of signs. We could speculate that in this event, a register of signs might be invented by children and adults too to establish contact as happens in dominant English. Presently, much of the attraction of ASL depends on it remaining low in the diglossic relationship it now has with oral and manual representations of English (Woodward, 1978; Hawkins, 1984). Diglossia is a term sociolinguists use to refer to the situation in a society where there are two or more forms of a language (High and Low German, for example) and one form has higher status than the other; or where there are two or more languages and one has higher status than the others. The concept is useful when applied to understanding the relationship between ASL and English. What seems to be true of sign language, as it is for other "low status" languages, is that it functions to impart a sense of belonging to its users partly because of its "low status."

I can now summarize the implications of varieties of conceptions of signs for replacement efforts. If ASL is conceived as structurally identical to spoken language, then bilingual educational policies are called for. These policies, at least in America, are, by and large, transitional — leading to a shift to English. If ASL is conceived as structurally similar to creoles, then the language will have no official status in an educational system. It could be tolerated or even appreciated through allowing it to be the language of contact among children and adults and even the subject of study. However, as long as educational institutions function as socialization agents for core values of American culture, it is likely that English will retain its role as chief channel to these values. Conceiving of signs as creoles implies their replacement.

THE RESILIENCE OF ASL

When one conceives of ASL as a language heavily oriented toward presence manipulation (a "contact language"), he or she is describing underlying sociological functions. Social functions often are latent and have indirect consequences for various groups implicated in a set of practices. Hence, an account of the persistence of ASL should attend to its functional consequences. ASL has survived almost 200 years of replacement efforts, it turns out, because of the latent functions it has for deaf communities.

Currently, no educational system in the United States uses ASL as an official language of instruction. It is also clear from the work of Erting, that the use of manual English in the classroom is quite different from the use of ASL. Children may well rely on their ASL competency to figure out what a teacher means or they may even depend on other deaf people (other children or a teacher's aide, for example) to reinterpret teachers' remarks and instructions. Still, the official language of the classroom is English. Perhaps a more accurate way to express this is that the children are dealt with in English. Therefore, although total communication approaches have become the approved pedagogy, this in no way represents a weakening of the replacement policy which underlies special education for the hearing impaired.

Table 2

Enrollment in Deaf Education

Date	Day Schools		Residential Schools		Total
1961	n = 9,132	% = 33	n = 18,457	% = 67	N = 27,589
1971	n = 28,975	% = 63	n = 17,100	% = 37	N = 46,075
1981	n = 33,684	% = 73	n = 12,572	% = 27	N = 46,256

Source: *American Annual of the Deaf,* Special issues on service

Statistics on enrollment and policy affecting the 47,000 hearing impaired children receiving special education in America at present gloss

over the amazing variety of manual and oral communication that actually takes place in the classroom (see Table 2). However, there has
been a dramatic change in these enrollments over the last thirty years
which does have implications for the maintenance of ASL. Many researchers, since the advent of sign linguists, have noted that residential
schools, even though many, if not most, forbade the use of ASL among
their pupils, provided the institutional bases for the learning of sign language. The typical experience of a deaf child thirty years ago was to
spend several frustrating years at oral education while living at home
and then to enroll at a very early age in the state residential school for
the deaf. We have seen how these schools in American society supported, at least tacitly, the use of signs. While it is true that the years
1940 to 1960 were years in which oral pedagogy dominated even these
schools, the roots of signing were deep and unbroken at these schools.
These same schools employ the largest portions of deaf teachers, have
deaf people working on staff and because of their long histories, the
communities in which they are located often have accommodated relatively large numbers of deaf people and at least tolerated institutional
supports for the deaf/sign community.

Support networks—in Washabaugh's terms, the contact function of
signing—were clearly in place at residential schools. Since 1960, however, a clear, strong and persistent trend in enrollment is toward more
and more deaf children entering and staying enrolled in day schools
while they live with parents or guardians year around. The opportunities for contact between deaf children are limited to a much greater extent than was the case in the residential school. Even though these day
schools may be using some kind of manual communicative system for
instructional purposes, the students receive limited exposure to signs.

However, the social functions which signs perform apparently remain unchanged in spite of the replacement policies of educational institutions. For example, Wilcox (1984) reports on how a group of high
school deaf students creatively modified the meanings of the sign
STUCK to express their dislike for school—their version of the predicament of being in school. They accomplished this communicative process
even though teachers were aware of the lexical item STUCK in sign language. They did this by applying some ASL rules which, of course the
teachers were not as competent in using as the students.

The sign STUCK is formed with the "v" hand shape and a movement
toward and even touching the throat. Its meaning is varied. It can be
used to refer to an object mired in the mud, to a predicament in which

one finds him or herself, or to simply being stymied by a problem (Wilcox, 1984). The deaf students at the high school Wilcox studied, however, used the sign more as a device to establish contact among themselves rather than to convey meanings to teachers or others. They modified the inflectional gestures associated with the sign to establish a sense of predicament in being "STUCK in school," but at the same time, a sense of having "caught" teachers and other students in this predicament. Students had changed the referent of the sign so that its use conveyed a sense of having "attacked" another person and somehow placed them in a sticky situation. Wilcox relates how over a period from 1981 to 1982, the students evolved the specialized use of STUCK as a way to insult and symbolically place teachers outside of the network of students. Hence, when teachers would ask students to provide answers to classroom lessons, they would invoke the special use of their sign so that they would sign "teacher STUCK" much to the delight of other students and to the puzzlement of the teachers. They were communicating a message to each other and the teacher "I've got power over you; I'm able to put you in your place." Wilcox reports that teachers never fully understood the use of STUCK, but did after a while come to think of it as a "dirty" sign. They forbad its use. Wilcox concludes that the students involved in this STUCK phenomenon were transfer students from residential schools and students who often had a reputation as "trouble makers." He also notes these same students comprise a large proportion of the total enrollment of hearing impaired students at this school (19 out of 39).

The detail of Wilcox's study provides us with some information about the fate of ASL in the trend toward the day school. As one might expect, ASL seems to once again function to establish contact among people who feel oppressed and STUCK in situations largely outside their control. Certainly, registers or argots of English which are used by young hearing students also function in this fashion. However, ASL becomes a strong identifier which persists as a channel for the establishment of symbolic networks in ways that argots or registers do not. In other words, ASL functions like a superordinate register binding people together with a master status of deafness (Higgins, 1980).

The trend to day schools does not necessarily mean replacement of ASL. Instead, it simply reinforces the contact function of ASL and ensures the continuation of the diglossic relationship between ASL and forms of signing which embody English.

Table 3

Recent Evidence on Maintenance and/or Spread of ASL

Findings	Implications for Maintenance and/or Spread	Source
Teachers of Deaf Assess Interpreting and ASL Instruction as Top Concerns of Next Decade.	Possibly Positive for Both	Prickett and Hunt, 1977
Majority of Canadian Teachers Believe ASL not Appropriate in Classroom. They do not Endorse Bilingual Educational Policies.	Neutral for Maintenance Negative for Spread	Steward, 1983
Teachers Endorse Sign English.	Negative for Both	Steward, 1983; Morres, 1978; Quigley, 1983
Enormous and Steady Growth in Sign Language Instruction (High School, Junior and Community Colleges).	Possibly Positive for Both	Delgado, 1984
Trend Toward Hiring Hearing Impaired as Sign Instructors (28% now Hearing Impaired).	Possibly Positive for Both	Delgado, 1984
Survey of Orally Schooled Adults Reveals They Know ASL.	Positive for Both	Arnold and Francis, 1983
Orally Schooled Adults Approve Oralism.	Negative for Spread	Ogden, 1979

Not only can a case be made for the maintenance of ASL, but there appears to be some spread of the language. The studies cited in Table 3 include several (Delgado, 1984 and Odgen, 1979 in particular) which indicate spread. Delgado's survey for instance, shows that instruction of sign language in post-secondary schools reaches approximately 30,000 students each year. Although we have no way of knowing exactly what variety of sign is being taught, the popularity of such texts as ABC's of MANUAL COMMUNICATION and several of Fant's texts suggest that at least hearing people who enroll in sign language classes using these texts do gain a measure of exposure to ASL. Delgado also indicated that his data measure a steady interest over the last ten years in sign language instruction. While it is true that may post-secondary schools do offer instruction in ASL, there are very few programs for the advanced study of ASL. Most people take an introductory class only. Still, the dramatic emergence of interest in ASL calls for an explanation.

DEAFNESS AND SYMBOLIC IDENTITY

First, some of the interest is due to the contributions of sign linguists. They whet the appetites of many people interested in varieties of human communicative modes. But, caution is warranted in attributing too much credit to academics and scientific research in this regard. A primary force behind increased interest in sign is the larger societal emergence of interest in ethnicity. Indeed, Erting (1978) has suggested that a proper way to understand the deaf community is as an ethnic group. In this fashion, she contends ASL can be recognized as a minority language. However, there are differences between minority linguistic speech communities and the sign community. The primary difference is, of course, in intergenerational ethnicity. Deafness is essentially a one generational phenomenon.

Nevertheless, there are enough similarities between deafness and ethnicity that changes in the distribution and meanings of ethnicity in American society have affected sign language maintenance and spread. In order to tighten the link between ethnicity and deafness, however, it is necessary to comment more specifically on issues related to the ethnic revival in American society.

Most minority language groups in America have shifted towards English within two to three generations, a process referred to as ANGLICISATION (Veltman, 1983:211-218). On the face of it, this seems to confirm a linear assimilation theory. But, there are social factors which apparently enhance the maintenance of ethnic mother tongue. One of these is income. For example, among the Chinese in America, Chinese persists for three or more generations among the rather well to do while it is lost by the second and third among the less well off (Lang Li, 1982). Indeed, even Japanese-Americans who are succeeding in business and education have recently manifested renewed interest in Japanese language maintenance, a remarkable trend given that few third generation Japanese know their ethnic mother tongue.

It seems that in spite of the continuing shift toward English among American linguistic minorities, there has been a corresponding interest in preservation of symbolic ethnicity including, of course, ethnic mother tongue. Several sociologists have attempted to account for why ethnicity has persisted in American society. Gans (1978) and Bell (1975), for instance, point to the essential correctness of the linear theory of assimilation. They cite the well documented trend in which generations of ethnics in American society seem to proceed in a more or less direct progression from the distinctiveness of their background in comparison to American cultural practices to less distinctiveness through a period of three generations. Certainly, this pattern of less distinctiveness between the original group and the general society is a part of the language shift phenomenon so solidly documented in sociolinguistic literature (Veltman, 1983).

According to Bell, the press toward similarity often becomes the grounds for efforts to reestablish distinctiveness among groupings of people based on ethnic heritages. He suggests that the pressures of modern social life force people to understand themselves and others in terms that are relevant to bureaucracy and shared routines of everyday life — the common general experiences of modern life. Yet, people want to belong to smaller units which are not as binding as, for example, a traditional family, which still meet the individual's desire for emotional attachments, and which can be defended politically. He writes

> What I think is clear is that ethnicity, in this context, is best understood not as a primordial phenomenon in which deeply held identities have to reemerge, but as a strategic choice by individuals who, in other circumstances, would choose other group memberships as means of gaining some power and privilege. . .And because saliency may be the decisive variable, the attachment to ethnicity may flush and fade very quickly depending on political and economic circumstances (Bell, 1975:170-171).

Following Bell, I suggest that the interest in signing is a small part of the general process taking place in American society whereby people are seeking to define their membership in terms of distinctive groups. Although surely only a very small number of peple who take a sign language course will find the identity of signer salient in their lives, it is their curiosity about how to so define identity that motivates them to take the classes. In short, they are curious about a group which in the midst of modern society looks very distinctive, but whose very distinctiveness is not fully ethnic and also not fully binding in the traditional sense. The sign community stands as a kind of model of distinctiveness, one in which individuals have devised strategic ways to establish contact with each other in the face of modern forms of oppression — namely, educational policies which do not match the "natural or primordial" needs of a group of people.

CONCLUSION

While interest in signs and deaf communities may well "flush and fade" with changes in society, sign usage will continue relatively unchanged. I have shown that replacement efforts have been strong and rational for the past 150 years, and these policies generally favor shift from sign to English, or even the oppression and cooptation of sign.

Recently, linguists and other scholars have used their research findings to support policies which promote maintenance of ASL. However, since ASL has been maintained in spite of and perhaps to a degree because of oppressive language policies, such official recognition of ASL may not be necessary, and could even have unintended consequences of changing the social functions of ASL. ASL functions as the cement of the community because of the symbolic identity it offers to deaf people — an identity which contrasts markedly with those they receive from having been members of educational institutions. Hence, most profoundly deaf people, regardless of the training they receive, learn to sign. They do so rather late compared with the "normal" pattern of language acquisition.

As long as deaf people feel a need to create for themselves distinctive identities, they will rely on ASL as their medium for social contact. Conversely, if ASL were to become an official language of instruction in special education programs in the United States, it might lose some of its power as a device for accomplishing a distinctive social identity.

REFERENCES

Arnold, P. and Francis, E.: Deaf peoples' views of speech and signing. *Journal of The British Association Of Teachers Of The Deaf, 7:*58-59, 1983.

Bell, Daniel: Ethnicity and social change. In Glazer, N. and Moynihan, D.: *Ethnicity: Theory and Practice.* Cambridge: University of Harvard Press, 1975, pp. 138-174.

Bellugi, U. and Fischer, S.: A comparison of sign language and spoken language. *Cognition, 1:*173-200, 1972.

Cokely, Dennis: Sign language interpreters: a demographic survey. *Sign Language Studies, 32:*261-286, 1981.

Delgado, G. L.: A survey of sign language instruction in junior and community colleges. *American Annals of The Deaf, 143:*38-39, 1984.

Erting, Carol: Language policy and deaf ethnicity. *Sign Language Studies, 19:*139-152, 1978.

Fischer, Susan: Sign language and creoles. In Siple P.: *Understanding Language Through Sign Language Research.* New York: Academic Press, 1978, pp. 309-331.

Gans, Herbert J.: Symbolic ethnicity: the future of ethnic groups and cultures in America. In Gans, Herbert J.: *On The Making Of America: Essays In The Honor of David Reisman.* Philadelphia: University of Pennsylvania Press, 1979, pp. 193-220.

Groce, Nora: Everyone here spoke sign language, *Natural History, 89:*10-16, 1980.

Grosjean, F.: *Life With Two Languages: An Introduction To Billingualism.* Cambridge: Harvard University Press, 1982.

Higgins, Paul C.: *Outsiders In A Hearing World.* Beverly Hills: Sage, 1980.

Hockett, Charles G.: In search of Jove's brow. *American Speech, 53:*243-313, 1978.

Kloss, Hans: "Abstand" language and "ausbau" languages. *Anthropological Linguistics, 9:*29-41, 1963.

Lane, Harland: A chronology of the oppression of sign language in France and the United States. In Lane, H. and Grosjean, F.: *Recent Perspectives On American Sign Language.* Hillsdale, Lawrence Erlbaum, 1980, pp. 119-161.

Li, Lang Wen: The language shift of Chinese-Americans. *International Journal of the Sociology of Language, 28:*109-124, 1982.

Llanes, Jose: The sociology of bilingual education in the United States, *Journal of Education, 163:*20-83, 1981.

Moores, Donald: *Educating Deaf Children.* Boston: Little, Brown, 1978.

Nash, Jeffrey E. and Nash, Anedith: *Deafness in Society.* Lexington, Lexington Books, 1981.

Odgen, P.: Experiences and attitudes of oral deaf adults regarding oralism. Unpublished Thesis, University of Illinois at Urbana, Champaign, 1979.

Prickett, H. and Hunt, J.: Education of the deaf — the next ten years. *American Annals of the Deaf, 122:*365-381, 1977.

Quigley, Stephen: *The Education of Deaf Children.* Baltimore: University Park Press, 1982.

Steward, D. A.: Bilingual education: teacher's opinions of signs. *Sign Language Studies, 39:*145-167, 1983.

Schein, Jerome D.: The Demographics of Deafness. In Higgins, Paul C. and Nash, Jeffrey E.: *The Deaf Community and the Deaf Population,* Social Aspects of Deafness Series, Washington, D.C.: Gallaudet College, 1982, vol. 3, pp. 27-62.

Stokoe, William C.: *Sign Language Structure,* (Revised Edition, 1978). Silver Spring: Linstok Press, 1960.

Interview with James P. Spradley. Tape in Possession of Author, 1976.

Stuckless, E. R. and Birch, J.: The influence of early manual communication in relation to the deaf child's intellectual, social and communicative functioning. *American Annals of the Deaf, 111:*452-462, 1966.

Veltman, Calvin: *Language Shift In The United States.* New York: Mouton Press, 1983.

Washabaugh, William: The manual-facturing of language. *Sign Language Studies*, *31*:291-330, 1981.

Sign language in its social context. *Annual Review of Anthropology*, *10*:237-252, 1982.

Wilcox, S.: "Stuck" in school: a study of semantics and culture in a deaf education class, *Sign Language Studies*, *43*:141-164, 1984.

Woodward, James: Historical bases of American Sign Language. In Siple, Patricia: *Understanding Language Through Sign Language Research*, New York: Academic Press, 1978, pp. 333-348.

CHAPTER 5

DEAFNESS AND FAMILY LIFE
IN MODERN SOCIETY

ANEDITH NASH AND JEFFREY E. NASH

SOCIOLOGISTS have very different ideas about the importance of family life in modern society. Some have declared that the family is an outmoded institution, stripped of its power to shape individual character and to perform its former functions of education, regulation of sexual activity and ascription of status to members in society. Amitai Etzioni (1977) has written that the forces of modern society have reduced the traditional family to a "memory," or symbol of how things used to be.

On the other hand, researchers like Theodore Caplow and his associates have discovered, in MIDDLETOWN FAMILIES (1982), what they believe is proof that families, at least in American society, have not changed fundamentally since the 1920s. Accordingly, they suggest that the family is still the backbone of society.

What has changed, they argue, is how people think about the family. Today people often "tell the story" of the decline of the family. These stories, or "sociological myths," as Caplow and associates have termed them, help us to understand the larger, complex society as well as strengthen the basis for our own personal — presumably better — versions of family life. While the narratives of the decline of the family may help individuals set themselves apart from "society," e.g., allow them to draw conclusions about how well off they are compared to other families, the stories do not accurately describe family life. The family has surely changed in some superficial ways, as Caplow and his associates concede, but these changes have not meant the weakening of roles and functions which families play in society. The debate about whether the institution

101

of the family retains its important functions in modern society is a significant one because it touches on issues central to a sociological perspective on families with deaf members. Since, by definition, institutions are societal, we would expect that the organization of social life in families with deaf members is very much like it is for society in general. To the degree that family life varies by class, ethnicity, and other sociological characteristics, we should expect these same variations in families with deaf members. There can be no question that deafness alters the experience of family life. But to assess the full impact of deafness in a family, we must first establish a baseline understanding of family life in general in American society today.

THE AMERICAN FAMILY SINCE MIDDLETOWN

In the 1920s, again in the 1930s and finally in the late 1970s, Muncie, Indiana, came under study by groups of sociologists interested in, among other things, the fate of the family in modern society. In the 1920s Robert and Helen Lynd (1929) first went to study the families of Muncie, expecting to find middle America on the verge of massive changes which could render the traditional family obsolete. Instead, they found family life well organized and intact. But they found the quality of family life less than idyllic. Marriage in Middletown, they observed, was a way of life without "delight, of fresh or spontaneous interest between husband and wife." At best, for many, "marriage seems to amble along at a friendly jog-trot marked by sober accommodation of each partner to his share of the joint undertaking of children, paying off the mortgage, and generally 'getting on' " (Lynd and Lynd, 1929:130).

Although Middletown families were surviving, the Lynds' conclusions, buttressed by a second study in the 1930s, left a legacy of suspicion about how well marriage and the institution of the family were faring in the modern world. Indeed, divorce rates did soar, and major changes were easy to document in the quality of marriage and the stability of family life.

The debate as to the health of the family was rekindled by Caplow and his colleagues when they returned to Muncie in the late 1970s to replicate the Lynds' studies. The return to Middletown finds families have weathered well the many changes in society brought on by the Great Depression, World War II, the Korean conflict, the war in Viet Nam and the general rapid rate of change during the 1960s. According to this recent study, there has been

> . . .no appreciable decline in the Middletown family during the past 50 years. Insofar as changes in the institutions can be measured, they seem to reflect a strengthening of the institutional form and increased satisfaction for participants. We have noted the likelihood that the trend for the entire country is similar (1982:329).

In the midst of the debate about change in family life several trends seem clear (cf. Smith, 1985): people still do marry, they still want and have children; and, they still believe the family is an essential component of a well ordered society. However, they seem to marry, have children, buy houses and do all these family things for dramatically different reasons in comparison to families in the early Middletown studies. Whereas in the society the Lynds studied, people felt marriage and family an inevitable part of life, today people think they are choosing the lives they want from a wide variety of options. Surely, there are still marriages of necessity and convenience, but more and more the hallmark of the modern relationship is choice. Both husband and wife choose to marry and decide when or if to have children and how many. They may even try to choose the sex of their children. And certainly, if they discover their marriage is not what they thought they had chosen or is not "working out," they choose to end it.

In addition to the belief that we are choosing life style and family form, the sociological myths about family today include a belief that our own families are strong while the institution of the family in general is in decline. This irony characterizing beliefs about family life in modern society is similar and connected to our belief in love and our chances for achieving it. That we have failed or have yet to find a loving relationship is not sufficient, in our minds, to warrant the conclusion that such relationships are not possible. When we learn about the failures of family by reading about high divorce rates and the prevalence of single parent families, or through personal knowledge of family problems of others, we tend to both acknowledge that decline seems to characterize the institution of the family and to deny that our personal experiences fit the norm.

While it is surely true that family life remains an important and salient part of everyday life in modern society, it seems equally clear that the basis of family life — the ideals upon which people try to construct and maintain relationships and families — has shifted from the fatefulness of marriage to the choice of it. Further, we expect our personal choices to "succeed," whether or not society trends indicate high rates of "failure" for others. Some scholars trace this shift back into the mid-nineteenth century, or even earlier (cf. Berger and Berger, 1982). But within the last thirty years, it has become a society-wide trend.

The shift in motivation for family life is clearly supported by strong demographic trends in family size. While family size has been declining in America since the nineteenth century, this trend has been quite pronounced recently. In 1984, the average size of an American family was 2.71 members. Equally as important is the trend toward more families headed by a single parent, 25.7% of all families. (US Census, Supplemental Report, 1985). Marriage has become "unnecessary" from the point of view of many single parents, an intolerable condition for many separated parents, and a serial arrangement of mates for the divorced and remarried. Statistics on family size, literature documenting changes in the organization of families and common sense knowledge confirm that whereas marriage used to be a "fact of life," it has become for many people an option in their menu of life choices. Changes that have occurred in family life condition the meanings of having a deaf person in a family and provide context for interpreting the experience of deafness in family life.

THE FIRST EXPERIENCE: THE DISCOVERY OF DEAFNESS IN THE FAMILY

Most parents of deaf children whom we have talked with over the years can relate vividly the exact moment when they realized that their child was deaf. They can recount in emotional detail this discovery, and they can trace major alterations in their plans for their child to those early moments. While there is considerable variation in how parents interpret the meanings of having a hearing impaired child — and an understanding of that variation is a part of the sociology of families with deaf members — all parents share a sense of the problematic in connection with the discovery of deafness in the family. Hence, within the context of modern family life — family by choice and the presumption of our family's success — the deaf child symbolically calls into question the expectations for and assumptions of normal family life.[1]

In no way does this statement mean that parents, if the family fits the norm, or the single parent, if it does not, do not love their deaf children. Nor, does it mean that they relinquish their exercise of choice in styles of life, childrearing techniques or any other matters of family life. It does mean, however, that the choices they thought they were going to have must be tempered and framed by new alternatives, alternatives which are in quality and range more limited than those the parents imagined for their child.

From the moment of diagnosis of deafness, parents are faced with a barrage of expert information, often none of it very intelligible to them, and sudden uncertainty about their child's future success in life. Their common sense knowledge about parenting, limited as it may have seemed to them anyway, is now almost inoperative. Everything they do with their child from now on will probably have a strained character of rote inadequacy and inflexibility coupled with a sense of guilt about not having ever done enough.

In her early work, Meadow (1968) explained that the diagnosis of deafness is so difficult for parents to understand partly because deafness itself is difficult to understand as a medical condition. While there are many special considerations associated with the diagnosis of deafness, Meadow demonstrates that the typical expectations parents have about how physicians examine, diagnose, treat and offer a prognosis is breached by the diagnosis of deafness. Rapidly in some cases, more gradually in others, medicine drops out of the choices a parent can make about "what to do" in the face of their child's deafness. Eventually, parents must come to grips with the social meaning of the disability for their child.

In our own research, we have tried to describe the complexity of the social meanings of deafness from the hearing parent's perspective (Nash and Nash, 1981). Early on, parents must decide about modes of communication, that is, which version of signing, speech and lipreading, or a combination of manual and verbal skills they will learn and use with their child. They will decide and form networks with one or more of many possible support groups. They must consider how much technology they will employ on behalf of their child (hearing aids and other forms of amplification). In addition, they must redefine the essential meaning of not hearing, or not hearing well enough to allow the normal parent-child relationship to develop. The choices parents make do have an organization to them, but the patterns themselves are not stable, particularly in modern society, where the structure of family life itself is not always stable.

A simple but powerful example of the complex rethinking a diagnosis of deafness occasions for the family is the effect of hearing impairment on choices of schooling. Especially among middle-class families, parents of "normal children" will carefully weigh the educational alternatives a community offers to their child. They can select public schools, within which there may be a variety of options from programs for gifted children to magnet schools which lure students with innovative programs. Private school choices may range from military to preparatory, Catholic or fundamentalist to liberal Christian, Montessori to Waldorf. Parents with a deaf child, however, may have to change place of residence just to find any school which has a program for their child.

Another example has to do with deciding how to relate to the larger community after the diagnosis of deafness in the family. Although such instances are very rare, parents of a deaf child may define the meanings of deafness as simply another life style—they may accept that deaf people have their own version of culture, their own language and social lives. And, if they are not deaf themselves and already members of the deaf community, they may adopt some, if not all, of the options of that life as their own whenever they are dealing with their children. However, hearing parents who accept "deafness as cultural difference," are still not assuming the identity of deafness in the same way their child will. While a parent can be a "friend of deaf people," that identity is not a core attribute of the parent in the way it is for deaf people, nor in the way it will become for their deaf child. Higgins (1980) documents a similar phenomenon which he calls "courtesy membership" in the deaf community. Deaf people, he observes, may allow hearing people some but not total access to the deaf world. Hearing parents of deaf children who are "friends of the deaf" are often merely managed courteously by deaf people with whom they interact. And the deaf children of hearing parents may early in their lives have only marginal acceptance among deaf adults.

While a hearing parent of a deaf child may well take on the identity of deafness, that identity is often specific to interactive encounters they have with others. On some occasions, parents may wish to evoke the deaf identity. In others, they may not. Of course, a deaf persons bears the identity in a different way—as a permanent feature of his or her self.

Identities in a modern world tend to be quite mutable (Zurcher, 1977). People change the ways in which they think of themselves according to how they perceive the demands of the social situation. People learn to take on the attitudes of others and learn to do this somewhat for the moment. We can not say how much a self concept can change without seriously affecting the integrity of the person, but it does seem that modern selves are easily changed. Of course, since deafness is, by nature, immutable, hearing parents may take on the identity of deafness only symbolically and for the purpose of specific interactive encounters. This fact is not lost on the deaf community.

From the family's first experiences with the meanings of deafness, the deaf child is a constant reminder of the immutability of not hearing. The range of life choices seems truncated and "success" of the family in many ways in question. Hence, there is a built-in social tension between modern parents and their deaf offspring which is not present in "normal families."

Of course, the phrase "normal family" brings to mind a host of questions about the quality of interactions taking place within the families of modern society. We do not mean that families with deaf members experience any more or less tension than other families, only that the source of the tension is qualitatively distinct from that experienced in most families. While rates of divorce may not be very dissimilar between families with deaf children and those with no handicapped children in them, while hearing siblings within families with deaf members may not suffer "ill effects" in terms of their own development (Freeman et al., 1979), these data do not mean that the tensions in families with deaf children are the same as those that other families deal with, nor that they are any more or less severe.

The crucial point with regard to understanding the tension deafness generates in families as they try to come to terms with and live out the social meanings of deafness, revolves around the physical bases of deafness: one does not choose deafness. A father can decide not to deal with his child or he can refuse to learn any communicative mode which would allow him some contact with his son. A mother may work for years to teach lipreading and speech skills to her daughter, but even if her child is proficient in verbal communication, the child can still be stigmatized (Goffman, 1963); i.e., she can be seen as "deaf" by others.

Hence, the diagnosis of childhood deafness in a family, within the context of modern society, calls into question fundamental assumptions people make about the meanings of their participation in social life. As a condition of life, deafness, from the parent's point of view, seems to cancel the power of rational decision making and, most importantly, of the control which they assume they have over the course of their own and a child's lives.

THE IMPACT OF THE DEAFNESS ON FAMILY LIFE

The sociology of deafness must address the ways that the organization of social experience is restructured in the face of the deafness. We will refer to this process as the impact of deafness on family life and its reciprocal process as coping with deafness. Our analysis recognizes that the meanings and subsequent actions of individuals vary from situation to situation and according to the sense of "lived time." That is, deafness impacts on family members differently at different stages in the life cycle of a family.

The idea of "lived time" refers to the social interpretations that people make about pace and tempo of life (cf. Lyman and Scott, 1970). People organize their experiences of time in many different ways, clock and calendar time being a base point in modern society. Family time is measured in the phases through which children move, the rhythms of the relationship between husband and wife, and the crises that every family faces. Of course, these senses of lived time vary considerably. For some families, the early stages of family life, characterized by attention to the quality of the primary relationship between husband and wife, may last many years, then be superseded by the problems of childrearing posed by the firstborn. In other families, there may be little or no time for exploring the meanings of living together before the arrival of children.

While social senses of time and social phases do function differently for different families, an outline of the form of social life of the family can be described. This form, in turn, becomes a useful guide for understanding how deafness breaches taken-for-granted assumptions about normal family life and how the problematic character of dealing with deafness continues and changes throughout the cycle of family life.

Cycles of family life move through phases from FORMATION in which the basic norms for life as a couple are built and practiced, to the FAMILY phase in which a child is introduced into the new form. The family phase can be prolonged by the introduction of more children. The MATURE FAMILY form operates when the norms and practices of the initial couple are taken for granted as the basic family functioning for all members. The last phase, the LAUNCHING phase, happens when children use the original form for their own efforts to establish new forms. They do this either by establishing separate households or modifying the original forms. This last phase evolves into a new form.[2]

Of course, any given family can end, truncate, or stall in a given phase. Nevertheless, when we see the family form in modern society as a consequence of decisions made in everyday life, and recognize that as a form it is mutable and transitory, we can better address questions about the impact on or breaches of form that deafness induces.

TYPICAL PROBLEMS OF DEAFNESS THROUGH THE CYCLES OF FAMILY OF LIFE

In order to show the consequences of deafness in the modern family, we will first describe typical problems within the context of family life cycles. The first problem has to do with the interpretation parents give to deafness. These interpretations are often problems because they are at odds with the articulated form of the family. The second is simply what to do with the deaf child and how choices are structured by answers to that question. The third is the general question of education for the deaf child, and the final, the problems of relationships between parents and their adult deaf children.

During the formation of a relationship, no matter how particularistic the reasons for the marriage, couples create norms and expectations about their lives together (Berger and Kellner, 1964). For example, increasingly, both partners in a marriage have employment outside the family, sometimes because they believe that work is a crucial social activity for their sense of self worth, or for a variety of other economic reasons. While the fact that an infant is a highly dependent creature must be known by couples or mothers, the practical consequences of the intrusion of such a creature upon the routines of marriage often are not fully appreciated until the problem is real, immediate and crying at 2:00 a.m., or too sick to go to day care.

The problems of intrusion are apparently so acute that all across America and Europe groups are being formed to help with the problems of coping with the first baby. Typically, these groups are composed of middle class, young parents who meet to discuss the "realities of night feedings and dirty diapers—and. . .feelings of inadequacy" (The Highland Villager, May 22, 1985). As a promoter of one of these programs remarked,

> A generation ago new mothers could turn to their neighbors for advice. Over morning coffee they could discuss toilet training, share ideas for coaxing their offspring to eat peas and compare notes on how to handle bedtime. . .But today's neighborhoods are pretty quiet. A mother looking for a little advice or just some moral support is likely to find her neighbors away at work, their children in day-care centers (Villager, Page 10).

The birth of a child changes a marriage. While all human infants require care, and while children are always problems in the sense that someone must mind them, in modern society they symbolize more, much more. Today they represent, under ideal conditions, a conscious decision to modify a marriage, rather than the reason for marriage itself. They are born into a more diffuse and complex role system in the family. Children, therefore, symbolize the specific values and decisional grounds upon which marriage is constructed. However, it is the nature of children that they do not, at least in this early phase, function as very good symbols. They become ill, they do not honor work schedules, they are ignorant of rationally contrived divisions of labor. By their very nature they intrude upon a marriage.

In the modern marriage, couples often discover they can, or perhaps, must, modify the traditional roles of mother and father. While there are great opportunities in this situation, there is also, as Weigert and Hastings (1977) point out, something paradoxical, for the requirements of "successful" family life often conflict with those of "success" in society. But, the paradox we identify here involves more than simple conflict between two social forms. It refers to a fundamental difference between life in family and life in society.

In order to understand this paradox consider the way family life functions to give to its members a strong sense of being "authentic" and "permanently" located in a social world. Presumably, a person's basic sense of self depends upon being able to retreat from society into the protection of the family. However, in modern society, the family is interconnected with other institutions and, hence, not well protected, nor particularly isolated. Of course, there is no paradox here as long as the interconnectedness does not call into question the foundations of the institution itself. But this is precisely what happens. Other institutions of society seem to require skills, values and action that are antithetical to family. A simple example is to look at cooperation and competition. The former, we suggest, is essential to family life the latter to, say, economic. Generally, competition among family members, especially, economically, does not promote family togetherness. On the other hand, cooperation among family members may well lower the earning power of all the members of the family.

Strong family commitments may take a person out of society. The more one invests in the family, therefore, the more likely it is that the sense of self one acquires there will be challenged and confronted in society, and the more likely within the context of the family those identities will be lost. While this idea of paradox is difficult, it is very important to understanding families with deaf children because the paradox is especially intense in these families. In order to deal with a deaf child, and develop a strong family, parents may have to "take themselves out" of society. Of course, such a response to deafness, may lead to "co-dependency" that sometimes develops among members of families with a deaf member. In its extreme form, "co-dependent" persons become unable to "function" outside the very small social world they have constructed.

A baby, but its very presence, serves as a symbolic reminder of the paradox of modern family life. While the infant must acquire a self, that self will be "inherently ambivalent" (Weigert and Hastings, 1977:1176) because it will consist of a family-based "archival sense" of self plus multiple senses of selfhood which it will acquire through contact with people outside of the family. The paradox of gaining and losing identity is built into the family, and, because of this, a baby intrudes upon the newly forming "museum of archival meanings" (Weigert and Hasting, 1977) which the couple has just put together from fragments of each others' past and from their "lives together." At a time when the function of imparting personal meanings is just beginning to operate for the couple, the baby comes. As we have described this phase of family life, one can see the amount of work required to interpret how the baby "fits in," and the stress this places on the newly forming sense of family which the couple is constructing.

Some practices exacerbate stress and strains even though they are instituted to relieve them. For example, increasingly, couples and single mothers depend upon day care as an institutional answer to their collective problem of continuing in their employment and self development in the social world. Day care facilities do not replace families. They do not care for sick children; rarely do they attempt to inculcate moral and religious values. We could easily characterize day care facilities collectively as incomplete institutions (cf. Cherlin, 1978). They work whenever things are normal — going as planned or, according to choice.

Since a deaf child is, by definition, outside the parameters of "normal" for a family, this child creates special problems. The pressure of the additional work that deafness necessitates in the forming of family is reflected in statistics which show mothers of hearing impaired children participate in the labor force at a lower rate than do mothers in general. 64% of mothers with school aged hearing impaired children are not in the labor force while the corresponding number is 53% for mothers with school aged children in the general population (ODS, Series R, 5 Gallaudet College and STATISTICAL ABSTRACTS, 1980).

Society offers incomplete institutional forms for the solutions of problems of everyday life, like what to do with a child while the parents are working. These incomplete forms are even more "incomplete" from the point of view of parents who have deaf children. For them, the presence of a baby is an acute reminder of the possibility of personal identity loss. In the process of imparting a biography of this new and "unusual" child, the archival sense of self which the couple or parent have invested in the new form of family is weakened and even lost. Deafness impacts this FORMATION phase of family life by exacerbating the predicament parents find themselves in when they try to exercise individual choice while serving as caretaker for a dependent child.

The question of what to do with the deaf child grows in intensity as the child becomes less dependent in the FAMILY cycle. And, in terms of the rich literature on the development of children, the era is marked by the onset of communicative problems. The well documented oralism/manualism/total communication debate is simply a gloss for the actual problems of families living with deaf members. We have suggested (Nash and Nash, 1981) that the choices which families make about how to communicate with a deaf child in their family are a function of attitudes toward language and toward the category "deaf people." When parents have strong attitudes about the appropriateness of standard English for social status maintenance and enhancement, when they are upwardly mobile themselves and wish their children to have a future at least as good as their present, they are apt to stress what they believe is a communicative system which is either English or some kind of reconstructed version of it. On the other hand, families in which sign language prevails are those composed of deaf parents, or those where the signing of the child happens in a most inadvertent way. Of course, there are always marginal parents — those who are poor, isolated culturally and educationally from mainstream society. They may not stress English because their own skills are marginal. Their deaf children may survive using forms of communication which reflect these marginal life circumstances. They may use "home signs" and rely on gestures to "get along" with others.

In any eventuality, the idea of choices as the hallmark of modern families is truncated. Parents are forced into a limited range of schooling opportunities for their children. Even if they live in large cities, they will discover that the special education facilities are centrally located and require that their child be bussed to them. However, a more salient comparison is between the matter of choice of schools and choice of socialization experience. The modern parent does not simply "send" his or her child to the local school. Increasingly, schools are seen as agents of socialization, and parents of "normal children" who have abdicated some of their control over the socialization of the child through their choices to remain employed and use institutional means to support that choice, try to regain a measure of that control with at least the impression that they have something to do with the training their child receives. They do this by carefully exercising options in the choice of a school for their child. Sometimes this exercise of control turns out to be largely symbolic. For example, a move to the suburbs to avoid the "undesirables" who live in the city may not be totally successful. Many of the problems which parents think they will avoid by living in the suburbs like drug dealing, they discover exist there too. However, the symbolism of the effort is clear, and important to maintaining an impression of control.

In every city in America, private schools have been founded to add to the range of menu selections from which a parent can design a tailor-made program for children. Often, the crucial matter in these schooling decisions hinges on the composition of the school's enrollment — who are the children with whom my child will be associating. While it is surely true that parents, in the final analysis, are relatively weak agents when it comes to controlling their children's friends and classmates, parents seem to think they can achieve a measure of control by choosing their child's school. Public schools also cater to this menu approach to schooling by offering parents "magnet" schools, flexible curricula and special options like self-directed science programs and computer classes.

Of course, in this sense, deafness severely restricts the range of choices which a parent can make for his or her child. Even for the mainstreamed child "special problems" emerge at every juncture in the world of modern education. A deaf child who needs signs in the classroom could qualify for a special computer class, for instance, but the school principal regretfully informs the parents that all available interpreters are already assigned. While there are exceptions and severely or profoundly deaf children may profit from participation in the new school options for education, most deaf children, as far as available evidence suggests (Erting, 1981), remain on the sidelines of education. Their performances on academic tests are still below normal, and while they are present in the same building with hearing students, they are socially and culturally separate from the majority of students, getting by without interpreting services in classes, in special programs and on athletic teams.

Parents find themselves faced with a dilemma with regard to how they answer the question "What will I do with my child?" The dilemma involves, on the one hand, providing for the child the optimal educational opportunities and, on the other, exercising control over the influences that shape and mold their child's "moral character." If parents select to mainsteam their child, they are following the rationale of menu driven modern approaches to education. However, to make this selection means either that the child must function as a "second-class" citizen in the school, or that the parent finds him or herself involved in the details of their child's education in ways that restrict their options to give socialization functions over to the school. In other words, the difficulty of the child's problems shift the responsibility back to the parents, who, of course, lacked the resources to deal with the problems in the first place. The problems of loss of control which the typical parents experience and which is a part of the motivation behind the "private school" movements and the tailored-made options approach to education are exacerbated for the parent of the deaf child, and they are confounded by the particular communicative needs of the child.[3] Resentment may build within the family as parents feel they must be involved in every aspect of their deaf child's life.

Although he did not have parents of deaf children in mind, Keniston's (1977) assessment of the predicament of the parent in modern society seems particularly descriptive of parents of deaf children. He writes that parents are like weak executives. They must make decisions about their children's social life, coordinate these services for their children among a variety of "experts" and technologies, and be accountable for the outcomes of these decisions and actions. However, parents have little power to supervise and control the ways in which their choices are carried out. The parent of the deaf child works from a menu with fewer choices and often is saddled with greater responsibility for the outcome of the choices. Further those responsibilities may conflict with expectations and roles the parent is responsible for outside the family.

Finally, during the LAUNCHING cycle of a family with a deaf member, there are typical problems with relationships between "adult" deaf people and their hearing parents. Generally, there is little research on the problem we now address either for deaf or hearing families. Partly this is because of the assumption of the prominence of the nuclear family. Sociologists, like everybody else, assume that when children are old enough, they will start their own families and the matters of socialization and family organization will shift to the next generation. However, at the level of individual choices, job opportunities, finances and other basic matters, life in modern society has become increasingly complicated and even chaotic. Hence, a trend toward greater and longer dependence of children on their parents has emerged. This trend does not signal a return to the "extended family," but rather it represents the use of the family form as a resource which young people can use to cope with the problems of "gearing into" a complex and competitive social world.

For example, after graduation from college, after the first marriage ends in divorce, after the first job lay-off, increasing numbers of "children" return to the nest to recuperate and gather resources to "try it again." A dependable retreat in the form of one's parents' paid-for home, can be a "safety net." Twenty-three year old children may maintain a come-and-go residence in their parents' home.

Parents of deaf children may find this societal trend exacerbates and confounds their problems. Like all parents whose children return to the nest, there are new problems of sharing household responsibilities and costs. And, there are the special problems of privacy and who can use the VCR or the family car, for what purposes and who pays? The returning children have become accustom to exercising their own powers of choice, and the ways they exercise choice may well clash with their parents' values. This can be a profound problem if the adult deaf child comes from a middle class family and has become a member of a clique of deaf people who follow routines of life which are typically associated by the parents with the "lower classes" of society. For example, middle class parents may have difficulty reconciling themselves to their daughter's social life which may consist of "hanging out" at an all night bowling ally in an "undesirable" neighborhood.

The reasons for the deaf child remaining in his or her parent's home well into adulthood include more than the regular "accounts" of how rough it is to pay for higher education, hold a job, or establish a family of one's own. Young deaf adults may well face problems of discrimination in employment, inability to adequately communicate on their own and lack of confidence outside the now scattered high school peer group. Tensions within the family and parents' resentment of the nesting deaf child may grow as the parents' worst fears seem to be coming true. Maybe this child really cannot make it on his or her own — ever. Even parents who have tried diligently to control and manage their deaf child's life harbor deep feelings of amorphous guilt and anxiety about not having done everything possible to insure this child's future. The deaf child returning or never leaving the family symbolizes a significant failure of family.

CONCLUSIONS

In this paper, we develop three aspects of the sociology of families with deaf children. First, the principle of the inseparability of individual and social context leads to a correction of the tendency in literature on deafness to see families with deaf children as "unique." While there surely are unique aspects to the social lives of people in such families, there are unmistakable features of life in any family derived from trends and forces in society.

Second, there is a wide range of interpretations about the meanings of change that have taken place in the organization of family life in American society. However, most researchers imply, and we contend, that individual choice has become the primary criterion and motivation for social action in modern society. Divorce rates, remarriage rates and other well-documented phenomena reflect attempts which people make under a variety of social conditions to exercise choice. These shifts toward voluntaristic bases for family life create paradoxical pressures within the institution of family.

Deafness creates distinctive problems in family life, problems calling for solutions which are not typical in modern family life. While parents in general spend less time with their young children now than did their mothers, at least, parents of deaf children are required to invest huge blocks of time in rearing their children. This may strengthen family life, but more often it increases the paradoxical nature of family life, making a parent's loss of identity in the outside world more likely. Likewise, at a time in history when parental involvement in children's development is becoming more "vicarious and symbolic" (paying for professional child caring, quality education and entertainment for their children), parents of deaf children become the center of their child's life far beyond the normal time span for such focus. Perhaps, most important, a deaf child in a family forces parents to restructure the choices they can make about what to do with a child.

Deafness exacerbates and confounds the paradoxical features of family life. The family imparts to children fundamental senses of who they are by giving them early life histories and details of their ancestry. In larger society, in modern times, these aspects of selfhood are not highly valued. For the deaf family member, the archival sense of self he or she may acquire in the context of family life is very fragile, and more likely to be challenged when that person engages in interaction outside the family. Of course, defenses like retreating into the family are also exaggerated. While families may appear to be strong and bonded by the experience of deafness, this may be simply the other side of the paradox. And, if Weigert and Hastings are correct, such seemingly bonded families might well raise the costs of the eventual loss of social identity.

Whereas a relationship between choice of schooling for a child and status of the family may be closely linked in a hearing family, that relationship is confounded in the family with deafness. To the well-to-do, highly educated family, for example, deafness may mean that the prep school or private college which father attended is not in the child's future. And on the other hand, in the poor family, a deaf child may receive attention from the school system which is clearly greater than that received by any other member of the family. In the first case, choice is truncated, and in the second it may even be expanded, though perhaps in ways that bring unwanted attention or intrusion to the family. Deafness changes everyday life. In the context of the family, these aspects of the meanings of not hearing are very clear. The taken-for-granted foundations of family life are challenged by the deafness of a member of the family.

The social approach to understanding deafness in family life should supplement other approaches by making us more aware of the role of societal factors in determining and shaping the experience of living with a deaf offspring. All too often, the hearing parent of a deaf child is portrayed in research literature in unflattering terms, especially when compared with deaf parents. While we take no exception to research results which show children of hearing parents lagging behind those with deaf parents in academic and social development, we believe that a more complete understanding of the differences between deaf and hearing interactive social contexts may help educators and professional human services people better appreciate the meanings and impact of the advice they give. For example, hearing parents may be advised to learn a new language, change friends and suspend deeply held values so that their deaf child may develop "normally," counsel they certainly will never feel entirely successful at following, even if they try. No easier is the way of intensive oral training that promises to make the child "as good as hearing."

Although the deaf child may profit from such various kinds of advice, the strains and stresses these recommendations place on an already fragile structure may have the effect of transforming a family into a form that probably is quite different from that envisioned and desired by the parents. Such a transformation may have profound effects on parents and children alike, effects difficult to anticipate and understand. A sociological perspective helps to highlight these issues and to suggest more informed and realistic policies for supporting families with deaf members.

FAMILY POLICY IMPLICATIONS

When we suggest that sociology inform family policy, we must be specific about the meaning of policy. First, the term implies some kind of formal organizational structure. People have opinions and attitudes, they act and interact, but we do not often think of them as having a policy unless they are in a position to influence formal organizations. On the other hand, schools and governments do have policies.

As small systems, families in modern society are becoming more dissimilar, more intimate and less integrated with other systems of society. Families do not and are not likely to have formal structures which link them in common causes or to shared goals and resources. Certainly, families can fire a social movement, like Mothers Against Drunk Drivers (MADD), or organizations of parents of school age hearing impaired. (We must add here that most of these organizations seem oriented toward children rather than families. It is easier to think of children as having needs than families.)

But, these "family" matters become effective in society to the degree that they become formal and organized. We have attempted to show that the experiences of parents with hearing impaired children vary greatly, from the abject sorrow that comes from seeing a child have all kinds of "troubles," to the joy of sharing in grand accomplishments. This kind of variation within and between families is characteristic of family life in modern society. It is not, however, the stuff of social movements, nor the building blocks of formal organizations. We should not be surprised to discover how difficult it is to organize parents to do anything as a group on behalf of each other's children.

What all this means is that no single organization sets policy for family life, but many organizations, schools and governments, have policies which affect family life. Parents, **as parents** react at the personal level to policies and their consequences within the context of their own family life. While some families adapt with amazing grace and strength to the impact of policy on their families, such reactions are patterned by forces which operate independently from the policy. These are the very forces which modern society has eroded and changed — authority, loyalty, obedience and family vitality. Of course, such situations give rise to "unintended consequences" of policy.

What sociology can do is help us understand the multifaceted impact of policy on family life. We may see, for example, that what parents want and need may not be what educators want, or even what children need. For example, early and intensive training of deaf children in language skills which educators regard as essential to successful education sets in motion forces that change the quality of family life. What may profit a child in an educational sense, may alter his or her family, transforming a mother into a teacher, or simply increasing the paradoxical predicament of family life in modern society.

What families need is more help, and more of it than most people imagine. This help must come from outside the institution of the family itself. Appropriately, it should come from the organizations which set policy. Educational organizations should assume greater responsibility for the socialization of hearing impaired children by increasing the scope of the care they offer, especially for very young children. Human service organizations must expand their services to include the hearing impaired whose numbers often do not make such specialized programs profitable. We have in mind here a system which parallels the vast one which is now emerging for the full range of problems families experience — drug treatment centers, houses for runaways, counseling for teenage mothers, and the like. The federal government must provide more money for the support of these and other programs. There should be, for example, day care facilities specially equipped and staffed for hearing impaired children.

Most of all, sociology can help people make associations between types of actions which individuals take and the social contexts and consequences of these actions. Such understanding could effect a major change in expectations people in policy-making positions now have. While it is surely true that "parents must do the work of socializing their hearing impaired child," it is no longer realistic to expect them to do it alone, or even to do most of it. Sociology can help to locate and depict forces affecting the lives of all those involved with the hearing impaired. By weighing these forces, we might be able to align needs with resources in more realistic fashion. With regard to families, we must come to understand that while parents of deaf children may play different roles than parents of "normal" children play, they, like all parents in modern society, cannot "do it all."

FOOTNOTES

1. Statistics show that the majority of deaf children are born to hearing families (see Schein, this volume). While the linguistic environment of deaf children born to deaf parents may be richer and more "normal," deaf parents are still faced with many decisions about childrearing and education, limitations on the possibilities for their child's future imposed by a hearing disability in a predominantly hearing world and all the other "normal" stresses that accompany childrearing in modern society. (For a fuller discussion of the family and language environments of deaf children in deaf families, see K. Meadow, this volume.) For purposes of this article, we will be primarily referring to families with hearing parents and deaf children, since they constitute the majority of families with deaf members. Nevertheless, the analysis can easily be applied to families that are all deaf, or families with deaf parents and hearing children.

2. There are many excellent discussions of the concept of family cycle. Most are informed by work showing that phases of development characterize both personality and social systems. We have oversimplified the idea of phases of family life in order to suggest how the concept might apply to understanding families with deaf members.

3. See the genre of "how we managed" books, which often include detailed and highly emotional personal accounts of the consequences, stresses and strains of deafness in a family. Some accounts in this genre are more "professional" than personal in orientation, but retain narrative style and are psychologically informative as well. While these books are often quite useful to parents encountering deafness, especially in the "formation" stage of life with a deaf family member, they do not cast the experiences they share in any sociological relief. Examples of these books include, WORDS FOR A DEAF DAUGHTER, by Paul West, and DEAF LIKE ME, by Thomas Spradley and James P. Spradley.

REFERENCES

Berger, Peter and Kellner, Hansfreid: Marriage and the construction of social reality. *Diogenes, 45:*1-25, 1964.

Berger, Peter and Luckmann, Thomas: *The Social Construction of Reality.* Garden City, Doubleday, 1976.

Caplow, Theodore et. al.: *Middletown Families: Fifty Years of Change and Continuity.* Minneapolis, University of Minnesota Press, 1982.

Cherlin, Andrew: Remarriage as an incomplete institution. *American Journal of Sociology, 84:*634-650, 1978.

Cicourel, Aaron: *Cognitive Sociology: Language and Meaning in Social Interaction.* New York, Free Press, 1974.

Erting, Carol: An anthropological approach to the study of communicative competence of deaf children. *Sign Language Studies, 32:*221-238, 1981.

Etzioni, Amitai: The family: is it obsolete? *Journal of Current Social Issues, 14:*4-9, 1977.

Freeman, Roger D., Malkin, S. F. and Hastings, J. O.: Psychosocial problems of deaf children and their families. *American Annals of the Deaf, 120:*391-405, 1979.

Higgins, Paul C.: *Outsiders In A Hearing World: A Sociology of Deafness.* Beverly Hills, Sage, 1980.

Keniston, Kenneth: *All Our Children: The American Family Under Pressure.* New York, Harcourt Brace Jovanovich, 1977.

Lyman, Stanford and Scott, Marvin: *A Sociology of the Absurd.* New York, Appleton-Century-Crofts, 1970.

Meadow, Kathryn: Parental responses to the medical ambiguities of deafness. *Journal of Health and Social Behavior, 9:*299-309, 1968.

Nash, Jeffrey E. and Nash, Anedith: *Deafness in Society.* Lexington, Lexington Books, 1981.

Smith, Mark C.: From Middletown to Middletown III: a critical review. *Qualitative Sociology, 7:*327-336, 1984.

Weigert, Andrew J.: Identity: its emergence within social psychology. *Symbolic Interaction, 6:*183-206, 1983.

Weigert, Andrew J. and Hastings, Ross: Identity loss, family and social change. *American Journal of Sociology, 82:*1171-1185, 1977.

Zurcher, Louis: *The Mutable Self: A Self Concept For Social Change.* Beverly Hills, Sage, 1977.

EDITOR'S INTRODUCTION

(FOR CULTURAL CONFLICT IN A SCHOOL FOR DEAF CHILDREN — CHAPTER 6)

I**N THE FOLLOWING** chapter, Carol Erting explores the cultural conflict that occurred between hearing educators and deaf parents in a school for deaf children, Jackson School, the fictitious name given to the school that she investigated. While Erting's discussion primarily focuses on one particular school, it may be usefully set within the larger social and historical circumstances of the education of deaf people. Further, her specific discussion about the cultural conflict between hearing educators and deaf parents of preschool deaf children informs us in broader ways about the education of deaf people.

EDUCATION OF DEAF YOUTH

The several hundred-year history of the education of deaf students is marked by controversy concerning the appropriate means for educating deaf children. Should deaf children be educated through oral means — speech, speechreading, and auditory training — or should sign language be the primary method (Bender, 1981; Lane, 1984; Neisser, 1983)? With the passage of a resolution that the oral method was to be preferred to that of signs at the International Congress of Milan in 1880, all countries except the United States adopted it as the preferred method (Bender, 1981:156). However, even in the United States, oralism spread throughout educational programs for deaf students. Within the United States in the past 100 years, sign language has not been universally used in educational programs for deaf students. Sign language was primarily used in state residential schools for deaf students, particularly with the older students, many of whom had not been successfully taught through

123

oral means when they were younger. Only since approximately 1970 has there been a growing emphasis on the use of sign language within the classroom; an emphasis on what is often called total communication (Jordan, Gustason, and Rosen, 1979). Yet even with that growing emphasis on sign language, the sign systems used have often been developed by hearing educators in order that they model more closely the oral, English language than does the native sign language of deaf people (see Woodward, 1982).

The controversy concerning the appropriate means for educating deaf students is part of a larger conflict between deaf and hearing people. Historically, hearing people have dominated the lives of deaf people. Oralism is taken by many deaf people as another means of domination, one that may also entail great frustration and few successes. While often well meaning, those who emphasize oral methods deny the validity of being deaf. Oralism holds out hope only to those deaf individuals who strive to be (and are successful in becoming) as much like hearing people as possible. However, through sign language, deaf people develop their own identities, culture, and communities. It is that fear that deaf people will live within, but also apart from, the hearing world that led one proponent of oralism, Alexander Graham Bell, to criticize residential schools, teachers of the deaf who were themselves deaf, reunions of former students, and the "gesture language" of the deaf. These and more were criticized because they constituted the:

> elements necessary to compel deaf-mutes to select as their partners in life persons who are familiar with the gesture language. This practically limits their selection to deaf-mutes and to hearing persons related to deaf-mutes. They do select such partners in marriages, and a certain portion of their children inherit their physical defect. We are on the way therefore towards the formation of a deaf variety of the human race. Time alone is necessary to accomplish the result (Bell, 1883:44).

As Erting's paper makes clear, that conflict between hearing and deaf perspectives of the world continues.

In the past decade in the education of deaf students, as well as in special education in general, students with special needs are increasingly being placed into the least restrictive educational environment. They are moving from residential facilities to day programs, from day programs to day classes within "regular" facilities, and into the mainstream of "regular" classes. PL 94-142, The Education for All Handicapped Children Act, was passed with controversy in 1975, and controversy continues to surround its implementation. For the education of deaf students the controversy involves many concerns. For example, some wonder whether adequate support services, such as interpreters, will be provided for the deaf child in a mainstreamed classroom (e.g., Jordan, Gustason, and Rosen, 1979). Others are concerned that those who are mainstreamed may not develop a strong sense of belonging with other deaf individuals (Vernon and Estes, 1975). And still others suspect that mainstreamed programs are yet another attempt to make deaf children hearing (Lane, 1984). Does mainstreaming provide the most appropriate educational environment for deaf youth (see *Gallaudet Today,* Winter 1986 for a variety of views)?

Presently, approximately 50,000 hearing-impaired children and youth in the United States receive some form of special education (*American Annals of the Deaf,* 1985:132). Those students are educated in a wide variety of public and private settings — residential facilities, day schools, day classes, and other programs. Where once residential facilities were the dominant setting for the education of deaf students (96% of all deaf students who received special education in 1890), today they no longer are (32% in 1984) (Higgins, n.d., and *American Annals of the Deaf,* 1985:132). Almost 60% of deaf students are educated in public day classes and approximately 44% are mainstreamed to some degree (*American Annals of the Deaf,* 1985:132; but also see Karchmer and Trybus, 1977; Jordan, Gustason, and Rosen, 1979). During the 1970s, residential facilities have come to serve an older group of students who are increasingly likely to be members of minority groups and to have multiple handicaps (Schildroth, 1980). In contrast, students who are mainstreamed are more likely to come from white, middle-class families whose parents are not deaf, to have less severe hearing losses, and to have more intelligible speech than those educated in other ways (Karchmer and Trybus, 1977; Wolk, Karchmer, and Schildroth, 1982; but see Allen and Osborn, 1984).

The students are educated by more than eight thousand teachers of deaf students. These teachers are overwhelmingly *young* (mean age 34), *white* (94%), *hearing* (86%) *females* (83%) (Corbett and Jensema, 1981). As are the students they teach, these teachers are located in a variety of settings. However, those teachers who are hearing impaired are more likely to be employed in residential facilities than those who hear (Jensema, 1977). While hearing-impaired students have moved into the mainstream, their hearing-impaired teachers have not to the same extent.

CULTURAL CONFLICT AT JACKSON SCHOOL

Jackson School is not the typical setting within which deaf students are presently educated. Further, it is not typical for half the deaf children of a program to have deaf parents as was the case in the preschool classes at Jackson. However, what is so typical is that Jackson School was staffed by those who were not deaf. Therefore, cultural conflict, which occurs between the hearing and deaf worlds, occurred in the school world as well.

However, Erting's examination of the cultural conflict between hearing teachers and deaf parents informs us not only of the conflict between adults but the developing conflict between adults and students. The view of the deaf parents can be understood as the concerns that gradually crystallized over the years as deaf youth were educated in programs run by hearing educators and as those youth became adults and dealt with the larger hearing world. When deaf students in a public high school program extend the semantic use of the ASL sign glossed "stuck" in order to tell particular teachers in the hearing-impaired program that "I've (the student) got power over you; I am able to put you in your place," then the emerging conflict between deaf and hearing people has become quite apparent (Wilcox, 1984:43). While such conflict disrupts the education of deaf students, it may increase the collective consciousness of deaf individuals as an oppressed group. That increased consciousness may ultimately serve to benefit deaf individuals as it becomes the basis for deaf people's active involvement in affairs that concern them. Thus, one of the deaf mothers involved in the cultural conflict at Jackson School became a teacher at the school and a catalyst for constructive changes. What follows is Erting's discussion of that cultural conflict.

REFERENCES

Allen, Thomas E. and Osborn, Tamara, I.: Academic integration of hearing-impaired students: demographic, handicapping, and achievement factors. *American Annals of the Deaf, 129:*100-113, 1984.

American Annals of the Deaf: Tabular Summary of Schools and Classes in the United States, October 1, 1984. *130:*133-134, 1985.

Bell, Alexander Graham: Upon the formation of a deaf variety of the human race. Presented to the National Academy of Sciences, 1883.

Bender, Ruth E.: *The Conquest of Deafness.* 3rd ed. Danville, Interstate Printers and Publishers, 1981.

Corbett, Edward E., Jr. and Jensema, Carl J.: *Teachers of the Deaf: Descriptive Profiles.* Washington, D.C., Gallaudet College, 1981.

Higgins, Paul C.: Employment trends of deaf and hearing teachers of the deaf in the United States. Unpublished.

Jensema, Carl: Three characteristics of teachers of the deaf who are hearing impaired. *American Annals of the Deaf, 122:*307-309, 1977.

Jordan, I. K., Gustason, Gerilee, and Rosen, Roslyn: An update on communication trends at programs for the deaf. *American Annals of the Deaf, 124:*350-357, 1979.

Karchmer, Michael A. and Trybus, Raymond J.: Who are the deaf children in "mainstream" programs? Series R, No. 4, Washington, D.C., Office of Demographic Studies, Gallaudet College, 1977.

Lane, Harlan: *When the Mind Hears: A History of the Deaf.* New York, Random House, 1984.

Neisser, Arden: *The Other Side of Silence: Sign Language and the Deaf Community in America.* New York, Knopf, 1983.

Schildroth, Arthur N.: Public residential schools for deaf students in the United States, 1970-1978. *American Annals of the Deaf, 125:*80-91, 1980.

Vernon, McCay and Estes, Charles C.: Deaf leadership and political activism. *The Deaf American, 28:*3-6, 1975.

Wilcox, Sherman: "Stuck" in school: A study of semantics and culture in a deaf education class. *Sign Language Studies, 43:*141-164, 1984.

Wolk, Stephen, Karchmer, Michael A., and Schildroth, Arthur: Patterns of academic and nonacademic integration among hearing impaired students in special education. Series R, No. 9, Washington, D.C., Center for Assessment and Demographic Studies, Gallaudet College, 1982.

Woodward, James: Some sociolinguistic problems in the implementation of bilingual education for deaf students. In Woodward, James: *How You Gonna Get to Heaven if You Can't Talk With Jesus: On Depathologizing Deafness.* Silver Spring, T. J. Publishers, 1982, pp. 21-50.

CHAPTER 6

CULTURAL CONFLICT IN A SCHOOL
FOR DEAF CHILDREN

CAROL J. ERTING

DEAFNESS HAS BEEN compared to ethnicity because the sociocultural processes involved when Deaf[1] individuals interact
with each other and with members of the larger hearing-speaking society
resemble ethnicity phenomena described by anthropologists such as
Barth (1969), Cohen (1974), and others (Erting, 1978; Johnson and Erting, 1984; Markowicz and Woodward, 1978). From such a perspective,
schools for deaf children are fascinating sociocultural environments in
which to study the interaction of language and social life. They are also
frustrating environments because of the conflict between two very different cultural systems—those of Deaf people and of hearing educators.

The conflict became apparent to me when I participated in a preschool parent education program as a sign language teacher for Deaf
parents of deaf preschool children. The fact that a normally hearing person was assigned to teach a sign language class for people who had been
using sign language as a primary language all or most of their lives
might seem strange, even absurd. Only by examining the sociocultural
dimensions of everyday life in the school can we begin to understand
how such an arrangement might come to be and how it might be viewed
by participants.

When this study began, I recently had joined the research department of Jackson School to begin a study of interaction between mothers
and their preschool deaf children. We were working closely with the pre-

school in order to contact families and arrange for their participation in the research. When the preschool needed a teacher for the Deaf parents' sign language class, the research department nominated me. I was an experienced teacher of preschool deaf children and had taught sign language classes to parents in the past. In addition, I had expressed interest in learning about the concerns and attitudes of Deaf parents. The newly formed research department saw this arrangement as a way to develop a collaborative, mutually beneficial relationship between researchers and teachers.

Because I was new to the school community, I was an unknown quantity to teachers and Deaf parents alike. From past experiences, I knew that teachers tend to be skeptical about researchers and the practicality of their work, and Deaf parents tend to be guarded and passive in their relationships with hearing people, especially educators. In spite of my training and experience, the teachers continued to relate to me as an outsider, or at least as a marginal member of the teaching team.

I gained some degree of acceptance from the Deaf parents' group because of one staff member, a mother of a preschool deaf child. After becoming acquainted with her the previous summer when she and her child were videotaped for our research project, she allowed me to interview her about her experiences as a Deaf person. She attended most of the weekly meetings of the Deaf parents' group and offered interpretations of behavior and conversations that occurred, as well as suggestions for improving my interaction with the Deaf parents. She was a respected member of the group and, early on, came to be seen as its leader.

The following discussion is a result of five years of participant-observation in one school for deaf childern. Prior to my experience at Jackson School, I had been involved for eight years with deaf children, their parents, and adult deaf communities in a variety of contexts. Through these experiences and the systematic analysis of field notes and interviews, it became clear that two themes structure the lives of deaf people in fundamental ways: deafness is primarily a visual experience; deafness results in dependence on those who are not deaf. These themes must be taken into account.

DEAFNESS AS A VISUAL EXPERIENCE

The world is structured by and for people who can both see and hear. Deafness, especially if it is profound from birth, drastically alters a person's perception of the world. No auditory information is available for development of either basic concepts or auditory-vocal language. Not only is lack of hearing annoying and inconvenient, it results in a different organizational structure for the lives of deaf people when compared with their hearing-speaking counterparts. To function successfully, deaf people, like all people, need to acquire information and communicative skills. Unlike most people, however, deaf individuals have only one major sense through which to do it — vision — the same sense they must rely upon for communication.

One effect of this single rather than dual channel capacity is a dramatic decrease in the amount of information easily accessible to deaf individuals when compared with their hearing counterparts. Because a deaf person requires as much information as a hearing person, a basic goal for deaf people is to acquire information and to communicate with others in the most efficient way possible, both to avoid visual fatigue and to free their visual attention for the next activity or demand. This goal is not peripheral; rather, it is a central organizing principle for their lives. Success in achieving it is necessary in a world in which effective information processing and management are keys to survival.

THE DEPENDENCY CONSTRAINT

At the same time that deaf people experience the world and structure their lives differently from people who are not deaf, they are forced to interact with and depend upon those who can hear and speak — people who know and understand very little about the deaf experience and the needs of people who depend solely upon vision. For most deaf people born to hearing parents, this dependence begins at birth. Their dependence on people who hear has its roots in the emotionally powerful and influential experiences of early childhood and the parent-child relationship. Dependence continues in the spheres of education, religion, employment, and in the acquisition of goods and services provided and controlled primarily by those who infrequently confront or even think about deafness as a life experience.

Along with dependence comes the need to play by rules and achieve goals that often have little or no meaning to deaf people or are unattainable. Attempts to meet hearing-world standards cause stress, but refusal to do so threatens survival. Although deaf individuals may expend great energy working toward meeting these standards, regardless of their success they continue to find their fate dependent, to a large extent, on the willingness of hearing people to interact with and accommodate them.

THE POLITICS OF THE EDUCATION OF DEAF CHILDREN

One fact above all others is helpful to keep in mind about the political context in which deaf and hearing people interact. That is the power differential. Hearing people have a great deal of power over deaf people's lives. In the wider society, life is structured according to the requirements of a hearing, speaking population. Deaf people earn a living, are consumers, and participate as citizens within a society that defines them as abnormal and is structured in ways that make it difficult for them to share equally with hearing people the benefits of that society.

Schools for deaf children are staffed primarily by people who are not deaf. Most teachers, administrators, counselors, researchers, and support personnel have normal hearing (Moores 1978:24-26). The Jackson Elementary School where this research was conducted is no exception. In fact, at the time this study began, the preschool department had only one faculty member who did not have normal hearing. By contrast, all of the 180 children enrolled in Jackson School had some degree of hearing loss, and approximately half of the 24 children in the preschool classes had deaf parents.

Schools for Deaf Children

Since most deaf children have hearing parents (Karchmer, Trybus, and Paquin 1978:3) and most of the school personnel controlling and allocating resources and making policy decisions are hearing people (Corbett and Jensema, 1981; Moores, 1978:24-26), school programs reflect the world view that hearing people take of deafness: Deafness is not a normal condition. In this view, the role of the school is to help deaf children become as much like normally hearing and speaking people as possible and to assist parents in helping their children to do so. Schools for deaf children vary with respect to the kinds of educational programs they provide. Because the single largest problem for hearing parents is communication with their child and, thus, integration of the child into the family unit and its world view, educational programs are built around various communication methods and definitions of deafness. Educators often refer to their methodology as a "way of life" or a "philosophy" that takes on the appearance of an ideology, offering solutions for deafness, a basic problem of human existence for these parents and children.

Currently, the majority of educational programs for deaf children can be categorized broadly as "oral-only" and "Total Communication" programs, the former barring any kind of visual-gestural communication system and the latter utilizing Simultaneous Communication as one of the key components of the communication environment. Simultaneous Communication is the speaking and signing of English simultaneously; it employs any one of several sign systems devised by educators to represent English manually and visually. These sign systems are not to be confused with the native sign language of Deaf Americans, commonly labeled American Sign Language or ASL. The former are invented systems that attempt to encode English; ASL is a language that developed over time through the social interaction of Deaf Americans. It is a language well-suited for its multidimensional visual-gestural modality, employing grammatical processes quite different from those of English, a linear, auditory-vocal language.

The Jackson School Program

Jackson School supports Total Communication as an educational philosophy. Parents and teachers are encouraged to use any and every means of communicating in order to achieve understanding. The central component of Total Communication as it is practiced in the school is Simultaneous Communication. The primary goal is to teach English, often referred to simply as "teaching language." Although American Sign Language is one of the stated components of Total Communication, most of the teachers and parents, both hearing and Deaf, do not accord it the same status as English (and most of the hearing people do not know ASL). Parents and teachers are encouraged to sign and talk simultaneously any time deaf children are present, even if they are talking among themselves, one hearing person to another. It is assumed that the more deaf children see manually encoded English (MCE), whether the communication is directed to them or not, the faster they will develop English and communication skills themselves. Furthermore, every conversational exchange with children is viewed as a potential English language learning experience. Teachers and parents are urged to sign every word they say, including the invented signs for the copula and selected grammatical affixes of English. School policy requires all children to wear some kind of hearing aid, and portions of the school day are set aside for specific work to develop auditory and speech skills.

The preschool program at Jackson School emphasizes the importance of the parent-child relationship in the educational and social-emotional development of deaf children. The school provides regularly scheduled home visits by teachers, weekly sign language classes and parent discussion groups, and monthly evening parent meetings. Hearing parents and deaf parents are separated for sign language classes. Both groups are taught by hearing people, and the signing taught is some kind of manual code for English. Although the Deaf parents are proficient in American Sign Language as well as in a variety of fluent English signing (sometimes labeled Pidgin Sign English), the school encourages Deaf parents to use manually encoded English with their children. However, many of the signs taught during these classes are viewed negatively by Deaf parents, either because there is an existing ASL sign that they use or because the invented signs feel or look awkward to them.

The parent program is designed to educate hearing and deaf parents about deafness and to provide emotional support, especially to hearing parents. Curriculum topics include medical aspects of hearing loss, the meaning of an audiogram, child development, language development, discipline, and speech development. Two counselors and two teachers (all of whom have normal hearing) are employed to address the informational and emotional needs of the parents. They are available upon request for individual meetings with parents and for the group meetings mentioned above. From time to time, mental health professionals are hired as consultants to work directly with parents and to advise counselors and teachers who work with parents.

DIFFERING VIEWS OF DEAFNESS

Hearing parents and Deaf parents come to the school with differing views of and experiences with deafness. There is a better match between the views of the hearing parents and those of the hearing educators than there is between the views of the Deaf parents and those of the hearing educators. These differences are important for several reasons, including the fact that the definition of deafness determines, to a large degree, the kinds of programs and services provided by the school. If there is a mismatch between the view held by those providing the services and those who are intended to benefit, it is not likely that the program will be successful from either point of view.

As Abner Cohen suggests, any political context is made up of "competing and quarreling groups" (1974:59); in the present context of the school, hearing parents, Deaf parents, and hearing educators are groups competing with each other and arguing about deafness—a particular problem of human existence all must confront every day. Deafness cannot be cured, except in the rarest of cases. Advances in technology have not eliminated completely the isolation it imposes nor the inconvenience. No method of education has been effective for the majority of deaf people: no method provides deaf children with native competence in English (or any spoken language); no method teaches the majority of deaf children to speak intelligibly, or to read above the fourth or fifth grade level as measured by standardized tests. The following summaries present the competing views of deafness taken by the three groups.

Hearing Parents

When hearing parents discover that a child is deaf, they face an abrupt change in their lives, one that challenges their understandings of themselves as parents and of what it is to be human. The diagnosis of deafness changes their role as parents to a new role, that of parents of a deaf child. Soon they discover there must be changes in their expectations for their child's present and future life. Free and easy communication between them and their child will not develop in the same way as with their own parents. Something as taken-for-granted and as seemingly natural as speaking with each other, as parent and child, is precluded by deafness. If anything that even approximates satisfactory communication is to occur, parents soon learn they must change their form of communication from spoken language to signed language.

The meaning of this challenge to the hearing parents' basic identity as hearing, speaking human beings can be grasped only when one understands the role of language as "the most important content and the most important instrument of socialization" (Berger and Luckmann, 1966:153). The language used by significant others is a part of the world that children internalize "as the world, the only existent and only conceivable world, the world **tout court**" (p. 154). Thus, a person's first language, through which primary socialization occurs, is inextricably part of that person's selfhood.

Hearing parents, unless they had deaf parents themselves, were socialized through spoken language. Being **speakers** of a language is fundamental to their understanding of themselves and their social world. Having a deaf child necessitates that they learn to use hands and bodies rather than voices to produce language, and that they rearrange notions of selfhood to take into account this fact. But an even more difficult challenge faces them. They must use this new form of language to communicate with and to socialize their child. If communication is to occur, they have no choice but to set aside their own first language, which is an integral part of their selfhood and their social world, replacing it with another that will become their child's first language. A hearing mother of a four-year-old deaf child described her early feelings about her daughter's deafness this way:

> When you [have] a child. . .you think of the future. . .they're going to do this, and they're going to do that. . .and all of a sudden it's this. . . your child's whole life is ruined. This is it. Here's this beautiful child that you love to pieces and. . .I can't do anything to help them. They have this terrible handicap and they're going to be stuck with it. . . .I just always ignored deaf people because I didn't know how to communicate with them and they scared me.

The child's father expressed his feelings about communication with his daughter and about his role as a parent:

> Kids are supposed to learn so much from parents through their conversation, what it's like to be an adult. And we aren't giving her that. (Sign language) is not a natural language.

The mother added:

> We sign to Cathy continuously, but we don't sign to each other. If we sit here talking, we just talk. It's so much easier. But she realizes. . . .Last week she sat here and I came in and sat down and started running my mouth and all of a sudden Cathy said, "My turn." And she goes, "Blah, blah, blah, blah." I asked Cathy what she was saying: "Use you signs." She just continued to talk. She said, "Mommy can do it. I can do it." She was really trying to get something across to us. She figured we should know what's going on and we didn't. . . .She says, "Same as Mommy and Daddy," and I thought, "You're right."

As Cohen points out, when change occurs people struggle "to preserve their identity, their selfhood, in the old traditional ways" (1974:57). Hearing parents struggle in the face of deafness to preserve their identities. Initially, this struggle may result in denial that their child is deaf (Luterman, 1981; Meadow, 1967). Subsequently, it may take a variety of forms (Nash, 1975). Hearing parents may refuse to use signed communication with their child, or they may accept and even actively advocate its use but insist that their child learn only an English variety of signing, perhaps also requiring the child's use of voice with the signing at all times. For example, the hearing parents quoted above described communication with their four-year-old deaf daughter like this:

Mother: Most of the time I talk to her and sign at the same time. But there are time I get angry and I talk. Or, there are other times I want her to lipread so I don't use it. But most of the time, I use. . .sign language and talking with her.

Father: If we know she can lipread it, we'll just talk to her. Other times we'll fingerspell because we're trying to get more fingerspelling in.

Mother: Cathy always uses her voice, 'cause we sort of ask for it, so she always uses her voice and signs. . . .She vocalizes with everything. . . . I guess we've given her that much.

Father: And we are learning her vocalizations. I mean, her "Daddy" doesn't sound like "Daddy." Her "Mother" is pretty good because she can say "ther" perfect and it's just a matter of getting the "mo-ther". . .so we recognize it and we know it's there.

Deaf Parents

In sharp contrast to hearing parents, Deaf parents often **expect** their children to be deaf, especially if they come from families with a history of deafness. Frequently, when expecting a child, they hope for a deaf child, rather than a normally hearing or a hard-of-hearing child. The following statements were made by Deaf parents of two deaf children who both have Deaf parents themselves:

Mother: If we had hearing children, maybe we would worry about speech development, because we can't hear and we're not talking. So with deaf children you don't have to worry about that. That's one advantage of having deaf children. We're able to share more fully with deaf children.

Father: I can share and discuss things with Steven easier. . .because I've had those same experiences. . . .I was deaf and I had Deaf parents. So you share similar experiences, and it's easier to communicate and share with the children.

A Deaf mother, whose parents are hearing and who has a Deaf husband and three deaf children, expressed her feelings about having deaf children:

We're happy that they have good health except deafness. That's OK. . . .We feel more comfortable communicating with them because they are the same. . . .When I was a little girl, I felt lost. All hearing people were around me. . . .I couldn't communicate with them. . .they couldn't communicate with me. So there's closeness because you are all deaf.

When Deaf parents express apprehension about having a deaf child, the concern usually is related to the difficulties they know the child will encounter in a hearing, speaking world, especially with limited job opportunities and educational problems. One Deaf father, who was fourth generation Deaf, hoped that his child would be born with normal hearing, "a break in our generations of deafness." However, when his son was born deaf, he accepted it saying, "I think we identify with him more because he is deaf like us." A Deaf mother with two deaf children, who was considering whether or not she should have another child, expressed the following concerns:

I am trying to think of the children's future. . . .Will they suffer more or less?. . .Will they accept deafness better than I do? I am trying to figure out what is the best in the future for them, what programs. If we live in the Midwest, I don't think I want to have any more children, because of the poor services there for deaf people.

In the case of Deaf parents, the birth of a hearing child is more likely to challenge their identities than the birth of a deaf child. As with the hearing parents who have a deaf child, the difficulties are especially evident in communication. One Deaf mother, who has Deaf parents and two deaf children, expressed these feelings about Deaf parents who had hearing children:

(My friends) who already had a hearing child around Michael's age. . . said, "You're lucky to have a deaf son. Now you will have no communication problems." They are worried about what to do with the hearing child about developing speech. . . .A few friends said, "I'm glad my son can hear." They were thinking about the phone. . . .I said, "Fine, but remember, teach your children sign language so that when they grow up you will have no communication problems."

Another Deaf mother, who has three hearing children said:

I remember the frustration I had in communicating with my hearing children when they were one or two years old. Even now, there is no problem in communication, but when the three are talking among themselves, I feel left out of what they are talking about. A lot of times they are bored. They don't want to tell me everything. They don't want to repeat. They say, "Oh nothing. It's not important."

The challenge that deafness presents to the deaf individual's notion of selfhood first occurs when it is perceived as an aspect of self not shared by the majority. Potentially the challenge recurs every time deaf individuals face deafness as a condition that makes them different, or that limits them in some way. Deaf adults have been meeting those challenges and living with deafness as part of their identities throughout their lives. Usually, having a deaf child is not a trauma for them and does not require a major rearrangement of their notions of selfhood. They know from experience what deafness means and they do not lack confidence in themselves as parents because of their deafness. Furthermore, their first language is usually some variety of sign language, acquired from their own parents if they were Deaf, or from Deaf peers, and it is the same language they use with their child from birth. Communication usually proceeds unhampered as the deaf child acquires competence in sign language.

For these parents, the deafness of their child brings a challenge to their identities as Deaf parents when they enroll their child in school and must interact with hearing educators. This interaction is problematic because of the differing definitions of deafness held by hearing educators, on the one hand, and by Deaf parents, on the other, and because hearing people are in a position of relative power and control over deaf people, in this case with respect to the education of the Deaf parents' children.

Hearing Educators

Teachers of deaf children are usually young, white, highly educated females with normal hearing (Corbett and Jensema, 1981). Their view of deafness has much in common with the view held by hearing parents. It is likely that their ideas about themselves as teachers as well as their experiences as hearing and speaking people are basic aspects of their identities. Most, if not all, of the training programs for teachers of deaf children have as their primary goal the training of teachers who will help deaf children develop the skills necessary to fit into the larger hearing, speaking society. The emphasis is on teaching children to use whatever residual hearing they have with the help of various kinds of hearing aids, teaching them to speak intelligibly, to speechread, and to be proficient in English.

Because the majority of deaf children do not perform successfully in these areas — according to the hearing teachers' criteria — the educators are constantly faced with a challenge. They must find a way to maintain their views of themselves as successful in the face of "failure" to produce a successful deaf child. Teachers' beliefs about the meaning of success for their deaf students derive from their identities as hearing, speaking individuals and from their socialization as educators. Thus, success is almost synonymous with English language competence, and even more specifically, spoken English language competence.

Hearing educators' identities are challenged not only by their deaf students, but also by Deaf individuals and occasionally by hearing individuals who do not subscribe to the definitions of success described above. For example, when Deaf parents call for the use of ASL in the classroom, or insist that their children not be required to use hearing aids, and when they express a different opinion about the role of speech in their children's lives, the hearing educators' identities potentially are threatened. Regardless of the impact of these challenges on the hearing teachers' notions of selfhood, there is also a potential threat to the job security of educators who have invested in the pursuit of a highly specialized career. When Deaf parents devalue the areas in which hearing educators have expertise — such as speech, auditory training, the use of hearing aids, and signing manually encoded English — and emphasize instead areas of expertise that few, if any, of the educators possess — such as fluency in ASL — hearing educators might well perceive a threat to their job as well as to their professional identity.

COMPETING DEFINITIONS OF DEAFNESS

Two contrasting views of deafness, as held by educators and Deaf parents, have important implications for the education of deaf children. These definitions of deafness are ideal types; not every hearing educator subscribes to the "educator view," not every Deaf parent would agree with the "Deaf parent" view. In fact, within the political arena of the school individuals may and do choose to align themselves with one view or aspects of one view in one particular situation, while aligning themselves with the opposite view or aspects of it in another situation. These ideal type definitions, however, represent the most frequent themes to emerge from the stated beliefs of educators and Deaf parents. A "hearing parent view" is not included, since most hearing parents still are formulating their beliefs and attitudes about deafness while their children are preschoolers and usually look to educators for direction.

The Educator View of Deafness

The first characteristic of the educator view is its terminology and categorization of deafness. Most educators prefer to use the term "hearing impaired" when referring to a child with a hearing loss. They define deafness in audiological terms according to hearing loss measured in decibels (units of amplitude of sound) at certain frequencies. Distinctions are made between hard-of-hearing children and deaf children, with each of those categories divided into subcategories: mildly hard-of-hearing, moderately hard-of-hearing, severely hard-of-hearing; or severely deaf, and profoundly deaf.

Etiology or cause of the hearing loss is another way educators categorize hearing impairment. For example, a child might have a hearing loss due to heredity, maternal rubella, meningitis, or birth trauma, or unknown etiology. A third aspect is age at onset. Hearing impairment can be congenital or acquired. The specific educational concern with this categorization of a hearing loss is its effect on language acquisition; that is, whether the hearing loss occurs before or after spoken language is acquired. Before the acquisition of spoken language, it is labeled prelingual deafness, postlingual deafness after spoken language is acquired. Finally, there is the distinction between sensori-neural and conductive hearing loss. The former is irreversible; the latter usually can be treated and often cured.

The second characteristic of the educator view is the definition of deafness as handicap: deafness prevents children from acquiring normal speech and language in the usual way. It is primarily a communication handicap that, in the teacher view, has ramifications for the child's academic future. Educators view deaf children as children without language and incapable of abstract thought simply because of the language deficit. In this context, language virtually always is equated with spoken language, which in the United States usually is English.

The Deaf Parent View of Deafness

The terminology that Deaf parents at Jackson School use when discussing deafness is quite different from that of the educators and hearing parents. Deaf parents rarely, if ever, use the term hearing impaired; children are either hearing, deaf, or hard-of-hearing. Even these labels have different references when Deaf parents use them than when educators use them. At times, the terms refer to differing attitudes or constellations of attitudes with respect to deafness; at other times, they may refer to something as specific as the person's ability to use the telephone. Deaf parents rarely discuss their children's deafness in terms of decibels or the characteristics of the audiogram. In identifying a deaf child, Deaf parents frequently refer to the child's parental hearing status—that is, whether the child's parents are hearing or deaf, and whether or not the child was deaf at birth.

The second way in which Deaf parents view deafness differently from educators is in the notion of handicap. Deaf parents do not view deafness primarily as a handicap or disability. It is a condition that creates a different way of life for them as compared to society's hearing majority. Deaf parents do not deny the difficulties and inconveniences that deafness imposes, but they emphasize their capabilities and the ways in which their lives are arranged to take account of the problems.

Deaf parents' and educators' views might seem to coincide in one detail. Most Deaf parents are concerned that their children develop good English skills. However, they also recognize that they have a language—sign language—that takes the place of spoken language for purposes of everyday communication. Regardless of the label they use to refer to this sign language, they regard it as more efficient, natural, and esthetically pleasing than manually encoded English signing. Here, of course, they are diametrically opposed to the educator view.

These two idealized views of deafness are composites of frequently expressed attitudes, beliefs, and opinions of hearing and Deaf individuals at Jackson School. Each is associated with clusters of symbols. Each symbol has the potential to call forth other symbols and to make a somewhat ambiguous reference during face-to-face interaction to what is assumed to be common or shared knowledge among educators and among Deaf parents. Part of that shared knowledge has to do with attitudes toward deafness and the types of symbols used by individuals during interaction, especially when parents and educators disagree with each other about definitions of deafness and compete for the resources the school provides. The following discussion describes some of the conflicts generated by the competing cultural systems of hearing educators and Deaf parents during everyday interaction.

DEAF PARENTS: A SPECIAL INTEREST GROUP

Although educators and counselors at Jackson School recognized a difference between the sign language needs of hearing and Deaf parents sufficient to warrant separate classes, they believed both groups needed instruction in manually encoded English as well as in counseling and basic information about deafness. These latter services were provided primarily through the weekly parent discussion group, which Deaf and hearing parents attended together immediately following their separate sign language classes.

The eight Deaf mothers who attended the weekly sign language class that I led did not know the purpose of the class and, once I explained it to them, did not agree with it. Nor did they define their needs or problems the same way the school did. In fact, the problems they identified — and eventually asked the school to address — were the very services being provided by the school. During the first five meetings of the deaf parents' sign language class, most of the issues around which the Deaf parents eventually organized were raised in one form or another. Three months later the Deaf parents called a special meeting with the administration of the school to present their grievances and demands. The remaining three months of the school year saw increasing alienation between the Deaf parents and the hearing educators.

Space does not permit a detailed description of the issues and social processes involved in the formation of the Deaf parents' special interest group. The following discussion summarizes some underlying cultural differences between the hearing educators and the Deaf parents, as revealed by an analysis of the differing ways in which the two groups discussed the recurring conflicts that arose between them. Frequently, the same linguistic symbols were used by members of both groups, but they often represented different, even contradictory meanings. Sometimes one or both of the participants in a discussion recognized the contradictions and misunderstandings, but most of the time it appeared they did not.

CULTURAL CONFLICT

One of the linguistic symbols that frequently carried different meanings for Deaf parents and hearing educators was the label **deaf.** As mentioned, educators tend to rely upon audiological definitions of deafness, whereas Deaf parents usually refer to behavioral and attitudinal indicators of deafness. When the Jackson School parents asked for a Deaf coleader for an evening parent meeting, the educators chose someone deaf according to their view but "not really Deaf" according to the parents' view. The women selected was audiologically deaf: she could not hear. But she had been able to hear as a child and had been socialized as a hearing person by hearing parents. She had acquired spoken English skills before losing her hearing and she had intelligible speech that she used simultaneously with manually encoded English. In the Deaf parents' view, she was more like hearing educators in terms of behavior and attitudes than she was like Deaf parents. The educators were pleased that they had been able to find a deaf counselor to satisfy the request of the Deaf parents. The Deaf parents were disappointed because in their view their request had not been satisfied. Few attended the meeting.

Counseling, a service the school personnel wanted to provide, was not a priority for Deaf parents. What they wanted was **information.** In their view, the school's responsibility was to provide the information necessary for decisions about their children's educational futures. A major complaint about the counselor and teacher was that the discussions they led were vague and never to the point. But the counselor and teacher did not view themselves as providers of information. Rather, they regarded themselves as facilitators for the parents. They defined their primary tasks in terms of a counseling paradigm to provide opportunities and environments that would encourage parents to grow, to discover their feelings and ways of dealing with them, and to take responsibility for themselves. Their view of repeated requests for information rather than counseling was that the Deaf parents were trying to avoid taking responsibility for their own lives. In addition, they stated that the parents were trying to avoid confronting uncomfortable feelings about themselves, about deafness, and about their children. In their view, it would have been a disservice to the parents to comply with requests that the majority of meetings be structured according to an education model rather than a counseling model.

Information was a word used frequently by the Deaf parents. It was their responsibility to keep each other informed; it was information they wanted from the school; and it was information they felt their children needed from their teachers. The Deaf mother who often acted as the spokesperson for the group frequently used the sign COMMUNICATION interchangeably with the sign INFORMATION when discussing the needs of preschool deaf children. The teachers in the preschool wasted time on language drill and cooking. In her view, precise English language skills would come with reading and writing as the children grew older. She emphasized that the important things during preschool years were to communicate, to give information, to challenge children, and keep them interested.

In this Deaf mother's discussions, Deaf teachers, communication, and information were all linked. She said most Deaf people preferred

Deaf teachers because they would deviate from the curriculum to teach children what they needed to know in order to survive in the world. They needed to know such things as how to buy a pair of shoes: that they had to ask for a specific size, and how to ask in an acceptable way. She stated that they needed to be taught how the system works and how to express their desires and questions without offending hearing people. In her own case, she related, Deaf teachers at her residential school had been helpful in giving information she needed to get a driver's license. Before they told her about a driver's license, she had had no idea that she needed one.

Most frequently, when the parents complained about the unmet needs of their children, those needs were discussed in terms of communication symbolism. This was especially true when Deaf parents expressed opinions to hearing educators. They made it a point to distinguish between COMMUNICATION and LANGUAGE. COMMUNICATION represented information exchange, concept development, receptive and expressive skills in sign language — all of which they associated with their experiences among Deaf rather than hearing people. LANGUAGE represented English language drills, memorizing English language patterns, boredom, failure, and difficult interactions among hearing people. On the other hand, hearing educators often used the terms communication and language synonymously; to them, both of these linguistic symbols usually referred to English or manually encoded English and rarely, if ever, to ASL. For example, if parents requested that a teacher concentrate on developing their child's communication skills, most teachers would assume that the parents meant manually encoded English, speech, and listening skills.

Educators and Deaf parents saw their interrelationship differently. Educators discussed their roles and involvement with the parents in terms of the symbolism of **contractual, single-stranded relationships.** They saw themselves as skilled professionals, paid to perform a service that required long and expensive training. But their jobs also required that they interact with the parents. Their contracts stipulated that they were employed for eight hours per day, five days per week. The time that they spent evenings and on weekends was time spent outside the working day, time they viewed as their own and for which they were not compensated.

Educators viewed their relationship with parents as one involving responsibility on both sides. They believed it was the parents' responsibility to participate, come to meetings regularly, contribute to discussions, and help make decisions about the programs within limits set by educators. The counselor and the teacher saw themselves as responsible for selecting the format of the meetings and the scope of the program. They decided on how many evening and weekend meetings would be held.

Another responsibility they defined for themselves was to set limits. They viewed themselves as the helpers in a helping relationship. That relationship often was discussed in terms of a parent-child model: the educators were the parents, the authority figures; the parents were the children, at times characterized as manipulative, naive and uninformed, experiencing growing pains and needing comfort, and unwilling to take responsibility and make decisions.

Deaf parents discussed their relationships with educators as contractual at times, but they also attempted to draw educators into **normative relationships** that were multiplex in nature. When parents met with the administration, they complained that the counselor was not doing her job. In their view, she was paid to provide parents with appropriate speakers and programs; parents should not be expected to tell her what they needed. She should know that by virtue of her professional status and should give parents something in return for her salary.

Deaf parents were annoyed at being used to educate hearing parents about deafness when the counselor and teacher were paid to perform that service. Educators viewed the Deaf parents' participation as their contractual duty, but the parents viewed the educators' expectations for their participation as inappropriate. They felt the school was taking advantage of them.

Deaf parents believed that they contributed to the school through their children and through their own association with hearing parents and teachers. Their children were the star pupils of the school. They were the children with the highest communication skills, and deaf children with hearing parents benefitted from interactions with them. Deaf parents saw themselves as experts on deafness. If it had not been for their interactions with the hearing parents, those parents would not have known what it was like to be a Deaf adult, according to the Deaf parents.

So, on the one hand, Deaf parents charged that the hearing educators were not fulfilling the contractual obligations that were theirs by virtue of the salaries they were paid. On the other hand, Deaf parents expected the educators to interact with them on the basis of normative relationships. For example, one Deaf mother suggested a Saturday evening get-together for teachers and parents and their families. She explained that such an event would provide an opportunity for the parents to interact with teachers outside the school context. There would be time for socializing and getting to know each other, followed by discussion of more business-like issues. She noted that Deaf and hearing parents do not get a chance to know each other as persons, in the context of their families, and that it is important to do so if there is to be comfortable and relevant communication during the group discussions. Her suggestions were met with negative response. The counselor said that the teachers would not be willing to give up a Saturday night because they were not compensated for evening or weekend meetings. The mother was upset that the counselor was so negative; she thought the suggestion should be brought before the teachers for their response. What was more important to them, the children or the money? If they really were concerned about the children, they would take the time.

Deaf parents seemed to expect educators to be involved in more ways than would be dictated by the single-stranded relationship of teacher-learner. They wanted to relate to teachers on the basis of roles they held in common, such as mother to mother, father to father, husband to husband, wife to wife. Such relationships would become multiplex and normative to some extent, moving toward the kinds of relationships Deaf parents have with each other. The educators did not expect to relate to the parents except on the basis of a contractual relationship. In most cases, they believed it important to separate professional roles from family and personal lives. The fact that Deaf parents and educators viewed their relationships so differently and had disparate expectations of each other led to misunderstandings and conflicts similar to those engendered by the cultural conflicts described earlier.

By the close of the academic year, Deaf parents and hearing educators were so alienated from each other that they stopped attending the parent meetings, and hearing educators openly expressed anger and resentment toward Deaf parents. The educators continued to use a mental health model, and interpretations based on their own experiences as hearing-speaking individuals, to produce explanations for behaviors of the Deaf parents. Deaf norms and categories — that is, Deaf parents' interpretations based on their experiences as Deaf individuals — were not recognized and thus could not be taken into account by the educators.

The Deaf parents' insistence on their need for information, rather than counseling, was a result of the lifelong difficulty they had experienced gaining access to everyday knowledge, much of which is available only in auditory form. They knew that information and knowledge were necessary prerequisites for daily decision-making and that the net result would be more control over their own lives and those of their young children. The counseling model not only failed to address their informational needs but also seemed to them to be based upon a view of deafness as pathology rather than as difference, which the Deaf parents rejected. It probably also was perceived as a way of perpetuating a feeling of dependence on hearing people that they had been living with all of their lives.

In much the same way, Deaf parents' emphasis on communication rather than language (structured English lessons) as a central part of the curriculum for preschoolers was a realistic response to the constraints imposed by deafness as they had experienced them. They remembered their own school experiences, the time spent day after day in drill and memorization of English sentences, which could have been spent acquiring knowledge and developing cognitive skills. They remembered their frustration and low self-esteem as they tried to attain the perfect speech and English skills their hearing teachers worked so hard to teach. In contrast, they remembered the freeing experience of communicating with other deaf people—perhaps their own parents, their peers, and Deaf teachers who often were responsible for rekindling curiosity and a desire for learning through information not previously accessible. They wanted their children to have this experience in their formative years so that they would develop the positive self-image and eagerness to learn important to their future academic and linguistic success.

Similar experiences and needs of Deaf people as they try to negotiate their everyday lives help bind them into a small scale, face-to-face community. It is important to their survival to know who is part of their group and who is not. They are well aware that simply to have a hearing impairment does not necessarily create the shared perspective necessary for community. But there is a shared perspective—a world view—held by those labeled REALLY DEAF. Within this face-to-face community, relationships are normative and complex. In this context Deaf people anchor themselves and develop positive, reciprocal relationships with others. When help is needed, they turn to each other. At times, this model of mutual support is the one they use to try to understand their relationship with school personnel.

Educators held different views of deafness, resulting in educational goals and strategies that, from the Deaf parents' point of view, were not successful. Their view of deafness as a condition to be corrected produced efforts aimed at changing characteristics of deaf people—such as their mode of communication, sign language, and behaviors—in order to match them as closely as possible to the hearing norm. Thus, even their signing needed to be changed to conform with sign systems developed by English speakers. From the educators' perspective, it was perfectly reasonable to assign a hearing person who was not a native signer to teach a sign class for Deaf adults. As the teacher of that class, my attempts to suggest alternative interpretations of the Deaf parents' behaviors to the educators usually were not successful. I was not viewed as an expert in the areas of parent counseling and education (in spite of my own background and training in those areas as well as in anthropology), but rather as an advocate for, or at least an ally of, the Deaf paents with whom they were so frustrated and annoyed.

I believe that any impact I had as an anthropologist, utilizing the tools and insights my profession has to offer, came as a result of the special relationship that developed between myself and one Deaf mother. She emerged as the leader of the Deaf parents and, two years later, started teaching in the preschool department. She focused her attention on the Deaf teachers in the school, and they formed an action group in much the same way the Deaf parents had. A change in the administration had occurred during the two-year interim, and a dialogue was established with the new principal. The result was a school-wide effort at improving communication between Deaf and hearing faculty members and between Deaf faculty and the administration. Demonstrating creativity, insight, and commitment to her goals, and utilizing some of the discoveries we made and understandings we achieved in our insider-outsider relationship, this Deaf woman was instrumental in effecting numerous changes in the educational environment of Jackson School.

FOOTNOTES

Acknowledgements. An earlier version of this article was presented at the annual meeting of the Society for Applied Anthropology, San Diego, March 1983. I am grateful to Joshua Fishman, Rachel Harris, Robert Johnson, Ruth Landman, Kathryn Meadow, and William Stokoe for helpful comments during discussions related to the development of the ideas expressed. I also would like to thank reviewers and editorial staff of **AEQ** for comments and suggestions. The responsibility for the content of the paper is, of course, solely my own.

1. I have adopted the use of "deaf" (with lower case **d**) as an adjective referring primarily to hearing loss, and the use of "Deaf" (with upper case **D**) as an adjective

referring to social collectivities and attitudes arising from interaction among people with hearing losses. This distinction was first made by Woodward (1972) and has become standard in much of the literature on the "Deaf Community."

REFERENCES

Barth, Fredrik: Introduction. In Barth, Fredrik: *Ethnic Groups and Boundaries*. Boston, Little, Brown, 1969, pp. 9-38.

Berger, Peter, and Luckmann Thomas: *The Social Construction of Reality*. Harmondsworth, Penguin, 1966.

Cohen, Abner: *Two-Dimensional Man*. London: Routledge and Kegan Paul, 1974.

Corbett, Edward, and Jensema, Carl: *Teachers of the Hearing Impaired: Descriptive Profiles*. Washington, D.C., Gallaudet College Press, 1981.

Erting, Carol: Language policy and deaf ethnicity. *Sign Language Studies, 19:*139-152, 1978.

Johnson, Robert, and Erting, Carol: Linguistic socialization in the context of emergent deaf ethnicity. Wenner-Gren Foundation Working Papers in Anthropology. Keith Kernan, ed. New York, Wenner-Gren Foundation, 1984.

Karchmer, Michael, Trybus, Raymond, and Paquin, Maurice: Early manual communication, parental hearing status, and the academic achievement of deaf students. Washington, D.C., Office of Demographic Studies, Gallaudet College, 1978.

Luterman, David: *Counseling Parents of Hearing Impaired Children*. Boston, Little, Brown, 1981.

Markowicz, Harry, and Woodward, James C.: Language and the maintenance of ethnic boundaries in the deaf community. *Communication and Cognition, 11:*29-38, 1978.

Meadow, Kathryn P.: The effects of early manual communication and family climate on the deaf child's development. Unpublished doctoral dissertation, Sociology Department, University of California, Berkeley, 1967.

Moores, Donald: *Educating the Deaf: Psychology, Principles, and Practices*. Hopewell, Houghton Mifflin, 1978.

Nash, Jeffrey: Hearing parents of deaf children: a typology. *Sign Language Studies, 7:*163-180, 1975.

Woodward, James C.: Implications for sociolinguistic research among the deaf. *Sign Language Studies, 1:*1-7, 1972.

CHAPTER 7

THE DEAF COMMUNITY

PAUL C. HIGGINS

D EAF PEOPLE do not live in isolation within the larger world peo-
pled by those who hear. Instead, some are members of deaf communities. While those who seek to understand deafness differ in how
they conceptualize deaf communities, all stress the interaction among
hearing-impaired (and possibly hearing) people with common ties.
These common ties bind together members of deaf communities as well
as partially separate them from the larger society. Through marriages,
friendships, formal organizations, publications, sign language, and
other means, hearing-impaired people create and maintain deaf communities. Deaf communities are both a response to the negative experiences encountered by hearing-impaired people in the larger society
and a positive means for deaf people to achieve a sense of wholeness and
belonging. While members of deaf communities are citizens of the larger
society, many hold to significant cultural beliefs and practices which differ from those of the larger society. In part, those beliefs and practices involve what is taken to be appropriate forms of communication. Most
hearing-impaired people, however, are not members of deaf communities. Membership is neither sought by nor granted to all who are deaf.
Further, (based on some conceptualizations) one need not be deaf (i.e.,
profoundly hearing-impaired) to be a member. Membership is an
achieved status, not an **ascribed** one. Those who are members are not
homogeneous. Through their actions and their attitudes, members of
deaf communities create differences among themselves. Members use
those distinctions in organizing their relationships with one another, and
their differing relationships help to maintain the significance of those
distinctions. While deaf communities are locally organized, members of

151

the communities are interconnected in a deaf network. That network helps to develop some sense of solidarity and shared identity among a widely dispersed population. This understanding of deaf communities has several important implications for those who are involved with or "work with" deaf people.

COMMUNITY

Social scientists use the term community in several ways. Somewhat obviously and commonsensically, they have termed towns and cities communities, but so too have they referred to prisons and religious groups as communities. Even corporations, factories, and trade unions have been referred to as communities (Minar and Greer, 1969). Consequently, one social scientist has lamented that the term "community" has fallen into that category of words, used routinely by social scientists, which "take on so many shades of meaning that it is difficult to endow them with scientific precision" (Poplin, 1972:3). However, while there certainly is not complete agreement, many social scientists use "community" to refer to people in "social interaction within a geographic area and having one or more additional common ties" (Hillery, 1955:111). This general perspective on community underlies how those who seek to understand deafness have conceptualized deaf communities.

Just as social scientists differ in their use of the term "community," so do those who seek to understand deafness differ in their conceptualization of deaf communities. Some students of deafness emphasize the language that people use. Those who use a common language are a community. Therefore, the use of American Sign Language (ASL) is taken to be the significant characteristic that defines members of deaf communities and binds them together (Schlesinger and Meadow, 1972; Padden and Markowicz, 1975; Markowicz and Woodward, 1978). Some further believe that attendance in residential schools, where competency in ASL is typically developed, is necessary as well (Stokoe et al., 1965 in Markowicz and Woodward, 1978).

Others stress the common goals shared by deaf and hearing people which bring them together. Those who are working together for what might be called the "betterment" of the lives of deaf people are part of deaf communities whether they happen to be audiologically or culturally deaf or not. Thus, within this perspective, a deaf community is a:

> group of people who live in a particular location, share the common goals of its members, and in various ways, work toward achieving

those goals. A deaf community may include persons who are not themselves Deaf (i.e., culturally deaf, in which ASL is a basic element of the culture), but who actively support the goals of the community and work with deaf people to achieve them (Padden, 1980:92).

At a very broad level, an important goal of deaf communities is to "achieve public acceptance of deaf people as equals—equals in employment, in political representations, and in the control of institutions that involve deaf people, such as schools and service organizations" (Padden, 1980:94).

A third perspective emphasizes the mutual identification of hearing-impaired people with one another. Based on shared experiences, some hearing-impaired people develop a sense of belonging among one another which leads to and is reinforced by participation with each other. From this viewpoint, deaf communities are local groups of hearing-impaired people who, based on shared experiences among each other and identification with one another, participate together in a wide variety of activities (Higgins, 1980: Chapter 2).

While these conceptualizations of deaf communities differ, they are also similar in important respects. Each emphasizes the interaction among one another of hearing-impaired (and perhaps hearing) people who share common ties—a language, goals, or experiences and identification. Each clearly indicates that however deaf communities are conceptualized, they are set apart from the larger hearing world. Yet, each would also grant that there are many important ties between deaf communities (and its members) and the hearing world. After all, deaf people live within the larger society even if they are not fully part of it. Conceptualizations are neither right or wrong. Instead, they are more or less useful; in this case more or less useful for understanding the lives of deaf people. The task is not to create correct conceptualizations which we impose upon the lives of deaf people, but to investigate and make sense of what deaf people do (Higgins and Nash, 1982:14). Conceptualizations aid in that task. In order to more fully explore deaf communities, I will use the third perspective discussed above, the one that emphasizes shared experiences, identification, and participation.

MEMBERSHIP

Deaf communities are local groups of hearing-impaired people, who based on shared experiences among each other and identification with one another, participate together in a wide variety of activities.

Shared Experiences

Members of deaf communities share many experiences. These similar experiences are due to the difficulties encountered in being hearing impaired in a hearing world and to being educated in special programs for hearing-impaired students. Out of these shared experiences, a mutual identification may develop. Out of variations in experiences, distinctions among members of deaf communities may arise.

Members of deaf communities have encountered many difficulties living in a hearing world. Those difficulties involve primarily problems of communication and identity. Throughout their lives members of deaf communities have experienced difficulty in communication with hearing people. Members share the frustration and embarrassments which often arise out of the awkward and inhibited interaction with hearing people. They share the loneliness of being left out by (even while they were in the presence of) hearing individuals—parents, and other family members, neighbors, co-workers, and even teachers. They endure the raised voices and exaggerated mouth movements of hearing people who have learned of their deafness. They silently suffer the misattributions made about them due to their often "unnatural" speech. Hearing individuals may think that they are foreign or that they are mentally retarded. Their inability to auditorily monitor their speech may lead to too loud or too soft speech, mispronunciations, and what might be called "deafisms": strange vocal sounds, clicking noises, grunts, or hums which may be made without awareness in conversation or in reverie. The interaction becomes further strained. While writing and gestures may aid in communication with hearing individuals, the encounters remain awkward and inhibited. Communication with hearing people is often an unsatisfying chore (Higgins, 1980: Chapter 6).

Technological devices of the hearing world, such as telephones and televisions, which are designed to improve the lives of its citizens, have often become sources of frustration and obstacles for members of deaf communities. Transactions that hearing people routinely conduct over the telephone, such as business, emergency, or social calls, cannot be taken for granted by members of deaf communities. Hearing family members, neighbors, or co-workers may be called upon. In the process, messages may be miscommunicated and feelings of dependency may be developed (or strengthened). While telecommunication devices for the deaf (TDD's) are greatly welcome, until they become widespread among deaf and hearing people and establishments, they serve to highlight the continuing difficulties while partially lessening them (Schein and Delk, 1974:71).

Television, a source of entertainment, news, and cultural information, is a major means of socialization in technologically advanced societies. Through watching television we, in part, become competent (some would also argue corrupted) members of our society. Through common experiences available on television (news programs, presidential debates, a big sports spectacular, a major entertainment program, and the like), members of society are partly bound together. Deaf people, children and adults, miss much of that. While they may enjoy television, without captions the subtleties and even the grossest meanings are lost.

Captioned programs have proved to be a welcome relief for some, but they are not a panacea. Captions do enhance the comprehension of programs and the ability to perceive emotional complexity among the characters (Murphy-Berman and Whobrey, 1983). However, while dozens of television programs are captioned and the support to do so is growing, only a fraction of programming hours is captioned. (Some may argue that this is a blessing in disguise.) Further, many deaf adults and certainly deaf children (as well as hearing adults and children) do not read well enough to fully understand the captions. In a world which revolves on the assumption that people can hear and can speak, members of deaf communities share the experiences of being the "odd ones out."[1]

Members of deaf communities also share the experiences of being stigmatized, of possessing a spoiled identity (Goffman, 1963). In a world which assumes that one must be able-bodied to be normal, deaf people are disvalued. As noted in the Introduction, deafness has typically been taken to be a deficit and deaf people to be defective. Members of deaf communities have experienced this stigmatization in many ways. As children, their parents may have tried to deny their deafness and denigrated their signing, and as parents, their own children may sometimes do the same. When signing in public, others may stare at or mockingly imitate them. If deaf people have been embattled when using sign language, the battle has only fortified some in its use. Instead of being treated as individuals who happen to have a hearing impairment, their hearing impairment becomes a **master status,** which overshadows their other characteristics (Hughes, 1945). Hearing people often act toward members of deaf communities based on the members' deafness (and assumptions that hearing people hold about deafness), not on their own attributes. Further, the actions of others who are deaf have often been generalized to them. Members may be "defined" by hearing people in terms of their deafness and treated as if all deaf people were the same. Thus, if one deaf student at a residential school gets into trouble at a local store, then other deaf students may be watched more cautiously by store personnel. Or, if a deaf employee does not work out satisfactorily at a business, then subsequent deaf applicants may find it difficult to get a "fair hearing." Because deafness is taken to be a deficit, deaf people may be scrutinized carefully by those who hear, whether it is a new employer or prospective parents-in-law whose betrothed child is hearing. And deafness is not just seen as a sensory deficit, but it is often viewed as a deficit of competence (see Introduction). In all these ways and more, members of deaf communities share the experiences of being "second-class citizens" (Higgins, 1980: Chapter 5).

However, in contrast to those difficulties experienced within the larger society, members of deaf communities share positive experiences, too. They typically share the easy communication, the camaraderie, and the beginning sense of belonging which grew out of being educated with other hearing-impaired students in special programs, particularly residential programs in the past. The often physical and social isolation of deaf students from the larger society (particularly in residential programs which were dominant in the education of deaf students until several decades ago), the ease of communication among one another, the friendships, and the wealth of everyday experiences which were shared became the basis for a developing commitment to the deaf world. The ties and the experiences which developed among the hearing-impaired students in these educational facilities provided a bridge from adolescence into the adult deaf community.

Identification

Out of the shared experiences of being hearing impaired, members of deaf communities develop an identification with one another. In part, they form a "moral" community which involves a "sense of identity and unity with one's group and a feeling of involvement and wholeness on the part of the individual" (Poplin, 1972:7). Within the community, members are individuals first, not first hearing impaired. However, most hearing-impaired people do not identify with the deaf world. Consequently, most are not members of deaf communities.

As suggested in Chapter 1 (see Table 3), approximately 17 million people in the United States have a detectable hearing impairment. Approximately two million people are profoundly hearing impaired. They are deaf; they cannot hear and understand speech. Those who were born with such a profound hearing impairment or who acquired it before the end of adolescence, the "prevocationally deaf," are a smaller group. They number approximately 480,000 people (Schein and Delk, 1972:2, 16). Most members of deaf communities are prevocationally deaf. Those who lack the experiences of an early (relatively) profound hearing loss, are unlikely to develop an identification with the deaf world.

Individuals with relatively minimal forms of hearing impairment are typically not members of deaf communities. They do not share the experiences of extreme communication difficulty (and its resulting social consequences) nor the experiences of being educated in special, often isolated, programs which underlie the moral community of deaf people. Those who become severely hearing impaired later in life, perhaps due to aging or an industrial accident, are not likely to identify with the deaf world either. While they may be more profoundly impaired than some of the members of deaf communities and now experience some of their difficulties, they grew up as hearing people. Their experiences and their identities are as hearing people. While no longer fully competent members of the hearing world, neither are they likely to become members of deaf communities.

Other individuals who have been significantly hearing impaired from birth or from an early age may also not have developed an identification with the deaf world. Those individuals with hearing parents and who were educated primarily with other hearing youth may not have developed an identification with members of deaf communities.[2] Nor may have some hearing-impaired youth who were educated with other hearing-impaired youth in oral programs. Those who were educated primarily with hearing youth may not have experienced very much friendship with other hearing-impaired youth that could lead to involvement in deaf communities. Some of those educated in oral programs, who may share many experiences of being hearing-impaired with those who become members of deaf communities, do not identify with the deaf world. Instead, given the strong emphasis in oral programs on speech and speechreading, on being as much like hearing people as possible, some identify with the hearing world. Others, however, do reject that emphasis and turn toward deaf communities after leaving school or transferring to a less oral program.

Those hearing-impaired individuals who do not identify with the deaf community may live as adults in various ways. Some live exclusively in the hearing world, whether satisfactorily or not. Others develop social relationships with similarly-minded hearing impaired people. A relative few may even join formal organizations, such as the Oral Deaf Adults Section of the Alexander Graham Bell Association. Some marginally participate in, but are not members of, deaf communities. They may participate in some of the activities of the deaf community such as religious services or large social gatherings, but they are not fully accepted by the members. Because they orient themselves to the hearing world, clinging to the emphasis on speech while rejecting sign language, they are not embraced by the members of deaf communities.

However, other individuals who are not profoundly hearing impaired may be members of deaf communities. Particularly, in the past when fewer and less specialized educational programs existed for hearing-impaired students, but even nowadays, children with various degrees of hearing impairments are educated together in special programs (Karchmer and Trybus, 1977). While not deaf, these less severely impaired youth share many of the experiences of their more profoundly impaired classmates both within and outside of the educational programs. Those similar experiences and school-age friendships become the basis for an identification with the deaf world, just as they do for more severely impaired youth.

Therefore, a hearing loss is not a sufficient condition for membership in deaf communities (Higgins, 1980; Padden, 1980). However, neither is an extremely profound impairment a necessary condition for membership (Furfey and Harte, 1964, 1968; Schein, 1968; Higgins, 1980). Membership is not an **ascribed** status. It is not assigned to all with a (certain severity of) hearing impairment. Instead, it is **achieved** through identification with the deaf world.

Participation

Participation of members of deaf communities with one another develops out of the shared experiences and mutual identification. In turn, participation leads to additional shared experiences and strengthens identification among the members. Through friendships, formal organizations such as churches, clubs, social activities, publications, and other means, members of deaf communities associate with one another. The "activities provide the body of the community, whereas the identification and shared experiences provide the soul" (Higgins, 1980:47).

Hearing people are also involved in activities of deaf communities. Family members of deaf individuals, interpreters, religious leaders, and other interested hearing people may participate in the activities of deaf communities. However, it is uncertain to what extent these hearing individuals are members of deaf communities. Different conceptualizations of deaf communities provide different responses. Observers who stress competency in ASL would argue that relatively few of these concerned hearing individuals are competent ASL users. Hence, their lack of fluency in ASL is a boundary between them and the members of deaf communities. The perspective explored in the previous pages, which emphasizes shared experiences and mutual identification, suggests that no matter how sympathetic or empathic these hearing people are, no matter that they may be close friends of particular members of deaf communities, they should not be viewed as full-fledged members of deaf communities. However, the perspective which stresses the sharing of common goals allows for hearing people to be members of deaf communities.

If observers of deaf communities differ in their assessment as to whether hearing people are or are not members of deaf communities, perhaps members do themselves. Hearing-impaired or hearing people may be accepted by some members of deaf communities but not by others. Perhaps it may be more useful to view people as more or less members of deaf communities depending on their own actions and attitudes and the actions and attitudes of others in the deaf communities. Or, perhaps deaf communities might be conceptualized as a network of ties among hearing-impaired and hearing people. Due to personal experiences and orientations, activities, and other existing ties, individuals would be tied more or less directly and more or less closely to one another. Wherever the boundaries would be drawn would be somewhat arbitrary. However, the above suggests that in whatever ways deaf communities are conceptualized and their boundaries drawn, many of their members are likely to share a culture which separates them from the larger society.

CULTURE

Members of deaf communities more or less share in the culture of deaf Americans. The culture of deaf Americans sets them apart from their hearing counterparts. While social scientists have conceptualized the concept of culture in various ways just as they have the concept of community, culture may be thought of as the "shared products of human society," the physical objects that people create and use such as clothing, tools, and buildings, and the abstract, often symbolic, creations of languages, ideas, beliefs, myths, rules, and the like (Robertson, 1977:51). Members of deaf communities share in much of the culture of their society, but some also produce and use a distinct culture, too. Three important elements of deaf culture are language, speech, and social relations (Padden, 1980:95-98).[3]

American Sign Language is an identifying feature of deaf culture (see Chapter 4). While not all culturally deaf people are highly competent in ASL, they use it and respect it. There is a "sacredness" attached to how the hands can be used to communicate" (Padden, 1980:96). Newly developed signs (often by hearing educators) which seem to force an oral conceptualization of language upon the deaf are resisted. Thus, a new sign for "carpet," which is the conjunction of long-used signs for "car" and for "pet," is seen as nonsensical (Higgins, 1980:99). A carpet is not conceptually a car and a pet though auditorily (or morphemically) it is similar to the conjunction of the two. These and other nonsensical uses of the hands in communication are not part of deaf culture (Padden, 1980:96).

While speaking may enable deaf people to navigate in the hearing world, those who share in deaf culture disassociate themselves from it (Padden, 1980:96). Exaggerated mouth movements are not acceptable among cultural members. Before the emphasis on total communication in the 1960s, signing with closed mouths was preferred. Older members may still do so, though younger members may modestly move their mouths. Mouth movement and the use of speech are part of the historical oppression of deaf people by those who hear. The oral emphasis is a denial of the worth of deaf people. It is an attempt to make deaf people into hearing ones. Hence, speech is seen as an unwanted vestige of that oppression.

Not surprisingly, there is a great stress on social activities and relations among deaf people. Here is where the easy communication and sense of belonging find expression. For those community members who live and work among hearing people most of the time, social activities with one another become particularly important.

SOCIAL ORGANIZATION

While many hearing people act otherwise, members of deaf communities are not homogeneous. Instead, they create and recognize differences among themselves. They use these differences in structuring relationships among one another—in developing friendships, deciding which organizations to join, and the like. These various relationships help to maintain the differences upon which the relationships are developed. Members of deaf communities use race, sex, and other social characteristics, such as where one attended school (Seidel, 1982), in distinguishing among one another and in structuring relationships within the communities (Higgins, 1980; Carmel, 1982; Layne, 1982; Zakarewsky, 1982). These characteristics are used by hearing people as well. Members also organize their relationships among one another according to communication preference. This distinguishing characteristic is related to members' status as outsiders in a hearing world.

Social Characteristics

Members of deaf communities grow up and live to a great extent within the larger society. While they are not fully part of the hearing world, they are socialized into it to a great degree. Consequently, they are likely to use characteristics in developing relationships among one another that are used by hearing people. For example, sex, race, educational attainment, and age are used by members of deaf communities in organizing relationships among one another just as they are by hearing people. Women may form coffee and bridge clubs, while men form poker groups or play on basketball teams. A fraternal organization of the deaf has had separate men's and women's groups. Race may be as divisive among deaf people as among those who hear. Interaction between white and black deaf is often minimal—friendships are not color blind, and clubs may be segregated (Anderson and Bowe, 1972; Carmel, 1982). Even their signs may differ (Woodward, 1976). Educational attainment also divides deaf communities. Friendships develop among members who have similar levels of educational attainment or "sophistication" (Carmel, 1982). Clubs are attended or not in part due to the sophistication of its members. Members of deaf communities who are not well educated (and most are not) may resent what they interpret to be the "air of superiority" put on by those with a college education. While shared experiences and mutual identification bind together the members of deaf communities, differing social characteristics divide them and help to structure relationships among them.

Age has a double significance for deaf communities. As in the larger society, deaf friends are often of similar ages, and members sort themselves out by similar age in activities and in organizations. A senior citizens' club for the deaf serves the needs of elderly members of the community (Becker, 1980). Athletic teams sponsored by clubs for the deaf are pitched toward younger members. However, age has a special significance as well.

Deaf communities are primarily adult communities. More than 90 percent of deaf children have hearing parents (Schein and Delk, 1974:36). Because their parents are hearing, few deaf children have much contact with deaf adults. Through teachers and other school personnel who are deaf (though they are relatively few outside of residential programs), through involvement in religious organizations which include deaf adults and in youth organizations such as the Junior National Association of the Deaf, and on other occasions, some deaf children become acquainted with deaf adults. These ties to the adult deaf world complement the shared experiences, friendships, and growing identification developed among deaf youth in special education programs. Those ties to the adult deaf world grow stronger as the youth grow older and become more independent of their hearing parents. Therefore, unlike racial or ethnic communities, where parents (and others) socialize their children into the communities, there is not a similar continuity from generation to generation for deaf communities and its members.

Communication Preference

Members of deaf communities associate with one another according to their communication preferences (Higgins, 1980; Carmal, 1982). Members who use sign language primarily interact with others who do too. Some of these members may speak and speechread quite well, but they embrace sign language as the appropriate means of communication within deaf communities. A small minority of deaf community members prefer to speak to their deaf friends. When communicating with those who depend on sign language, they will sign some but not fluently. Those who completely reject signing are not members of deaf communities. While those who embrace signing and those who favor speaking recognize each other as members of the same community, they distinguish between each other, too. Each group is not quite comfortable with how the other communicates. Consequently, while they do associate with each other, particularly at more general gatherings—a senior citizen's club or a community-wide affair—they do not interact as much as they do among one another. They may create and attend separate social clubs or organizations (such as local divisions of the National Fraternal Society of the Deaf), which respect and reinforce their differences in communication preferences. However, not only do distinctions exist between these segments of deaf communities, but so may mistrust as well.

Those who embrace sign language may question the identification with and commitment to the deaf community of those who do not. Historically, sign language has been denigrated by educators, by parents, and by the public. Instead, deaf individuals were to be molded in the image of hearing people through an emphasis on speech and speechreading. Those who embrace sign language, however, disavow the stigma of deafness and of sign language. Further, many older members of deaf communities who use sign language were educated, at least partly, in oral programs. These programs were dominant in the education of deaf students throughout this century until the development of total communication in the 1970s. Oral programs emphasized speech and speechreading while excluding sign language. Many of these older members progressed poorly in the oral programs. Upon leaving school, they gravitated toward those who signed. Consequently, they are adamantly opposed to oralism because they perceive themselves as the victims of it. Therefore, those who embrace sign language question whether those who prefer to speak are fully committed to the deaf world or not. Are they trying to hide their deafness, or are they still under the influence of the hearing world?

LOCATION

Deaf communities exist in towns and cities throughout the country. However, unlike in many ethnic and minority group communities where members often live in well-defined locations, members of deaf communities are scattered throughout the communities' locales. There is no equivalent to an ethnic neighborhood or a minority group ghetto within deaf communities. Deaf communities do not exist as easily identified areas of cities or towns. Instead, they exist through the interaction and identification among its members.

Deaf communities vary according to their locations (Padden, 1980:93). The larger population and the prevailing social institutions and activities of the locales influence deaf communities as they do hearing communities. Deaf communities in large cities have more organizations and activities and a wider variety of them than do deaf communities in small towns. The organizations and activities in the larger deaf communities may serve the needs of special segments of the deaf communities. For example, senior citizen's groups and well organized specialized activities for elderly deaf individuals exist in large cities but are unlikely to in small towns. With fewer members, small deaf communities may not be able to specialize quite as much as larger ones do in developing associations and activities among its members. The composition of the local population also influences deaf communities. Deaf communities in the West and in the Southwest will have Mexican-American members (as well as likely divisions between Anglo-American members and Mexican-American members); those in the upper great plains may have few black members; and those in the large cities of the east, midwest and the south may experience tension between white and black members. Separate white and black deaf communities may even exist (Higgins, 1980:50-53). Whether they cater primarily to deaf individuals or not, important institutions and organizations are likely to influence greatly local deaf communities. One would expect to find more highly educated deaf individuals who are more likely to be employed in professional and managerial jobs in locations where there are colleges for deaf individuals and opportunities for such employment. They may even be more politically active. For example, due to Gallaudet University, the federal government, and other institutions and opportunities that exist in the Washington, D.C. metropolitan area, members of that deaf community are better educated and are more likely to work in professional and managerial positions than are deaf individuals throughout the United States (Schein, 1968:58, 63; Schein and Delk, 1974:52, 82). The locations of deaf communities influence their composition and character.

While members of deaf communities are scattered throughout the communities' locales and the communities themselves are scattered throughout the country, the members and their communities are interconnected in a deaf network. Beginning at the local level and building to the state, regional, and national level (even the international level), widely dispersed deaf people are in contact with one another. The local associations and activities link together members of individual deaf communities. State, regional, national and even international associations and activities, such as a state association of the deaf, a regional athletic tournament, a national association of the deaf, and the World Federation of the Deaf, bring together widely dispersed deaf individuals. Through those occasions and organizations from the local to the national (and even international) level, through telecommunication devices for the deaf and publications such as *The Deaf American,* and through deaf relatives, friends, and former classmates who have moved or who travel, deaf communities and their members who are widely scattered are in contact with one another.

These interconnections among deaf people, from the local level to the national (and even international) level are significant. As in a small town, where residents may know each other's affairs, information about events within a local deaf community may spread throughout the community. However, unlike in a small town, where residents can easily escape their pasts by moving away, members of deaf communities may find it more difficult to escape their pasts. News may spread beyond the local deaf community to others. Thus, members of deaf communities may find it difficult to control information about themselves. However, this network also helps deaf people who are widely dispersed to develop a sense of solidarity and unity among themselves. Thus, this deaf network is both a drawback and a blessing (Higgins, 1980:69-74).

IMPLICATIONS

A social understanding of deaf communities has implications for those who are not part of the community but who interact or "work with" those who are—parents of deaf children, educators, counselors, interpreters, and others (as well as for those who are part of the community). These implications vary according to the relationship one has with the deaf community.

Hearing people are likely to be seen as outsiders to those who are members of deaf communities. Members may question their motives for being involved in the community. Are the hearing people sincerely interested in deaf people as self-determining individuals or are they here to "help" on their own (hearing) terms? Concerned hearing people should not expect to be greeted with open arms until their intentions become more fully known to members of deaf communities.

Not only may members of deaf communities be skeptical of hearing people who are involved in deaf people's affairs, but some members may be concerned that their personal affairs may become public knowledge. Some deaf individuals are reluctant to become too involved in community activities for fear that private concerns will become publicly known. There is simply too much "gossip" for these members. Hearing interlopers may be seen as possible transmitters of private information. Interpreters, counselors, and other concerned hearing people are potential publicists of private matters and troubles. Consequently members of deaf communities may once again be skeptical of hearing people who seek to be involved in deaf communities. Members need to satisfy for themselves that the hearing individuals can be trusted.

Hearing people with minimal sign language skills are likely to be able to communicate more easily with the more oral members of the deaf communities. Communication difficulties are likely to be fewer and those members' orientations toward the hearing world will be more similar to the orientations used by hearing people. However, those most accessible are not most representative of the community. While they may speak well, they certainly do not speak for all. Members of deaf communities even resent that spokespeople to the larger hearing world have often been atypical of members of deaf communities. There is growing demand that those without good oral skills assume leadership and other more public positions.

Further, just as those members of deaf communities who speak well do not speak for all members, all members are not the same. While there is a commonality of experiences and a shared identity among the members of deaf communities, there are also important differences. The community is heterogeneous, not homogeneous. One should not expect all members of a deaf community to rally together on whatever issue confronts them. They are even likely to disagree on what issues confront the community. As in most communities, relatively few members of deaf communities will be active in promoting change. Most will simply be managing everyday as best they can.

For those who intend to "work with" deaf individuals, there is a danger of "doing for" deaf people instead of enabling deaf people to do what they wish themselves. Of course, this stance of "saving" deaf people stems from the historical assumption that deafness is a deficit and deaf people are defective. Many members of deaf communities will greatly resent such a stance. Those who fully take pride in being deaf and who have cast off the shame placed upon them by the hearing world will not accept any paternalism heaped upon them.

Because deaf communities are primarily adult communities, those who are involved with deaf children and youth confront a special obligation and challenge. Not knowing any deaf adults, some deaf children wonder what they will become as adults. They may wonder if they will become hearing. Even with the advances of medical technology, obviously very few will. Instead, many will become adult members of deaf communities, a potentially satisfying position to have. Many hearing people who are involved with deaf children and youth, particularly parents and teachers, have little contact with deaf adults. Parents, wanting their children to be as much like hearing individuals as possible, are often uncomfortable around deaf adults. Teachers, many of whom were trained to use an oral education approach and only "recently" began to sign, may be uncomfortable as well. The obligation that those who are involved with deaf children and youth face is not only to prepare them to do well in the hearing world (e.g., as competent citizens and valuable employees), but to introduce them to the deaf community, to assist in building the bridge for those youth to the deaf community.

The challenge that is faced is to do so without burning the bridges which tie the deaf children and youth to the hearing world, particularly through their parents. For too long, for too many deaf people, the move into the deaf community was greatly due to and further enhanced their estrangement with the hearing world, particularly their parents. They became socialized into deaf communities not by their parents but often in opposition to and with opposition from their parents. Of course, the assumptions and actions of hearing people, including parents, that indicated that deaf people were defective had much to do with that estrangement. Thus, the challenge faced by those who are involved with deaf youth will be more likely met successfully if those debilitating assumptions and handicapping actions are challenged themselves.

Finally, deaf communities face an uncertain future. With a governmental emphasis on fiscal restraint which entails cuts in social services, with an emphasis on federalism (a return of responsibilities to states), and with what appears to many to be a lessening concern with the rights of minorities, the recent gains made by and for members of deaf communities (and others with disabilities) are unlikely to be matched in the future. Present gains may even be in jeopardy. For example, a recent attempt to deregulate P.L. 94-142, The Education for All Handicapped Children Act, has been defeated but attempts do continue (Smith and Tawney, 1983; Kimball et. al., 1984). Recent court decisions may enable administrators to be more cost conscious and less child conscious (McCarthy, 1983). Members of deaf communities and others concerned with the welfare of deaf people will need to be vigilant.

With changes in education, deaf communities face uncertain futures, too. Residential schools, which used to be the primary settings within which deaf youth received special education, have been superseded by day schools and programs where hearing-impaired youth have much more contact with hearing youth. While many have fought long for this change in special education, which is (somewhat mistakenly) characterized simply as mainstreaming, others are not so sure. Within deaf communities, some are concerned that deaf youth in "integrated" programs will not develop the "closeness to other deaf people that can be so valuable" (Vernon and Estes, 1975:4). If they do not, will they become fully part of the hearing world, or might they become marginal to the deaf and the hearing worlds, lacking a sense of belonging in both? Ironically, as deaf communities and other agents of social change achieve some success in enabling deaf people to participate more fully within the hearing world, they may also be diminishing one of the bases for deaf people to be involved in deaf communities.

Technical changes that enhance the lives of members of deaf communities may also change the character of the communities. TDD's provide much easier communication among community members than driving to someone's house. In the comfort of their homes, members may watch captioned television programs and movies, but in the process they participate less in clubs and social affairs. Those technological changes lessen the personal, face-to-face relations among members, a hallmark of deaf communities (Nash and Nash, 1981; Emerton, Foster, and Royer, 1986). These and other concerns challenge members of deaf communities and others involved with them. An understanding of deaf communities helps us to understand those challenges and perhaps to meet them more successfully.

FOOTNOTES

1. A recent study indicated that 23% of hearing-impaired citizens watched between 0-2 hours of television per day, 43% watched 3-4 hours, and 35% watched 5 or more hours per day (Blatt and Sulzer, 1981). The national average in America is more than 6 hours per day.
2. See Karchmer and Trybus (1977), Wolf, Karchmer and Schildroth (1982) and Allen and Osborn (1984) for recent findings and estimates of what percentage of hearing-impaired youth are educated with hearing youth. Youth who are more profoundly impaired are less likely to be educated with hearing students.
3. In Jack R. Gannon's (1981) *Deaf Heritage, The Deaf American,* the *National Theater of the Deaf,* and similar publications and organizations, the culture of deaf Americans is preserved, displayed, and even created.

REFERENCES

Allen, Thomas E. and Osborn, Tamara I.: Academic integration of hearing-impaired students: demographic, handicapping, and achievement factors. *American Annals of the Deaf, 129:*100-113, 1984.

Anderson, Glenn B. and Bowe, Frank G.: Racism within the deaf community. *American Annals of the Deaf, 117:*617-619, 1972.

Becker, Gaylene: *Growing Old in Silence.* Berkeley, University of California Press, 1980.

Blatt, Joseph and Sulzer, James S.: Captioned television and hearing-impaired viewers: the report of a national survey. *American Annals of the Deaf, 126:*1017-1023, 1981.

Carmal, Simon J.: Diversity within an American deaf community. In Higgins, Paul C. and Nash, Jeffrey E.: *The Deaf Community and the Deaf Population,* Social Aspects of Deafness Series, Washington, D.C., Gallaudet College, 1982, vol. 3, pp. 193-231.

Emerton, R. Greg, Foster, Susan, and Royer, Harriette: The impact of changing technology on older deaf workers. Presented at the Second Research Conference on the Social Aspects of Deafness, Washington, D.C., Gallaudet College, June 8-10, 1986.

Furfey, Paul Hanly and Harte, Thomas J.: *Interaction of Deaf and Hearing in Frederick County, Maryland.* Washington, D.C., Catholic University of America, 1964.

Furfey, Paul Hanley and Harte, Thomas J.: *Interaction of Deaf and Hearing in Baltimore City, Maryland.* Washington, D.C., Catholic University of America, 1968.

Gannon, Jack R.: *Deaf Heritage: A Narrative History of Deaf America.* Silver Spring, National Association of the Deaf, 1981.

Goffman, Erving: *Stigma: Notes on the Management of Spoiled Identity.* Englewood Cliffs, Prentice-Hall, 1963.

Higgins, Paul C. *Outsiders in a Hearing World: A Sociology of Deafness.* Beverly Hills, Sage, 1980.

Higgins, Paul C. and Nash, Jeffrey E.: Introduction: understanding deafness through a sociological imagination. In Higgins, Paul C. and Nash, Jeffrey E.: *The Deaf Community and the Deaf Population,* Social Aspects of Deafness Series, Washington, D.C., Gallaudet College, 1982, vol. 3, pp. 1-26.

Hillery, George A., Jr.: Definitions of community: areas of agreement. *Rural Sociology, 20:*111-123, 1955.

Hughes, Everett Cherrington: Dilemmas and contradictions of status. *American Journal of Sociology, 50:*353-359, 1945.

Karchmer, Michael A. and Trybus, Raymond J.: Who are the deaf children in "mainstream" programs? Series R, No. 4. Washington, D.C., Gallaudet College, Office of Demographic Studies, 1977.

Kimball, Walter H., Heron, Timothy E. and Weiss, Adele B.: New federalism and deregulation: impact on special education. *Remedial and Special Education, 5:*25-31, 1984.

Layne, Charles A.: The Deaf Way: An ethnography of a deaf adult. In Higgins, Paul C. and Nash, Jeffrey E.: *The Deaf Community and the Deaf Population,* Social Aspects of Deafness Series, Washington, D.C., Gallaudet College, 1982, vol. 3, pp. 169-191.

McCarthy, Martha M.: The Pennhurst and Rowley decisions: issues and implications. *Exceptional Children, 49:*517-522, 1983.

Markowicz, Harry and Woodward, James: Language and the maintenance of ethnic boundaries in the deaf community, *Communication and Cognition, 11:*29-38, 1978.

Minar, David W. and Greer, Scott: *The Concept of Community: Readings with Interpretation.* Chicago, Aldine, 1969.

Murphy-Berman, Virginia and Whobrey, Linda: The impact of captions on hearing-impaired children's affective reactions to television. *Journal of Special Education, 17:*47-62, 1983.

Padden, Carol: The deaf community and the culture of deaf people. In Baker, Charlotte and Battison, Robbin: *Sign Language and the Deaf Community: Essays in Honor of William C. Stokoe.* Silver Spring, National Association of the Deaf, 1980, pp. 89-103.

Padden, Carol and Markowicz, Harry: Cultural conflicts between hearing and deaf communities. Linguistic Research Laboratory, Gallaudet College, Washington, D.C., 1975.

Poplin, Dennis E.: *Communities: A Survey of Theories and Methods of Research.* New York, Macmillan, 1972.

Robertson, Ian: *Sociology.* New York, Worth, 1977

Schein, Jerome D.: *The Deaf Community: Studies in the Social Psychology of Deafness.* Washington, D.C., Gallaudet College, 1968.

Schein, Jerome D. and Delk, Jr., Marcus T.: *The Deaf Population of the United States.* Silver Spring, National Association of the Deaf, 1974.

Schlesinger, Hilde S. and Meadow, Kathryn P.: *Sound and Sign: Childhood Deafness and Mental Health.* Berkeley, University of California, 1972.

Seidel, John V.: The points at which deaf and hearing worlds intersect: a dialectical analysis. In Higgins, Paul C. and Nash, Jeffrey E.: *The Deaf Community and the Deaf Population,* Social Aspects of Deafness Series, Washington, D.C., Gallaudet College, 1982, vol. 3, pp. 131-167.

Smith, Jonathan and Tawney, James W.: Compliance monitoring: a dead or critical issue. *Exceptional Children, 50:*119-127, 1983.

Stokoe, William C., Casterline, Dorothy C. and Croneberg, Carl G.: *A Dictionary of American Sign Language on Linguistic Principles.* Washington, D.C., Gallaudet College, 1965.

Vernon, McCay and Ester, Charles C.: Deaf leadership and political activism. *The Deaf American, 28:*3-6, 1975.

Wolk, Stephen, Karchmer, Michael A., and Schildroth, Arthur: Patterns of academic and nonacademic integration among hearing impaired students in special education. Series R, No. 9, Washington, D.C., Center for Assessment and Demographic Studies, Gallaudet College, 1982.

Woodward, James C.: Black southern signing. *Language in Society, 5:*211-218, 1976.

Zakarewsky, George T.: A discussion of deafness and homosexuality. In Higgins, Paul C. and Nash, Jeffrey E.: *The Deaf Community and the Deaf Population,* Social Aspects of Deafness Series, Washington, D.C., Gallaudet College, 1982, vol. 3, pp. 233-254.

CHAPTER 8

THE SILENT MINORITY: THE SOCIOECONOMIC STATUS OF DEAF PEOPLE

JOHN B. CHRISTIANSEN AND SHARON N. BARNARTT

THE SOCIOECONOMIC STATUS OF DEAF PEOPLE

IN THIS CHAPTER we will examine some of the data that have been collected throughout this century which document the socioeconomic status (SES) of the deaf population of the United States.[1] The focus will be primarily on the SES of pre-vocationally deafened individuals, since almost no socioeconomic information is available on people deafened later in life.[2] We will also compare these data to similar data for the general population and other physically disabled minorities, in an attempt to assess the overall socioeconomic status of deaf people.[3]

In addition to this descriptive material, we will suggest a theoretical perspective that appears to be a useful way to help explain the comparatively low SES of deaf people. While a minority group perspective is certainly not new, its application to the study of persons with disabilities is relatively recent, and we feel that it has much to offer in this context. Finally, we will look at some of the implications of viewing deaf people as a minority group. Not only does this perspective encourage the collection of data which can assist those interested in collective action among deaf people, but it also calls into question some of the underlying assumptions of those who tend to see solutions to problems of inequality in personal, rather than social, terms.

Educational Attainment and Academic Achievement

During the years of the Great Depression in the United States, deaf people completed approximately the same number of years of school as

171

those in the general, hearing population. For example, a survey of approximately 20,000 hearing impaired people conducted in the mid-1930s found that almost 50% had completed elementary school (or less), about 38% attended high school, and slightly less than 13% attended college. These achievements were similar to those of the general United States population in 1940 (Martens, 1937, p. 20; U.S. Bureau of the Census, 1958a, p. 111).[4]

While it is clear that the educational attainment of deaf people has improved significantly in the United States since the 1930s, the improvement registered by the general population has been even greater. In the early 1970s the median years of schooling completed by deaf people was 11.1, compared to 12.1 for the general population. These numbers, however, mask the fact that significantly fewer deaf adults have completed college or more, and significantly more have finished high school or less, than is true of hearing adults (Schein and Delk, 1974, p. 52; U.S. Bureau of the Census, 1973, p. 115).

In addition to grade-level comparisons between deaf people and the general population, research has also focused on the question of comparative academic achievement. For many years the reading, writing, and mathematical abilities of deaf and hearing students have been analyzed and compared. Virtually all studies have found that the majority of hearing impaired students leaving school in their late teens are at a severe educational disadvantage compared to hearing students.

The Gallaudet Center for Assessment and Demographic Studies (CADS) is one organization which periodically assesses the academic achievement of the approximately 90,000 hearing impaired students in the United States between the ages of five and seventeen. CADS uses the Stanford Achievement Test (hearing impaired edition) in this effort. Data collected for the 1982-83 Annual Survey of Hearing Impaired Children and Youth show, for example, that in reading comprehension the median score for deaf students aged 15-17 is equivalent to slightly above a third grade level for hearing students. In mathematics, deaf students did slightly better, performing close to a seventh grade equivalency level (CADS, 1985). These results are similar to those found by Mindel and Vernon during the 1970s. In an extensive study which included 93% of deaf students 16 years of age and older in the United States, they found that only five percent achieved at a tenth grade level or better, that 60% were at grade level 5.3 or below, and close to 30% were basically illiterate (Mindel and Vernon, 1971, p. 94).

It is reasonably clear, then, that while the grade-level attainment rates for deaf people have generally improved during the past half century in America, and are now only slightly below those enjoyed by their hearing peers, the academic achievement of deaf students remains quite poor.

Labor Force Participation and Unemployment

For a variety of reasons, it is difficult to evelute the accuracy of studies concerning the participation of deaf people in the civilian labor force in America that were undertaken prior to the National Census of the Deaf Population (NCDP) in the early 1970s.[5] Nevertheless, it is probably safe to conclude that during the first half of the twentieth century deaf people were not employed at rates equal to the hearing population.[6]

In the early 1970s, the labor force participation rate for deaf men was higher, and the unemployment rate lower, than for their hearing counterparts. Recent data show that, for both deaf and hearing men, the labor force participation rate decreased, and the unemployment rate increased, during the 1970s. However, it is apparent that deaf men experienced a more unfavorable change than did hearing men. Among deaf men, the labor force participation rate decreased by almost 8% from 1972 to 1977, while the decrease for hearing men was only a little over 1%. Similarly, the unemploymet rate for deaf men increased over 7% during this period (to 10.2% in 1977), while the unemployment rate for hearing men increased only 1.3% (to 6.2% in 1977). Thus, by 1977, deaf men were clearly at a relative disadvantage compared to hearing men for both of these variables. In fact, by 1977, the unemployment rate for deaf men was even higher than it was for hearing women.

Hearing women were the only group to improve their labor force participation in the 1970s, recording a 4.6% increase from 1972 to 1977. Like the other three groups, though, their unemployment rate increased during this period, exceeding 8% in 1977. Among deaf women, their labor force participation rate declined more than 2% from 1972 to 1977, while, at the same time, their unemployment rate increased by almost 2% (to 12% in 1977). By 1977, then, while the labor force participation rate for deaf and hearing women was about the same, deaf women experienced a significantly higher unemployment rate than their hearing peers. It is readily apparent, then, that deaf workers of both sexes were somewhat worse off in 1977 compared to hearing workers than they were earlier in the decade (U.S. Department of Labor, 1980, pp. 8-9, 68; Schein and Delk, 1974, p. 75; 1978, pp. 73, 75).

Occupational Status

It is clear that before the 1970s there were large occupational differences between deaf and hearing workers.[7] Among males, hearing men were more than twice as likely as deaf men to hold white collar jobs.[8] In 1920, almost 8% of the former held white collar jobs compared to less than 3% of the latter. Similarly, in the 1950s, almost 36% of the hearing men were found in white collar positions while the comparable figure for deaf men was less than 14%. Furthermore, while almost three-quarters of the deaf men held blue collar jobs before 1970, this was true of only about half of the hearing men.

Between 1972 and 1977, however, the occupations held by deaf and hearing men became more similar. In 1972, for example, almost 40% of hearing men had white collar positions compared to approximately 20% of deaf men. By 1977, though, while the figures for hearing men increased by only 1%, the percentage of deaf men in white collar positions jumped to more than 31%. Given the biased nature of the sample used in the 1977 study, though, these figures must be used cautiously. However, if they reflect real improvements for deaf men, their occupational disadvantage compared to hearing men decreased substantially during the mid-1970s.[9]

Differences in the principal occupations held by deaf and hearing men have remained larger than those between deaf and hearing women, although deaf women do remain at somewhat of a disadvantage compared to hearing women. Both groups of women have followed a similar pattern of vastly increasing white collar participation, decreasing blue collar participation, and somewhat increasing pink collar participation since 1920. By the 1970s, over 60% of hearing women worked in white collar jobs compared to about 40% of deaf women. There are, however, large differences between deaf and hearing women within the white collar category. While about 22% of hearing women worked in professional, technical, managerial, or administrative jobs in 1977, this was true of less than 9% of deaf women. The largest percentage of workers in both groups work in clerical jobs. However, it was only in 1977 that clerical work surpassed factory work as the largest employer of deaf women, even though it has been the largest employer of hearing women since before 1950. Deaf women continue to work in blue collar positions more than twice as often as hearing women, a fact which has been true since at least the mid-1950s. The participation of deaf women in service jobs increased substantially between 1972 and 1977, bringing them to about the level of hearing women. Overall, it is clear that the occupational status of deaf women has remained disadvantaged compared to hearing women throughout the 1970s. (Best, 1943, p. 233; Lunde and Bigman, 1959, p. 21; Schein and Delk, 1974, p. 82; 1978, p. 83; U.S. Bureau of the Census, 1957, p. 12; 1973, p. 233; 1978a, p. 418.)

Income Characteristics[10]

Income distributions for the late 1930s for the deaf and hearing population of the United States suggest rough parity between deaf and hearing men, while deaf women actually seemed to have slightly higher incomes than hearing women (Martens, 1937, p. 74; U.S. Bureau of the Census, 1954, p. 318). In 1956 it was found that the median income of deaf workers (both sexes combined) was actually higher than that of the general population ($3465 compared to $2818). This rather unexpected finding probably reflects the fact that the sample used in the 1956 study of hearing impaired people was essentially limited to white deaf adults. This study also found that females of both hearing statuses had incomes which were much less than those of either hearing or deaf men. For example, while only about 28% of deaf males and slightly less than 37% of hearing males earned less than $3000 per year, approximately 75% of both groups of women earned less than this (Lunde and Bigman, 1959, p. 27; U.S. Bureau of the Census, 1985b, p. 46).

The availability of median income figures for 1971 and 1976 makes the comparisons between deaf and hearing workers much clearer for these years. In 1971 deaf workers of both sexes earned about 75% of the income of their hearing counterparts, while both groups of women earned about 60% of the income of their male counterparts. By 1976, deaf males had lost a little ground compared to hearing males, but the difference is small enough that it would not be worthy of much attention were it not for the upward educational bias, and apparent occupational improvement, of the 1977 sample (see footnote 3). Deaf women lost substantial ground compared to hearing women, decreasing from earning about 75% of hearing women's income in 1971 to earning about 60% of their incomes in 1976. Moreover, deaf women's median income dropped from about 60% to about 56% of deaf men's during this period (Schein and Delk, 1974, p. 102; 1978, p. 90; U.S. Bureau of the Census, 1972, p. 105; 1978b, pp. 192-201).

Thus, although the quality of the data do not permit us to make generalizations with as much certainty for the earlier years of this century as for the 1970s, we would at the very least suggest that the incomes of deaf workers have decreased compared to hearing workers since the Depression years. With the recent, more reliable data we can clearly see the extent of deaf workers' relative income disadvantage, and we can see that this disadvantage, if anything, increased during the 1970s. A paucity of data, however, prevents us from saying anything about the income situation during the 1980s.

Non-White Deaf Persons

Virtually all of the national and regional studies of the grade-level attainment of deaf persons done in the United States this century have shown that non-white deaf persons have, on the average, not completed as many years of school as white deaf persons (for example, Best, 1943; Lunde and Bigman, 1959; Schein, 1968; Schein and Delk, 1974). In recent years, however, this finding seems to be confined primarily to deaf males (Schein and Delk, 1974, p. 52). In the 1950s, for example, while approximately 10% of white deaf persons attended college, less than 2% of non-white deaf males (90% of whom were black) did so. Virtually no non-white deaf females attended school beyond high school (Lunde and Bigman, 1959). By the time the NCDP was conducted in the early 1970s, non-white deaf males attended school for a fewer number of years than white deaf males, but non-white deaf females had a slightly higher level of educational attainment than their white counterparts. It is unknown whether this change was due to a sampling bias or whether it actually represents a dramatic improvement for non-white deaf women during the late 1950s and throughout the 1960s. It is also worth noting that, within each racial category (white and non-white), sex differences in grade-level attainment have not been very significant for the past 30 years.

In addition to studies which have examined educational attainment, other reports have consistently documented the lower academic achievement of non-white deaf students compared to their white peers (for example, Furfey and Harte, 1968; Bowe, 1971; Moores and Oden, 1977). A study conducted in 1975, for example, discovered that Hispanic deaf students had lower academic achievement levels than whites in vocabulary and reading comprehension (Jensema, 1975). Furfey and Harte, in their study of deaf persons in Baltimore, found that about half of the non-white deaf people in their sample were so poorly educated that they were virtually social isolates; they could not communicate with average ability with either other deaf persons or with hearing individuals (Bowe, 1971, p. 359).

It is apparent that, among both males and females, unemployment rates for non-white deaf persons in the United States have traditionally been higher than for their white colleagues. In a study of the deaf community in Washington, D.C., conducted in the early 1960s, for example, it was found that the unemployment rate for non-white deaf men (predominantly black) was four times the rate for white deaf men. Also, while 10% of white deaf women were unemployed, about 50% of non-white deaf women could not find gainful employment (Schein, 1968).

The NCDP discovered that, while the unemployment rate for non-white deaf women was not as bad nationally in the early 1970s as it was in Washington, D.C., ten years earlier, it was still higher than for white deaf women. Similarly, the unemployment rate for non-white deaf men was higher in 1972 than it was for white deaf men. The small follow-up study in 1977 of a sample of those who were included in the original NCDP study revealed that the unemployment rate was slightly lower in the late 1970s than it was in the early 1970s for non-white deaf males. Since the non-white sample in this follow-up study was quite small, these apparent changes may be due to sampling error and should consequently be interpreted with caution. Unfortunately, since no national socioeconomic data have been collected in recent years, it is simply not known whether unemployment rates of non-white deaf persons are still higher than those of their white peers. Further, most of the information about the unemployment rates of non-white deaf people is limited to blacks, and virtually nothing is known about the unemployment rates of deaf members of other minority groups (Schein and Delk, 1974, 1978).

In addition to experiencing higher unemployment rates, non-white deaf people have traditionally been found in lower status occupations than white deaf persons. For example, in 1920 it was reported that, while more than 20% of white deaf men were employed as craftsmen, fewer than 4% of non-white deaf men were so employed (Best, 1943). Fifty years later, the NCDP revealed that white deaf men were being employed as craftsmen at a rate that was still twice that of their non-white counterparts Among deaf females, the NCDP found that, while non-whites were more likely to be employed in professional and technical positions than were white deaf women, they were also more likely to be found in semi-skilled and unskilled positions than their white colleagues (Schein and Delk, 1974).

While the occupational situation for non-white deaf people in the United States appears to be quite dismal, it is important to note that there are indications that this situation may be improving somewhat. For example, in one study of deaf professionals in the early 1960s, no black professionals other than teachers were located (Crammatte, 1965). By the early 1980s, though, a number of black, Hispanic, Asian American, and Native American professionals were found (Crammatte, 1985). While this is a significant improvement in the twenty years separating the two studies, the number of non-white deaf professionals is still small compared to the number of white deaf people in professional occupations. However, in spite of this progress, it is clear that in the blue collar occupational world where deaf people have traditionally found jobs, non-white males and females are still more likely to be confined to semi-skilled and unskilled positions than are their white peers.

Given this picture of the occupational situation faced by non-white deaf people, it is certainly not surprising to discover that their incomes have generally lagged behind those enjoyed by white deaf people through this century. In 1920, for example, while approximately one-third of the white deaf male population earned more than $1200 per year, less than 13% of the non-white deaf male population did so. Non-white females also earned less than their white peers (Best, 1943).

In his regional study of the deaf community in Washington, D.C., in the early 1960s, Schein (1968) found that in 1962 non-white males earned only 40% of the income of white males. He also discovered that non-white females earned only 28% of the income enjoyed by their white counterparts. The NCDP found that, in general, non-white deaf males earned approximately 57% of the income enjoyed by white deaf males. Non-white deaf women, in contrast, earned approximately 72% of the incomes of white deaf women in the United States in the early 1970s (Schein and Delk, 1974).

Whatever else these more recent comparisons might show, compared with the figures for 1920 they seem to indicate that the income gap between white and non-white deaf persons in the United States, while still wide, is perhaps not quite as wide as it once was. Unfortunately, as there is little current information available about occupational problems facing deaf people, especially deaf members of specific minority groups, there is also little contemporary income data available. We simply do not know whether the income situation for non-white deaf people has improved or deteriorated since the 1970s.

Comparative Inequality: Deaf People Vis-a-Vis Other Physically Disabled Minorities

Little research has been done which compares the socioeconomic characteristics of people with different types of physical impairments. Not only do we lack sufficient data to make these comparisons, but the data which are available have not been appropriately analyzed. However, if we are to examine comprehensively the socioeconomic status of deaf people, it is important to compare their socioeconomic status with those of groups characterized by other types of physical impairments. We know, of course, that the physical consequences of the various types of impairments are different. For purposes of developing appropriate public policies and otherwise assessing the needs of different groups, knowledge of potentially different socioeconomic effects for those with different physical impairments is also needed.

In this section we will examine this issue. However, because our data are less than optimal, our conclusions must be regarded as tentative. The biggest problem is that there are no data for the different groups from the same year. Thus, we are forced to depend upon 1971 data for deaf people, 1976 data on visually impaired people, and 1972 data for the general population of people with disabilities. Figures for the non-impaired (i.e. general) population used here are from 1971 and 1976. While we recognize that such a comparison is severely limited, we think it does at least begin to address the issue raised above.

The educational attainments of the four groups by sex are shown in Table 1. Among males, those who are hearing impaired have the lowest rate of post-high school attainment, while those who are visually impaired or in the general disabled category have rates which are several percentage points above deaf males. All the groups, however, are substantially below the general U.S. population in post-high school attendance. At the other end of the spectrum, a smaller percentage of deaf men attended fewer than 8 years of schooling than did either the visually impaired or general disabled groups. Again, however, all the groups with physical impairments have much larger percentages than does the general population. The percentage of hearing impaired men who graduated from high school is actually about the same as it is for the general population and is much higher than for the other two groups.

The pattern for women is about the same as for men. Although the percentages are slightly different, it is clear that a larger percentage of hearing impaired women than visually impaired women or generally disabled wo-

Table 1

Percentage Distribution of Educational Attainment by
Disability Status and Sex (Selected Years)

Sex	Disability Status	Educational Attainment (years)			
		Less than 8	8-11	12	13+
Males					
	Hearing Impaired[a] (1971)	17.2	33.6	35.4	13.7
	Visually Impaired[b] (1976)	25.0	33.0	25.0	18.0
	Disabled[c]	22.0	32.5	27.6	19.9
	General Population[b] (1976)	7.0	21.0	35.0	37.0
Females					
	Hearing Impaired[a] (1971)	15.1	35.0	38.3	11.7
	Visually Impaired[b] (1976)	27.0	36.0	25.0	13.0
	Disabled[c]	20.5	35.3	32.4	11.9
	General Population[b] (1976)	6.0	22.0	43.0	29.0

Sources:

[a]Data from the NCDP (percentages obtained by authors). Ages 18-64.

[b]Kirchner and Peterson (1981, p. 269). Ages 18-64.

[c]Calculated from Ferron (1981, pp. 33-34). Ages 20-64.

men have either completed high school or pursued some type of post-secondary education. However, this percentage is still much lower than that for the general population. Thus it seems that hearing impaired people have a slightly higher average educational attainment than do people with other types of physical impairments, although their educational attainment is still lower than that of the general population.

The labor force participation rates for each group are found in Table 2. For both sexes, the rate for hearing impaired people is closest to that of the general population. The rate for the visually impaired group is the lowest, while the rate for the general disabled group is about halfway between the hearing impaired and the visually impaired groups. Again, however, even labor force participation rates for those with impaired hearing are about 10% below those for the general population for each sex.

Income data for hearing impaired people and for the general disabled population in 1971 and 1976-1977 are presented in Table 3. The table does not include the visually impaired group, since data for them are not available. While the figures for the two groups are not exactly comparable,[11] they do suggest a similar pattern. In 1971, the incomes of both hearing impaired males and hearing impaired females were higher than

Table 2

Labor Force Participation by Disability Status and Sex (Selected Years)

Sex	Disability Status	% In Labor Force	Year
Males			
	Hearing Impaired	82.7%[a]	1972
	Visually Impaired	43.0%[b]	1976
	Disabled	69.6%[c]	1971
	General Population	93.6%[c]	1971
Females			
	Hearing Impaired	49.4%[a]	1972
	Visually Impaired	20.0%[b]	1976
	Disabled	36.5%[c]	1971
	General Population	59.3%[c]	1971

Sources:
[a]Schein and Delk (1974, p. 75)
[b]Kirchner and Peterson (1979, p. 240)
[c]Ferron (1981, p. 133)

those of the general disabled population of the same sex. That was also true for females in the 1976-1977 comparison, although it was not true for males. However, given the one year time difference, the relatively small dollar difference between the two groups of males can probably be interpreted as indicating relative parity.

Table 3

Median Incomes of Disabled and Hearing Impaired
People by Sex (Selected Years)

Year	Males	Females
1971		
Disabled[a]	$ 4,352	$ 2,800
Hearing Impaired[b]	7,084	4,306
1976-1977		
Disabled (1977)[c]	10,799	2,858
Hearing impaired (1976)[d]	9,449	5,411

[a]1972 Survey of Disabled and Nondisabled Adults (Ferron, 1981, p. 161). Includes only unmarried people since incomes reported for married people include earnings of all family members.
[b]1972 National Census of the Deaf Population (Schein and Delk, 1974, p. 102).
[c]1978 Survey of Disability and Work (Lando et al., 1982, pp. 231-2).
[d]1977 Follow-up of 1972 NCDP (Schein and Delk, 1978, p. 78).

These figures, then, suggest that hearing impaired people have a somewhat higher average educational level than do people with other types of physical impairments, at least in terms of number of years of school completed. They are more likely to be in the labor force than are people with other physical impairments, and their incomes are as high or higher than those of people with other physical disabilities. Although we cannot minimize the limitations of our data, we have to conclude that, based upon available information, type of physical impairment does seem to make a socioeconomic difference. The figures presented here suggest that people with impaired hearing may experience somewhat less of a socioeconomic disadvantage than do those with other physical impairments. However, these figures also reinforce the fact that physical impairment in our society carries with it a socioeconomic disadvantage for people with all types of disabilities.

TOWARDS AN EXPLANATION OF THE SES OF DEAF PEOPLE

While several theoretical perspectives have been used by sociologists examining issues related to disability in general and deafness in particular, it seems to us that a "minority group perspective" is most appropriate for explaining the relatively low SES of deaf people. Other perspectives, such as those which view people with physical disabilities as sick or deviant, while occasionally helping us understand certain features of the lives of deaf people, are not particularly useful for explaining socioeconomic issues.

A minority group perspective has traditionally been applied to groups which are of lower socioeconomic status, politically powerless, culturally different, negatively stereotyped, discriminated against, and aware of this discrimination (see, for example, Bayes, 1982; Deegan, 1981; Stroman, 1982; Safilios-Rothschild, 1976). This perspective has been applied most frequently to racial or ethnic groups, with the result that the terms "ethnic group" and "minority group" have become almost synonymous. Several authors have suggested that this perspective could also be fruitfully applied to people with physical impairments (Deegan, 1981; Higgins, 1980; Stroman, 1982; Wright, 1960).

The minority group perspective focuses on the extent to which social barriers and practices (the social structure) handicap deaf people. Instead of "blaming the victim" for lower socioeconomic status, this view turns our attention to the society. Since it emphasizes social structural rather than personality explanations, institutional change rather than behavioral modification is suggested as appropriate public policy. Such a view also emphasizes the proposition that while programs such as vocational rehabilitation may provide piecemeal solutions to individual problems, they will not bring about greater equality in the absence of broader institutional changes. What, then, are some of the explanations suggested by a minority group perspective that might help explain the low SES of deaf people?

The Effect of Education

Type of Education

Deaf children face a considerable number of educational barriers during their formative years. For example, disagreement continues among deaf educators and other professionals concerning the most appropriate mode of communication in classrooms where deaf children are present. Some educators believe that oral methods are preferable, while others favor some variant of manual communication. In addition, most parents of deaf children have normal hearing, and have no experience with deafness or deaf people before the birth of their hearing impaired child. Thus, they are frequently at a loss as to how to communicate with their deaf child. One consequence of this is that the deaf child may not be exposed to any language other than homemade "gestures" until the optimum time for language development has passed, and may enter school with virtually no communication skills at all. The lack of adequate communication skills, including basic fluency in the English language, while hardly the fault of the deaf child, obviously makes "normal" academic progress extremely difficult.

Parents also experience considerable confusion and anxiety about the most appropriate educational setting for their child.[12] Deaf students may attend residential schools for hearing impaired children, regular public schools with or without one of the many types of special programs for hearing impaired children, or day schools for hearing impaired children. Residential schools were the type of school attended by most deaf children in the past. Of the adults responding to the 1972 NCDP, about 52% reported having attended residential schools exclusively (Barnartt, 1985). With the passage in 1975 of PL 94-142, the Education for All Handicapped Children Act, this is no longer true. Karchmer et al.,

(1979, p. 100) report that by the 1977-78 school year, only about 30% of hearing impaired children were enrolled in residential schools.

Not much information exists which evaluates the socioeconomic consequences of the different types of educational programs which are available. However, research by one of the present authors has shown that, at least before 1972, while type of education did not make much difference for either the type of job or the income level of deaf people, amount of education had a significant effect on both of these variables (Barnartt, 1985).

Amount of Education

Barnartt (1985) has shown that deaf men who attended college, and deaf women who at least finished high school, were much more likely than other deaf workers responding to the 1972 NCDP to hold white collar jobs. She also showed that there was a clear and statistically significant improvement in their incomes with increasing years of education. For example, the average 1971 income of deaf men who had less than a high school education was $6253 compared to an average of $7135 for deaf men who had attended some college. For women the averages were $3413 and $5019. Clearly, more education, and especially post-secondary education, leads to higher socioeconomic status for deaf workers.

The lower relative socioeconomic status of deaf workes can, then, be at least partially explained by the relatively few deaf students who seek post-secondary education in academic programs. Why is this so? To some extent, fewer deaf students are able to seek post-secondary education because of poor academic preparation in primary and secondary schools. However, for many students, appropriate post-secondary programs simply are not available. Moreover, many of the post-secondary programs which are oriented to the special communication needs of deaf students are vocationally oriented. For those deaf students who do attend a post-secondary academic program, various services (such as interpreters or notetakers) which most deaf students need in order to be successful in classroom settings are frequently not available.

If we look even further and consider graduate school programs, we find very few which offer these services, and these tend to be in social work and counseling. A deaf student, therefore, either has to be exceptionally intelligent, or willing to fight for needed services, or both, in order to become qualified for most professional or managerial jobs. Thus, the lack of viable post-secondary educational opportunities helps to explain why so few deaf people hold professional or managerial white collar jobs.

The evidence suggests that the amount of education deaf workers have, as well as barriers to their improved educational attainment, are important determinants of their socioeconomic status. However, amount of education is not as strong a predictor of the socioeconomic status of deaf workers as it is for hearing workers. Barnartt (1985, 1986b) showed that, for hearing males, amount of education was one of the strongest predictors. For both deaf males and deaf females, on the other hand, it was one of the weakest of the statistically significant predictors. Consequently, while amount of education is important in determining the socioeconomic status of deaf workers, other factors are also important.

The Special Problem of Non-White Deaf Education

It is clear that a special problem confronted non-white deaf students, primarily blacks, until quite recently. That was the system of segregated residential schools established in many states. According to the Babbidge report issued in the mid-1960s, in 1949 there were separate residential schools for white and black deaf students in thirteen states (Babbidge, 1965). By 1963, almost ten years after the Supreme Court declared such segregated schools to be unconstitutional, eight states continued to maintain separate, and inferior, schools for black deaf students. While these eight schools had desegregated by 1970, several states still maintained two residential schools at least into the early 1970s. One of these institutions was invariably smaller, older, and staffed with fewer qualified teachers than the other. Not suprisingly, this was the institution attended by most of the non-white deaf children of the state. Moreover, most of the schools for black students emphasized vocational training in areas such as shoe repairing, tailoring, barbering, or hair dressing (Hairston and Smith, 1983). Nationally, in the early 1970s, at least five residential and day programs had no white students, and more than 130 had no minority students (Moores and Oden, 1977; Ries et al., 1975).[13]

Career Choice Patterns

Several other factors have been suggested to explain various aspects of these patterns of socioeconomic disadvantage experienced by deaf people. The first of these is career choice patterns. There is substantial evidence that deaf teenagers hold strong stereotypes, both about those occupations which they feel are appropriate for males and females, and about those which they feel are appropriate for deaf or hearing workers. Because sex stereotyping is so pervasive among teenagers, it is also likely that, for deaf boys, traditionally female white collar jobs, and, for deaf girls, traditionally male blue collar jobs, will be perceived to be "off limits" for them because of their sex. Additionally, deaf adolescents of both sexes erroneously perceive very few occupations of any type to be viable options for deaf people. For example, while young deaf males cited 31 occupations as being a realistic option, deaf workers are actually found in over 500 different occupations (Cook and Rosset, 1975; Egelston-Dodd, 1977). It seems, then, that deaf adolescents' occupational aspirations (and, perhaps, those of older deaf people as well) may be severely limiting their occupational choices.

The Effects of Occupational Segregation

Another factor which affects the occupational distribution, and therefore the incomes, particularly of deaf women, is occupational segregation by sex. The fact that they are deaf does not exempt deaf women from experiencing patterns of occupational segregation similar to those which characterize hearing women. The enormous increase in the number of white collar jobs in the past 35 years, many of which are traditionally female jobs, has clearly benefited deaf women (deCesare, 1975). They have moved out of blue collar jobs and into white collar jobs at a much higher rate than have deaf men. However, deaf women also suffer from the subtle discrimination which arises from the fact that traditionally female occupations undervalue "women's" skills (such as typing) and consequently pay less than male occupations which demand the same or similar qualifications. This lack of equal pay for jobs of comparable worth puts deaf women at the same sort of income disadvantage compared to deaf men which hearing women, whether white or black, experience compared to their male counterparts (see Almquist, 1977; Almquist and Wehrle-Einhorn, 1978; Epstein, 1973; Duncan, 1984; Tremain and Hartmann, 1981; Barrett, 1979).

Discrimination

Finally, we cannot ignore the obvious possibility that there is still a considerable amount of discrimination against deaf workers of both sexes. Both the increase in deaf male unemployment at a time when the unemployment rate decreased for other groups (deaf females as well as hearing males and females), and the reduced labor force participation rates for deaf workers of both sexes, support the discrimination hypothesis. Although such discrimination ought to have become illegal with the passage of the Rehabilitation Act of 1973, Barnartt (1982a) has argued that both demographic and social changes may have increased the probability that such discrimination occurs. Additionally, Barnartt and Seelman (1985) show that the scope of the law is restricted to a small number of employees, and that other laws and court decisions do not fill in the gaps. Thus, both overt and covert discrimination by many employers in all aspects of employment is still legal, and it must be considered to be a factor in explaining the lower SES of deaf workers of both sexes.

CURRENT ISSUES AND IMPLICATIONS

The use of a minority group approach to studying deaf people raises several points which deserve further attention. First, the utilization of this perspective necessitates continuous, comprehensive and appropriate documentation of the extent to which a group retains its minority status. For deaf people, this means that we need socioeconomic data comparable to those available for many other minority groups. Between the cost of securing national socioeconomic data about sub-populations such as deaf people which are not identified by the U.S. Census, and the decreasing interest of the Federal Government in supporting large scale data collection (McNeil, 1981), we are faced with an appalling paucity of data about deaf people. We are approaching the 15th anniversary of the 1971-72 NCDP without any indication that a follow-up study is even being considered.

Those few national data which are available assume the sick role perspective rather than a minority role perspective. Currently, most data about deaf people are collected either as part of the Social Security Administration's surveys of disability (see, for example, U.S. Department of Health and Human Services, 1981; 1982) or as part of the National Health and Nutrition Examination Surveys (see, for example, U.S. Department of Health, Education, and Welfare, 1980). The disability surveys assume that deafness is a work-limiting disability (Altman, 1982). The other two surveys assume that deafness is a sickness-related condition. While the disability surveys do obtain minimal socioeconomic data, their published reports categorize people by degree of disabiilty rather than by type of impairment (see, for example, U.S. Department of Health, Education, and Welfare, 1979a, 1979b, U.S. Department of Health and Human Services, 1982). Reports based on the NHIS or NHANES surveys tend to focus on variables other than socioeconomic ones. Also, unlike the National Census of the Deaf Population, these surveys include many people whose hearing loss occurred in adulthood, since these are, in fact, the majority of hearing impaired people (Reis, 1985). While this is desirable from a demographic point of view, these are the people who are least likely to consider themselves to be deaf, and thus the subjective component of minority group status is likely to be ignored by these methods of data collection. Thus, the use of the minority group perspective suggests that both more data and different data are needed about deaf people as well as other persons with physical disabilities.

Further, a minority group perspective encourages us to become more aware of the beginnings of collective action. In recent years, many groups, including ethnic minorities, gay people, and women have documented and protested the extent of their disadvantages. During the last 15 years people with physical disabilities have also become more cognizant of the extent to which they have been victims, and have begun to protest this situation. The Independent Living Movement, which got its start in Berkeley and Boston in the early 1970s, is a response which reflects this developing consciousness. Within the deaf community the popularity of phrases like "deaf pride" and "deaf power," as well as the growth of groups involved in advocacy, are manifestations of this emerging awareness.

This suggests that a new social movement is occurring which deserves further sociological analyses. In addition, sociological analyses could assist in the development and mobilization of this movement in the same ways that sociological data revealed the forms and extent of discrimination experienced by blacks or women. In particular, sociologists may assist if they can document non-economic forms of discrimination faced by deaf people, including their differential power, sources of the insensitivity displayed by some members of the helping professions (Safilios-Rothschild, 1976; Scott, 1981), and linguistic discrimination. This last point, which involves the use of American Sign Language (ASL), is a particularly important issue in the deaf community at this time.

As deaf people come to view themselves as members of a minority group, the formation of coalitions with other minority groups is likely.

This would not necessarily include only other disabled groups, although, as the Independent Living Movement shows, this has usually been the first step.[14]

For those involved in working with deaf people, the inequality of the deaf has serious implications. An explanation of inequality which focuses on social structural variables implies that potential solutions to the educational, occupational, and income inequities faced by deaf people which focus only on personality variables are likely to be incomplete.

This is particularly important for practitioners in the area of rehabilitation. Albrecht (1976) has noted that the traditional goals of rehabilitation are to help persons with disabilities return to work, to maximize independence, to improve the self-image of the individual, and to increase respect for life. It is readily apparent from this list that the focus is on changing or helping the individual in some way rather than on changing the society (e.g., eliminating architectural barriers, changing laws which discriminate against those with disabilities, or revising job requirements which unfairly and inappropriately exclude qualified candidates with disabilities). A minority group perspective implies that we should be trying to change the social structure in order to make it easier for deaf people, as well as others with physical disabilities, to participate fully in the labor force. It is quite clear that one way to encourage recalcitrant employers to recruit, hire, and promote qualified deaf people is to make it economically painful for them not to do so. The successful bus boycotts and sit-ins during the 1950s and 1960s have demonstrated that discrimination tends to diminish somewhat when an employer's livelihood is in jeopardy. Thus, we would argue that rigorous enforcement of existing legislation, especially the Rehabilitation Act of 1973, would alleviate some of the employment (and subsequent income) difficulties faced by deaf people. Moreover, the Education for All Handicapped Children Act of 1975 could, with rigorous enforcement and adequate teacher training, help bridge the academic achievement gap between deaf and hearing children.

We are not suggesting that rehabilitation counselors are wasting their time trying to assist deaf clients who come to local vocational rehabilitation office seeking help. Clearly, people in need of services should be assisted if at all possible. Indeed, since the Rehabilitation Act of 1973 requires that rehabilitation agencies give priority to those who are severely disabled, agencies continue to be obliged to become substantially involved in the rehabilitation of individual deaf clients and others seeking their services (Higgins, 1985).

We are suggesting, however, that this "personal" approach is not likely to lead to much improvement in the dismal occupational and income statistics presented above. Many deaf people, particularly those who are poorly educated, inexperienced in the work world, impoverished, or members of racial or ethnic minority groups, may be unaware of vocational rehabilitation services, or may be reluctant to contact a large, intimidating bureaucracy. Further, even individuals who receive retraining at one of the over 3,000 vocational rehabilitation workshops in the United States are quite unlikely to be able to find jobs. Gliedman and Roth (1980) note that of the half million workers with disabilities who received such retraining during the 1970s, only about 10% subsequently found employment. Moreover, there is evidence that those selected for vocational rehabilitation programs are the very people who need it least: those who are most likely to be successfully placed in the workforce after completing the program (Nagi, 1965; Safilios-Rothschild, 1970; Sussman, 1969, 1976). One consequence of this, of course, is that many of those who might benefit from such services are not in appropriate programs.

It is also important to note that many scholars have suggested that rehabilitation agencies in the United States are generally organized to perpetuate dependence and compliance on the part of those seeking their services (for example, Sussman, 1965; Albrecht and Levy, 1981; Scott, 1965, 1981). Further, it is apparent that the typical rehabilitation bureaucracy can actually reduce the range of possibilities open to the client and, because of the vagaries of public funding, keep them in a dependent status longer than necessary (Sussman, 1969, 1976). Thus, while a single individual might actually be helped in such a setting, the price paid, in terms of one's self image, could be quite high.

In sum, the minority group approach emphasizes social structural rather than personality variables, and it posits an active rather than a passive or sick individual. It is an approach which raises some interesting basic and applied sociological questions, and it highlights social changes which are beginning to occur so that persons with physical impairments can become equal participants in the world that the temporarily able-bodied take for granted. It suggests that concerted social action will be needed to raise the low socioeconomic status of deaf workers above what it has been in the past in the United States.

FOOTNOTES

1. The term socioeconomic status has been used by sociologists and other social scientists for more than half a century to describe, primarily, the income, occupational, and educational characteristics of a group of people.

2. It is important to emphasize that the nationwide studies of the deaf population in the United States have often been conducted in very different ways using very different definitions of deafness. For example, the deaf population, especially as defined in studies conducted before 1970, often included persons who were hard-of-hearing in addition to those who were deaf (especially Martens, 1937, and Gentile, et al., 1967). Further the age of respondents included in each study varies somewhat. Also, since it is frequently difficult to locate deaf persons who do not participate actively in the life of the deaf community, many hearing impaired persons may have been inadvertently omitted from these earlier studies. Consequently, comparative comments are, at best, tentative. Nevertheless, these are the only data we have. Thus, while it would be inappropriate to dwell on exact percentage change over the years, it seems appropriate to suggest general trends when data from a variety of national and regional studies point in the same general direction.

3. The major nationwide studies of the deaf population used in this chapter are as follows: a) A survey of 19,580 deaf and hard-of-hearing people, who were or had been employed, conducted by the Office of Education as a Civil Works Administration project in 1934 (Martens, 1937). b) A national stratified sample of 10,101 deaf people who were surveyed in 1956 (Lunde and Bigman, 1959). It is likely that this sample was somewhat biased toward higher socioeconomic status, since many hard-of-hearing people were included, and almost 10 percent of the respondents indicated that they had attended college when this was true of only 14 percent of the general population. c) The National Census of the Deaf Population (NCDP), which was conducted in 1972. This census began its sampling process with the identification and location of all known prevocationally deafened individuals (about 400,000), and ended up with a stratified sample of 1,876 people (Schein and Delk, 1974). d) A small follow-up study which included 476 of the original respondents in the NCDP was conducted in 1977 (Schein and Delk, 1978). This sample was clearly skewed toward respondents who had higher incomes and educational levels than the 1972 sample, although they were similar in terms of race and sex.

4. For a more detailed discussion of the educational attainment of deaf people during the 20th century, see Christiansen (1982, 1986a).

5. It is important to note that the concept "labor force participation" includes only those individuals who are working or who are unemployed and actively seeking a job. People who are not actively looking for work are not counted as being unemployed.

6. For a more detailed discussion of specific labor force participation and unemployment rates of deaf people see Barnartt and Christiansen (1985).

7. More detailed discussions of the occupational status of deaf workers can be found in Christiansen (1982, 1986a), Barnartt (1982a, 1982b, 1985, 1986a), and Barnartt and Christiansen (1985).

8. White collar occupations include professional and technical, managerial and administrative, sales and clerical workers. Blue collar occupations include crafts workers, operatives (both transit and non-transit) and laborers (both farm and non-farm). Pink collar includes general service and private household workers.

9. As noted in footnote 3, deaf persons with relatively high educational attainment were overrepresented in the small 1977 follow-up study of the NCDP. Nevertheless, the fact that the improvement for deaf men was so much larger than that for

deaf women, even though there is no evidence that the male respondent group is any more skewed than the female respondent group, suggests that a real change occurred. However, the fact that most of the other 1972-1977 changes were not positive raises questions about what is really happening. (For further discussion of these changes see Barnartt, 1982a).

10. Additional information about income characteristics of deaf people can be found in Christiansen (1982, 1986a), Barnartt (1982a, 1982b, 1985, 1986a) and Barnartt and Christiansen (1985).

11. In particular, the 1972 Survey of Disabled and Nondisabled Adults (Social Security) data being used here only report earned income for families. Thus, only the incomes of unmarried people represent individual incomes and so could be compared to the 1972 NCDP data. However, since unmarried people tend to be younger, and to differ in other ways from married people, any comparisons using these data must be made with great caution. Also, the NCDP follow-up (which has limitations mentioned above) asked about 1976 income, while the 1978 Survey of Disability and Work (Social Security) asked about 1977 incomes. However, we do not feel that a one year difference should make a huge amount of difference in the patterns.

12. See Spradley and Spradley (1978) for a sensitive, moving discussion of the experiences of one family confronted with this situation.

13. See Christiansen (1986b) for a more thorough discussion of some of the problems faced by non-white deaf people.

14. On the other hand, as Deegan (1981) points out, the development of a minority group consciousness also fosters a "us versus them" mentality, which, especially in a time of limited economic resources, mitigates against coalition formation. Davis and Heyl (1978) point out that, in the past at least, the National Federation of the Blind has resisted forming coalitions with groups representing other people with disabilities. Safilios-Rothschild (1976, p. 45) also points out that people with unseen disabilities are frequently prejudiced against those with visible disabilities. Thus, patterns of potential and actual coalition formation deserve futher theoretical and empirical attention.

REFERENCES

Albrecht, G.: Socialization and the disability process. In Albrecht, G.: *The Sociology of Physical Disability and Rehabilitation*, Pittsburgh, University of Pittsburgh Press, 1976.

Albrecht, G., and Levy, J.: Constructing disabilities as social problems. In Albrecht, G.: *Cross National Rehabilitation Policies: A Sociological Perspective*, Beverly Hills, Sage, 1981.

Almquist, E.: The disadvantaged status of black women. In Glazer, N. and Waehrer, H.: *Women in a Man-made World*, Chicago, Rand-McNally, 1977.

Almquist, E., and Wehrle-Einhorn, J. L.: The doubly disadvantaged: minority women in the labor force. In Stromberg, A. and Harkness, S.: *Women Working*, Palo Alto, Mayfield, 1978.

Altman, B.: Disabled Women: Doubly Disadvantaged Members of the Social Structure? Paper presented at the annual meeting of the American Sociological Association, San Francisco, 1982.

Babbidge, H.: *Education of the Deaf in the United States: Report of the Advisory Committee on Education of the Deaf.* Washington, U.S. Government Printing Office, 1965.

Barnartt, S. N.: The Socio-economic Consequences of the Rehabilitation Act of 1973 for Deaf Workers. Paper presented at the annual meeting of the American Sociological Association, San Francisco, 1982a.

Barnartt, S. N.: The Socio-economic Status of Deaf Women: Are They Doubly Disadvantaged? In Christiansen, J. and Egelston-Dodd, J.: *Socioeconomic Status of the Deaf Population,* Washington, Gallaudet College, 1982b.

Barnartt, S. N.: Predictors of the Occupational and Income Status of Deaf American Workers. Paper presented at the International Congress on Education of the Deaf, Manchester, England, 1985.

Barnartt, S. N.: Deaf population: deaf women. In *The Gallaudet Encyclopedia of Deafness and Deaf People.* New York: McGraw-Hill, 1986a.

Barnartt, S. N.: Disability as a Socio-Economic Variable: Predicting Deaf Workers' Incomes. Paper presented at the annual meeting of the American Sociological Association, New York, 1986b.

Barnartt, S. N., and Christiansen, J. B.: The Socioeconomic Status of Deaf Workers: A Minority Group Approach. *Social Science Journal, 22:*19-32, 1985.

Barnartt, S. N., and Seelman, K.: Is it Better to be Black or Blind: A Comparison of Federal Policies Toward Disabled and Minority Groups. Paper presented at the annual meeting of the American Sociological Association, Washington, 1985.

Barrett, N. B.: Women in the job market: occupations, earnings, and career opportunities. In Smith, R. B.: *The Subtle Revolution: Women at Work,* Washington, The Urban Institute, 1979.

Bayes, J. H.: *Minority Politics and Ideologies in the United States.* Novato, Chandler and Sharp, 1982.

Best, H.: *Deafness and the Deaf in the United States.* New York: Macmillan, 1943.

Bowe, F.: Non-White Deaf Persons: Educational, Psychological, and Occupational Considerations. *American Annals of the Deaf, 116:*357-361, 1971.

CADS: *Today's Hearing Impaired Children and Youth: A Demographic and Academic Profile.* Center for Assessment and Demographic Studies (CADS), Gallaudet Research Institute. Washington, Gallaudet College, 1985.

Christiasen, J. B.: The socioeconomic status of the deaf population: a review of the literature. In Christiansen, J. and Egelston-Dodd, J.: *The Socioeconomic Status of the Deaf Population,* Washington, Gallaudet College, 1982.

Christiansen, J. B.: Deaf populations: socioeconomic status. In *The Gallaudet Encyclopedia of Deafness and Deaf People.* New York: McGraw-Hill, 1986a.

Christiansen, J. B.: Deaf population: minorities. In *The Gallaudet Encyclopedia of Deafness and Deaf People.* New York: McGraw-Hill, 1986b.

Cook, L., and Rosset, A.: The Sex Role Attitudes of Deaf Adolescent Women and their Implications for Vocational Choice. *American Annals of the Deaf, 120:*341-345, 1975.

Crammatte, A.: *The Formidable Peak: A Study of Deaf People in Professional Employment.* Washington, Gallaudet College, 1965.

Crammatte, A.: Personal communication, 1985.

Davis, F. J., and Heyl, B. S.: Approaches to Needed Sociological Research on the Physically Handicapped. Paper presented at the annual meeting of the American Sociological Association, San Francisco, 1978.

Deegan, M. J.: Multiple Minority Groups: A Case Study of Physically Disabled Women. *Journal of Sociology and Social Welfare, 8:*274-295, 1981.

deCesare, C. B.: Changes in the Occupational Structure of U.S. Jobs. *Monthly Labor Review, March:*24-34, 1975.

Duncan, G. J.: *Years of Poverty, Years of Plenty.* Ann Arbor, Institute for Social Research, University of Michigan, 1984.

Egelston-Dodd, J.: Overcoming Occupational Stereotypes Related to Sex and Deafness. *American Annals of the Deaf, 122:*489-491, 1977.

Epstein, C. F.: Black and Female: The Double Whammy. *Psychology Today, August:*57-61 +, 1973.

Ferron, D. T.: *Disability Survey 1972: Disabled and Non-Disabled Adults,* Research Report No. 56, SSA Publication No. 13-11812. Washington, U.S. Government Printing Office, 1981.

Furfey, P. H., and Harte, T. J.: *Interaction of Deaf and Hearing in Baltimore City, Maryland.* Washington, Catholic University of America, 1968.

Gentile, A., Schein, J. D., and Haase, K.: *Characteristics of Persons with Impaired Hearing: United States, July 1962-July 1963,* NCHS Series 10, No. 35. Washington, U.S. Department of Health, Education, and Welfare, 1967.

Gliedman, J., and Roth, W.: *The Unexpected Minority.* New York: Harcourt, Brace, Jovanovich, 1980.

Hairston, E., and Smith, L.: *Black and Deaf in America: Are We That Different?* Silver Spring, T.J. Publishers, 1983.

Higgins, P.: *Outsiders in a Hearing World: A Sociology of Deafness.* Beverly Hills, Sage, 1980.

Higgins, P.: *The Rehabilitation Detectives: Doing Human Service Work.* Beverly Hills, Sage, 1985.

Jensema, C.: *The Relationship Between Academic Achievement and the Demographic Characteristics of Hearing Impaired Children and Youth.* Washington, Office of Demographic Studies, Gallaudet College, 1975.

Karchmer, M. A., Milone, M. N., and Wolk, S.: Educational Significance of Hearing Loss at Three Levels of Severity. *American Annals of the Deaf, April:*97-109, 1979.

Kirchner, C., and Peterson, R.: Employment: Selected Characteristics. *Visual Impairment and Blindness, 73:*239-242, 1979.

Kirchner, C., and Peterson, R.: Men, Women, and Blindness: A Demographic View. *Visual Impairment and Blindness, June:*267-270, 1981.

Lando, M. E., Cutler, R., and Gamber, E.: *1978 Survey of Disability and Work Data Book.* Washington, U.S. Government Printing Office, 1982.

Lunde, A. S., and Bigman, S. K.: *Occupational Conditions Among the Deaf.* Washington, Gallaudet College, 1959.

Martens, E.: *The Deaf and Hard-of-Hearing in the Occupational World,* Bulletin 1936, No. 13. Washington, U.S. Government Printing Office, 1937.

McNeil, J. M.: Factors Affecting the 1980 Census Content and the Effort to Develop a Postcensus Disability Survey. Paper presented at the annual meeting of the American Public Health Association, Los Angeles, 1981.

Mindel, E., and Vernon, M.: *They Grow in Silence.* Silver Spring, National Association of the Deaf, 1971.

Moores, D. F., and Oden, C. W.: Educational Needs of Black Deaf Children. *American Annals of the Deaf, 122:*313-318, 1977.

Nagi, S.: Some Conceptual Issues in Disability and Rehabilitation. In Sussman, M.: *Sociology and Rehabilitation,* Washington, The American Sociological Association, 1965.

Ries, P.: The demography of hearing loss. In Orlans, H. P.: *Adjustment to Adult Hearing Loss,* San Diego, College-Hill Press, 1985.

Ries, P., Bateman, D., and Schildroth, A.: *Ethnic Background in Relation to Other Characteristics of Hearing Impaired Students in the United States.* Washington, Office of Demographic Studies, Gallaudet College, 1975.

Safilios-Rothschild, C.: *The Sociology and Social Psychology of Disability and Rehabilitation.* New York: Random House, 1970.

Safilios-Rothschild, C.: Disabled persons' self-definitions and their implications for rehabilitation. In Albrecht, G.: *The Sociology of Physical Disability and Rehabilitation,* Pittsburgh: University of Pittsburgh Press, 1976.

Schein, J. D.: *The Deaf Community Study of Metropolitan Washington, D.C.* Washington, Gallaudet College, 1968.

Schein, J. D., and Delk, M. T.: *The Deaf Population of the United States.* Silver Spring, National Association of the Deaf, 1974.

Schein, J. D., and Delk, M. T.: Economic status of deaf adults: 1972-1977. In Schein, J. D.: *Progress Report #12,* New York, New York University, 1978.

Scott, R. A.: Comments about interpersonal processes of rehabilitation. In Sussman, M.: *Sociology and Rehabilitation,* Washington, The American Sociological Association, 1965.

Scott, R. A.: *The Making of Blind Men: A Study of Adult Socialization.* New Brunswick, Transaction Books, 1981 (also published by the Russell Sage Foundation, 1969).

Spradley, T. S., and Spradley, J. P.: *Deaf Like Me.* New York, Random House, 1978.

Stroman, D. F.: *The Awakening Minorities: The Physically Handicapped.* Washington, University Press of America, 1982.

Sussman, M.: Occupational sociology and rehabilitation. In Sussman, M.: *Sociology and Rehabilitation,* Washington, The American Sociological Association, 1965.

Sussman, M.: Readjustment and rehabilitation of patients. In Kosa, J., Antonovsky, A., and Zola, I.: *Poverty and Health,* Cambridge, Harvard University Press, 1969.

Sussman, M.: The disabled and the rehabilitation system. In Albrecht, G.: *The Sociology of Physical Disability and Rehabilitation,* Pittsburgh, University of Pittsburgh Press, 1976.

Tremain, D. J., and Hartmann, H. J.: *Women, Work, and Wages: Equal Pay for Jobs of Equal Value.* Washington, National Academy Press, 1981.

U.S. Bureau of the Census: *Statistical Abstract of the United States: 1954.* Washington, U.S. Government Printing Office, 1954.

U.S. Bureau of the Census: *Current Population Reports: Labor Force,* Series P-57, No. 175. Washington, U.S. Government Printing Office, 1957.

U.S. Bureau of the Census: *Statistical Abstract of the United States: 1958.* Washington, U.S. Government Printing Office, 1958a.

U.S. Bureau of the Census: Income of Families and Persons in the United States, 1956, *Current Population Reports: Consumer Income,* Series P-60, No. 27. Washington, U.S. Government Printing Office, 1958b.

U.S. Bureau of the Census: Money Income in 1971 of Families and Persons in the United States, *Current Popoulation Reports: Consumer Income,* Series P-60, No. 85. Washington, U.S. Government Printing Office, 1972.

U.S. Bureau of the Census: *Statistical Abstract of the United States: 1973.* Washington, U.S. Government Printing Office, 1973.

U.S. Bureau of the Census: *Statistical Abstract of the United States: 1978.* Washington, U.S. Government Printing Office, 1978a.

U.S. Bureau of the Census: Money Income in 1976 of Families and Persons in the United States, *Current Population Reports: Consumer Income,* Series P-60, No. 114. Washington, U.S. Government Printing Office, 1978b.

U.S. Department of Health and Human Services: *Disability Survey '72: Disabled and Non-Disabled Adults,* Research Report #56. Washington, Department of Health and Human Services, 1981.

U.S. Department of Health and Human Services: *1978 Survey of Disability and Work,* SSA Publication #13-11645. Washington, U.S. Government Printing Office, 1982.

U.S. Department of Health, Education, and Welfare: *1974 Follow-up of Disabled and Non-Disabled Adults: Work Experience of the Disabled, 1972 and 1974,* SSA Publication #13-11725. Washington, U.S. Government Printing Office, 1979a.

U.S. Department of Health, Education, and Welfare: *1974 Follow-up of Disabled and Non-Disabled Adults: General Characteristics.* SSA Publication #13-11725. Washington, U.S. Government Printing Office, 1979b.

U.S. Department of Health, Education, and Welfare: *Basic Data on Hearing Levels of Adults 25-74 Years, United States, 1971-75.* DHEW Publication No. (PHS) 80-1663. Washington, U.S. Government Printing Office, 1980.

U.S. Department of Labor: *Handbook of Labor Statistics.* Washington, U.S. Government Printing Office, 1980.

Wright, B. A.: *Physical Disability: A Psychological Approach.* New York, Harper and Row, 1960.